1,000 STORIES AND QUOTATIONS
OF
FAMOUS PEOPLE

1,000 STORIES AND QUOTATIONS OF FAMOUS PEOPLE

Compiled by Wayne E. Warner

BAKER BOOK HOUSE
Grand Rapids, Michigan

Copyright © 1972 by
Baker Book House Company

Paperback edition issued December 1975

ISBN: 0-8010-9581-6

Library of Congress Catalog Card Number: 72-85670

PHOTOLITHOPRINTED BY CUSHING - MALLOY, INC.
ANN ARBOR, MICHIGAN, UNITED STATES OF AMERICA
1975

To Mom and Dad Warner

INTRODUCTION

Henry Wadsworth Longfellow, that great American poet of the nineteenth century, captured the enduring value of a good example:

> Lives of great men all remind us
> We can make our lives sublime,
> And, departing, leave behind us
> Footprints on the sands of time.

In compiling this sourcebook, I have attempted to give you a quick reference to some of the inspiring stories and quotations great men and women have impressed in the sands to which Longfellow referred. They can be used to illustrate your speech, sermon, debate, or writing. Or they can be used to make you a more interesting conversationalist. Through timely use of stories and quotations your speech or writing will sparkle; your hearers or readers will come alive with rapt attention. And they will remember what you said.

Taking a quick look at the contents you will find men and women representing various professions, diverse religious and national backgrounds, different social and educational levels, and a time period stretching from the fifth century B.C. to the present. There are politicians, preachers, scientists, entertainers, writers, editors, a pilot, a missionary, soldiers, inventors, a nurse, and others who in a great measure have helped shape history. The entries are arranged in alphabetical order — Aesop through Woodrow Wilson.

In limiting a book of this type to forty-four famous people, the compiler is confined to but a fragment of history. One could easily select another forty-four or four hundred and forty-four who have contributed as much or more than the ones who make up this book.

You won't agree with every position our selected people have taken. Perhaps their political or religious persuasions are not identical to your own. Nevertheless, they did something and said something worthwhile. And what they did and said can be used effectively in your work.

Each entry features a handy biographical sketch so you won't have to consult other reference books for this help. Then there are stories by or about the featured personality, followed by quotations from his speeches or writings. A topical index in the back will help you quickly find the stories and quotations you need.

I am indebted to a great number of authors and compilers whose works are given in the bibliography, to whom credit (where known) is given. To my wife, Joy, and daughters — Lori Lee, Avonna Marie, and Lolisa Joy — I can only say a big thanks for their understanding and cooperation during the time I took from normal family activities and devoted to this work.

Despite the usual careful research, every writer is fearful that misquotes and other errors will creep into his work. It seems fitting, therefore, to borrow a prayer Geoffrey Chaucer wrote for one of his books:

> Go, little book; God send thee good passage, and especially let this be thy prayer, unto them all that thee will read or hear, where thou art wrong, after their help to call, thee to correct in any part, or all.

WAYNE E. WARNER

CONTENTS

Stories and Quotations of:

Aesop	11	Abraham Lincoln . . .	183
Augustine	17	Charles A. Lindbergh . .	191
Francis Bacon	23	David Livingstone . . .	199
✔ Clara Barton	29	Henry W. Longfellow . .	209
William Booth	37	Douglas MacArthur . .	215
John Bunyan	45	✔ Henrietta C. Mears . . .	225
Andrew Carnegie . . .	53	Dwight L. Moody . . .	235
George Washington Carver	61	Richard M. Nixon . . .	241
Sir Winston Churchill . .	69	Louis Pasteur	249
Charles Dickens . . .	77	J. C. Penney	257
Walt Disney	87	Will Rogers	267
Benjamin Disraeli . . .	93	Theodore Roosevelt . .	273
Thomas A. Edison . . .	99	Charles H. Spurgeon . .	281
Dwight D. Eisenhower .	107	Adlai E. Stevenson . . .	289
Benjamin Franklin . . .	115	Thomas à Kempis . . .	299
Billy Graham	125	Leo Tolstoy	303
Horace Greeley	135	Wernher von Braun . .	311
Jerome Hines	141	George Washington . .	319
J. Edgar Hoover . . .	149	Daniel Webster	327
Lyndon B. Johnson . .	155	John Wesley	333
Samuel Johnson . . .	163	Woodrow Wilson . . .	341
✔ Helen Keller	169	Bibliography	349
John F. Kennedy . . .	175	*Index*	353

AESOP
(ca. 620–560 B.C.)

Aesop was a Greek slave who was known as a skillful storyteller. He is not given credit for the origin of all the stories attributed to him, but he was the person who gave them their popularity. It has been said that Aesop's wit and wisdom so impressed one of his masters that he gave him his freedom. The enduring value of his writings is evidenced by their continuing popularity through 2,500 years.

AESOP SAID IT

1
Greed

Once upon a time a dog was crossing a bridge over a small river and carrying a piece of meat in his mouth. Seeing his own reflection in the water, he thought that he saw another dog with a bigger piece of meat. In an attempt to snatch the bigger piece of meat away from the other dog, he opened his mouth and dropped out the piece of meat that he already had.

The result was that he had nothing. He couldn't get the other piece of meat because it didn't exist; and his own piece of meat, which fell out of his mouth, was swept down the stream by the swift current.

2
Selecting Associates

Once upon a time there was a man who intended to buy a donkey. He took it home on trial and put it into the corral with his own donkeys. The new donkey turned its back to all of the donkeys except one, which was the laziest and the greediest of the whole lot. The new donkey stood close beside the lazy one and did nothing. So the man put the bridle back on the donkey, took it to its owner, and told the man that he had decided not to buy it. "I am sure," he said, "that this donkey is just like the one that it singled out for a companion in my corral."

3
Complain

As some oxen were dragging a wagon along a heavy road, the wheels set up a tremendous creaking. "Brute!" cried the driver to the wagon. "Why do you groan, when they who are drawing all the weight are silent?" Those who cry loudest are not always the most hurt.

4
Contentment

A donkey, belonging to a gardener, having little to eat and much to do, besought Jupiter to release him from the gardener's service, and give him another master. Jupiter, angry at his discontent, turned him over to a potter. He now had heavier burdens to carry than before, and again appealed to Jupiter to relieve him, who accordingly contrived that he should be sold to a tanner. The donkey having now fallen into worse hands than ever, and daily observing how his master was employed, exclaimed with a groan, "Alas, wretch that I am! It had been better for me to have remained content with my former masters; for now I see that my present owner not only works me harder while living, but will not even spare my hide when I am dead!"

5
Deceit

A wolf, once upon a time, resolved to disguise himself, thinking that he would thus gain an easier livelihood. Having, therefore, clothed himself in a sheep's skin, he contrived to get among a flock of sheep, and fed along with them so that even the shepherd was deceived. The wolf was shut up with the sheep and the door was locked. But the shepherd, wanting something for his supper and going to get a sheep, mistook the wolf for one of his flock and killed him on the spot.

6
Gratitude

Some travelers on a hot day in the summer spotted a tree and made straight for it. They threw themselves on the ground and rested in its shade. Looking up toward the tree as they lay, they said one to another, "What a useless tree to man in this barren plain!" But the tree answered them, "Ungrateful creatures! At the very moment you are enjoying benefit from me, you rail at me as being good for nothing."

7
Rescue Before Lecture

A boy was swimming in a river but got out too deep and was at the point of sinking when he saw a traveler coming by. He called out for help with all his might. But instead of the requested help the man began to give the boy a lecture for his foolhardiness. The boy cried out, "Oh, save me now, sir; and read me the lecture afterwards."

8
Gratitude

Gratitude is the sign of noble souls.

9
Favoritism

Once upon a time a monkey gave birth to twins. It so happened that the mother monkey gave all of her love to one of the twins while she constantly corrected and criticized the other. One day the mother held the favorite monkey to her breast so tightly that he smothered and died. The twin that was rejected grew to maturity and lived a happy and useful life.

10
Sharing the Load

Once upon a time a horse and a donkey were taken on the same trip by their master. The donkey, who carried all the supplies, said to the horse, "If you would take a share of my load, it would save my life." But the horse refused to help, and it was not long before the donkey was worn out with fatigue and fell down and died. Then the owner took all the supplies off the dead donkey's back and put them on the horse's back, plus the hide of the donkey.

Then the horse began to complain, saying, "Look at me now. I wouldn't take the light load when I had a chance and now I have to carry everything — including the donkey."

11
A Victim of His Own Trap

Once upon a time a goat and a donkey were kept in the same barn by their owner. The goat became very jealous of the donkey because the donkey always had food enough and some to spare. So to taunt the donkey the goat said, "Your life is one of never ending work, what with turning the millstone all day and carrying heavy loads. Take my advice. Pretend to trip and fall down every once in awhile so that you can rest."

The donkey took the goat's advice but was seriously injured when he fell. The owner sent for the veterinarian and after looking at the donkey, he prescribed a broth made from goat's meat as a cure. So they killed the goat to heal the donkey.

12
Look Before You Leap

Once upon a time a fox fell into a well, and although the well was not too deep, he was unable to get out. After the fox had been in the well for what seemed to be a long time, a goat came by to get a drink. The goat thought that the fox had gone down into the well to drink and asked if the water was any good. "Why, it's the best in the whole country," said the sly fox. "Why don't you jump in and have some?"

The thirsty goat quickly jumped in and began to drink. Just as quickly the fox jumped on the back of the goat and from there leaped out of the well. The silly goat now realized what a predicament he was in. He begged the fox to help him out, but the fox was already running off into the woods.

As he ran he turned back and said, "If you had half as much sense as you have beard, you would have thought about how to get out before you jumped in."

13
A Good Combination
Good manners and soft words have brought many a difficult thing to pass.

14
Two Different Scales
The injury we do and the one we suffer are not weighed in the same scales.

15
Excuses
Any excuse will serve a tyrant.

16
Substance and Shadow
Beware lest you lose the substance by grasping at the shadow.

17
Coward
Only cowards insult dying majesty.

18
Someone Worse Off
There is always someone worse off than yourself.

19
Poor Substitute
Outside show is a poor substitute for inner worth.

20
Humility
It is better to be humble and bend gracefully when it storms than to be proud and stiff and break when adversity comes.

21
Sour Grapes
It is easy to despise what you cannot get.

22
Contentment
Be content with your lot; one cannot be first in everything.

23
Misrepresentation
We can easily represent things as we wish them to be.

24
Jealousy
People often begrudge others what they cannot enjoy themselves.

25
Liar
A liar will not be believed, even when he speaks the truth.

26
Folly
Men often applaud an imitation, and hiss the real thing.

27
Advice Not Recommended
Never trust the advice of a man in difficulties.

AUGUSTINE
(354–430)

The brilliant Augustine was born in North Africa. His father gave him the best possible education; but, unfortunately, his youthful years were marked by licentious living. He became a Christian in 384 at Milan, where he came under the influence of Saint Ambrose, bishop of Milan. He was ordained a priest in 391 and in 395 became bishop of Hippo. He is regarded as one of the greatest leaders in church history. Two of the most popular religious writings of all time are his City of God *and* Confessions.

28
A Praying Mother

Patricius, a pagan living in the fourth century in North Africa, married a seventeen-year-old Christian by the name of Monica. The world has read much about their famous son Augustine. His youthful sins and later virtues combined to make an extreme that has scarcely ever been equaled. Patricius was a wicked man and the generation gap between him and his son was wide. Yet in spite of the hatred Augustine had for his father, he followed his example. Monica's pain was almost unbearable as she watched her son read everything and then try everything. But even though she suffered as she saw the direction her son was going, Monica never ceased to pray for his conversion. One day she poured out her heart to an elderly bishop. He sensed the mother's love and devotion; he comforted her with a prayer and a prophecy: "Go thy way and God bless thee, for it is not possible for the son of these tears to perish."

Monica has gone down in history as a faithful, praying mother who was passionately interested in the salvation of her son. As Susanna Wesley was to become centuries later, Monica was an important link in the church history chain.

29
Man's Free Will

As a young man Augustine turned away from his mother's Christianity for Manichaeanism, a pagan religion that rejected what it considered the objectionable commandments of Christianity. Its followers considered God as being both evil and good. They believed that the evil half of God dominated most men; there was no choice in the matter for the man. The young Augustine liked the philosophy because it gave him an excuse for his sinful ways.

But Augustine slowly discovered that even though there was a force tempting him to sin, he himself was granting the permission. He discovered his free will. Later in his *Confessions* he wrote: "And just this was my incurable sin that I thought myself not to be a sinner. What raised me into light was that I knew as well that I had a free will, as I knew that I lived."

> Out of my bondage, sorrow and night,
> Jesus, I come, Jesus, I come;
> Into Thy freedom, gladness and light,
> Jesus, I come to Thee.

30
Effects of Christian Hymns

Augustine gives an account of the effect that the singing of Christian hymns had on him at the time of his baptism:

"Oh, how freely was I made to weep by these hymns and spiritual songs; transported by the voices of the congregation sweetly singing. The melody of their voices filled my ear, and divine truth was poured into my heart. Then burned the sacred flame of devotion in my soul, and gushing tears flowed from my eyes, as well they might."

> — From *450 True Stories from Church History*, by J. Vernon Jacobs. Wm. B. Eerdmans Publishing Co. Used by permission.

31
The New Augustine

There is a legend that Augustine, accosted on the street by a former mistress shortly after his conversion, turned and walked in the opposite direction. Surprised, the woman cried out, "Augustine, it is I."

But Augustine, proceeding on his way, cried back to her, "Yes, but it is not I."

What he meant was that there was a new Augustine, and that this new Augustine would avoid the very territory and appearance of evil.

> — From *Macartney's Illustrations,* by Clarence E. Macartney. Copyright 1945 by Whitmore and Stone.

32
Good Works of Unbelievers

There were always some among the ancient pagans who felt they were good enough without becoming Christians. They hadn't committed any gross crimes, and morally compared favorably with believers.

Augustine answered them thus:

> It is not only important *what* a man does, but what *object* he has in view in doing it. Let the captain of a vessel understand perfectly how to manage it, but if he does not know the direction of the port he is sailing to, of what use is it that he can sail hither and thither as he pleases? He knows how to protect the vessel from the fury of the waves, to turn and to back about just as he may think best; but if asked, Whither are you sailing? he answers, I do not know; or, instead of saying that, he says, I am sailing to yonder port, and then runs not into the port, but against the rocks. . . . So it is with the man who, if he runs ever so well, has lost the right path. Would it not be better if the captain were not so vigorous, if he steered the vessel with labor and some difficulty, and yet pursued the right track; and would it not be better for the traveler if he were weaker and slower, but yet in the right way, rather than be running in the wrong direction?

> — From *450 True Stories from Church History,* by J. Vernon Jacobs. Wm. B. Eerdmans Publishing Co. Used by permission.

33
Humility

Augustine believed that there were three requirements necessary to be a Christian. The first was humility, the second was humility, and the third was humility. And this man brought many more men to Christ by his humble confession than by his brilliant theological works that have assisted all Christendom so mightily to understand the mystery of "the City of God."

> — David A. Redding, *What Is the Man?*

34
Augustine No Phony

Following Augustine's conversion and his subsequent rise to become the Bishop of Hippo in North Africa, he refused to be a pretender, or as some would say today, a phony. He stripped away the facade that others had built around the bishops of his day by confessing that he still had sinful thoughts. Moreover, he argued that no saint ever became perfect in this life — not even the pope. Although he confessed he still had weaknesses, Augustine knew God's grace was sufficient for him and any others who would humbly bow before God.

35
Conviction of the Holy Spirit

When Augustine, of Hippo, was teaching in Milan, he became convinced of the errors of his way, and was torn between the desire to continue in evil living and definitely accepting Christ.

One day, when his soul was in great distress, he went out into the garden, and cast himself under a fig tree, giving vent to his emotions in tears. Just then there came from the neighboring yard the voice of a little child, which repeated monotonously, "Take up and read; take up and read."

Feeling that it was a command of God, he opened his Bible, and his eyes fell on Romans 13:13, 14 which smote his heart with telling conviction, and led to his decision to enter into the new life.

—J. Vernon Jacobs

AUGUSTINE SAID IT

36
God

God is more truly imagined than expressed, and He exists more truly than He is imagined.

37
Pride and Humility

It was pride that changed angels into devils; it is humility that makes men as angels.

38
Holy Spirit

O Holy Spirit, descend plentifully into my heart. Enlighten the dark corners of this neglected dwelling and scatter there Thy cheerful beams.

39
Faith

Faith is to believe what we do not see; and the reward of this faith is to see what we believe.

40
Habit

Habit, if not resisted, soon becomes necessity.

41
Love

He that is not jealous is not in love.

42
Avoid Self-Satisfaction

Be always displeased with what thou art, if thou desirest to attain to what thou art not; for where thou hast pleased thyself, there thou abidest. But if thou sayest I have enough, thou perishest. Always add, always walk, always proceed. Neither stand still, nor go back, nor deviate.

43
Something Missing

I have read in Plato and Cicero sayings that are very wise and very beautiful; but I never read in either of them: "Come unto me all ye that labour and are heavy laden."

44
Confession

The confession of evil works is the first beginning of good works.

FRANCIS BACON
(1561–1626)

Few men in history can be remembered for outstanding contributions in so many fields as Francis Bacon. He was an English philosopher, statesman, scientist, writer, and jurist. His essays are widely read even today. He is recognized for the publicity he gave to the inductive method of research. He was a member of Parliament and held other key positions in England's government. As a judge in 1621, he was accused of and confessed to taking bribes. The king, however, pardoned him. Bacon died while making an experiment on the use of snow as a food preservative.

45
Too Large for the House

When Queen Elizabeth visited Lord Bacon at his house in Hertford soon after she had created him chancellor of England, she remarked, "This house is too small for a man like you."

"Madam, it is Your Majesty's fault," replied Bacon with a bow; "for you have made me too large for the house."

46
Treason or Plagiarism?

After having heard suspicious reports about Haywood's *The Life of Henry IV*, Queen Elizabeth summoned Lord Bacon to ask him about the book since she knew her chancellor would have read it.

"Tell me, my lord," she inquired, "is it true that there is treason in this book of Haywood's?"

"No, Your Majesty," replied Bacon, "but there is felony in it, for he has stolen most of it from Tacitus."

FRANCIS BACON SAID IT

47
Building and Tearing Down

He that gives good advice, builds with one hand; he that gives good counsel and example, builds with both; but he that gives good admonition and bad example, builds with one hand and pulls down with the other.

48
Books

Some books are to be tasted; others swallowed; and some to be chewed and digested.

49
Misery

It is a miserable state of mind to have a few things to desire, and many things to fear.

50
Making Opportunities

A wise man will make more opportunities than he finds.

51
Vainglory

Vainglorious men are the scorn of the wise, the admiration of fools, the idols of paradise, and the slaves of their own vaunts.

52
If a Man . . .

If a man be gracious and courteous to strangers, it shows he is a citizen of the world, and that his heart is no island cut off from other lands, but a continent that joins to them.

If he be compassionate toward the afflictions of others, it shows that his heart is like the noble tree that wounds itself when it gives the balm.

If he easily pardons and remits offences, it shows that his mind is planted above injuries, so that he cannot be pained.

If he be thankful for small benefits, it shows that he weighs men's minds, and not their idle talk.

53
Prosperity and Adversity

Prosperity is not without many fears and distastes; and adversity is not without comforts and hopes. The virtue of prosperity is temperance, but the virtue of adversity is fortitude, which in morals is the more heroical virtue.

Prosperity is the blessing of the Old Testament, adversity is the blessing of the New, which carrieth the greater benediction, and the clearer revelation of God's favor.

54
Conformed to Christ

If he [a man] have St. Paul's wish to be *anathema* from Christ for the salvation of his brethren (Romans 9:3), it shows a nature that has a kind of conformity with Christ Himself.

55
Speech

Discretion of speech is more than eloquence; and to speak agreeably to him with whom we deal is more than to speak in good words.

56
Past Is Irrevocable

That which is past and gone is irrevocable; wise men have enough to do with things present and to come.

57
Making the Man

Reading maketh a full man; conference maketh a ready man; and writing maketh an accurate man.

58
Acting According to Custom

Men commonly think according to their inclinations, speak according to their learning and imbibed opinions, but generally act according to custom.

59
Health

A healthy body is a guest-chamber for the soul; a sick body is a prison.

60
Folly and Fortune

The folly of one man is the fortune of another.

61
Man Related to God

They that deny a God destroy man's nobility; for certainly man is of kin to the beast by his body; and, if he be not of kin to God by his spirit, he is a base and ignoble creature.

62
No Limit

God has placed no limit to intellect.

63
Knowledge

For knowledge, too, is itself a power.

64
A Little Philosophy Dangerous

A little philosophy inclineth man's mind to atheism; but depth in philosophy bringeth men's mind about to religion.

65
Christianity

There was never law, or sect, or opinion did so much to magnify goodness as the Christian religion doth.

66
Revenge

In taking revenge a man is but equal to his enemy, but in passing it over he is his superior.

67
Superstition

The general root of superstition is that men observe when things hit, and not when they miss; and commit to memory the one, and forget and pass over the other.

68
Young Men

Young men are fitter to invent than to judge; fitter for execution than for counsel; and fitter for new projects than for settled business.

69
Study

Natural abilities are like natural plants; they need pruning by study.

70
Wisdom

A prudent question is one-half of wisdom.

CLARA BARTON
(1821–1912)

A one-time quiet school teacher is today best remembered as the woman who founded the American Red Cross. She first gained attention as a nurse in the Civil War. At first she was denied access to the battlefields, but later the government relented and she was given official permission to help the wounded in the battles and was called the "Angel of the Battlefield." She also served on the battlefront of the Franco-Prussian War. After the American Red Cross was organized, she became its president and helped in many natural disasters. Her entire life — some ninety-one years — was devoted to helping others.

71
Beat Him at His Own Game

Clara Barton was a schoolteacher before she became known as the "Angel of the Battlefield." But she was a timid teacher, she later admitted. Her first school had a reputation of being tough to handle. The last teacher — a strong, mature man — had been run off by four big boys in the school. Clara did well by winning the confidence and respect of the students except Nate, the bully of the playground. One day there was a showdown. Clara told the pupils what games they would play, only to have Nate turn on her and glare. "I'm the boss around here," he snapped. "You are?" inquired Clara. "And why is that?" Nate told Clara that he was boss because he happened to be the best horseshoe player in the school. "Go on now, mind your own business," he said to Clara. But Clara wasn't through. She challenged the bully to his own game — and won.

The bully's rule on the playground was broken and Clara gradually won his friendship too.

72
A Belief in Equal Opportunity

During her teaching career, Clara Barton took a position in Bordentown, New Jersey, at a private school. She wanted to open a public school in the town when she saw the many children who had no school to attend. But she received no encouragement from the chairman of the school committee. Her persistence finally paid off and she was given official sanction to begin a public school which she herself would teach. On the first day of school she had "six bright renegade boys" to greet her. At the end of the first year she was in a new school building and had six hundred students enrolled. Bordentown had a public school simply because one woman was convinced that some idle, renegade boys needed an education.

73
Courage and Compassion

Why would Clara Barton, a single woman of almost forty, leave the security of the Patent Office and plunge into a nursing job on the battlefields of the Civil War? Probably a combination of courage and compassion, for on the battlefields she had opportunity to demonstrate those two traits many times. Early in the war she wrote her father: "We are ready to bind the wounds or bear them of our own, if necessary. I shall remain here while anyone remains, and do whatever comes to my hand. I may be compelled to *face* danger, but *never fear it,* and while our soldiers can stand and *fight,* I can stand and feed and nurse them." And according to the men on the battlefields, that is what Miss Barton did; her tender care went to all — Northern and Southern, black and white.

74
Her Place Was at the Front

Clara Barton battled government red tape and customs to get to the battlefields at the beginning of the Civil War. At first she was forbidden to go. Finally, after months of persistent effort, Clara was permitted to go with supplies to the battle of Cedar Mountain. She knew there was a need for nurses and she went. She told about the events of Cedar Mountain: "I broke the shackles and went to the field.

Five days and nights with three hours' sleep — a narrow escape from capture — and some days of getting the wounded into hospitals at Washington. . . . And if you chance to feel that the positions I occupied were rough and unseemly for a *woman* — I can only reply that they were rough and unseemly for *men*. But under all, lay the life of the nation. I had inherited the rich blessing of health and strength of constitution — such as are seldom given to woman — and I felt that some return was due from me and that I ought to be there."

75
Not for Sale

During the Spanish-American War of 1898, two of the most famous Americans in history served in Cuba — one a nurse and the other a soldier: Clara Barton and Lt. Col. Theodore Roosevelt, later the twenty-sixth president of the United States.

Early one morning Colonel Roosevelt approached Clara Barton and her Red Cross unit. "I have some sick men with the regiment who refuse to leave it," the colonel said. "They need such delicacies as you have here, which I am ready to pay for out of my own pocket. Can I buy them from the Red Cross?"

Dr. Joseph Gardner, one of Clara's associates, replied, "Not for a million dollars!"

"But my men need these things," the colonel explained. "I think a good deal of my men. I am proud of them."

"And we know they are proud of you, colonel. But we can't sell Red Cross supplies."

Finally, Colonel Roosevelt got the message. "Just ask for them, colonel," Dr. Gardner said.

76
Sharing with Unfortunate

America in the "Gay Nineties" was generally a nation of plenty. But not so in other parts of the world, particularly in Russia where massive crop failures occurred in 1889–1892. Some thirty-five million people were facing starvation. Clara, her humanitarian spirit still strong at seventy, rose to the occasion and organized American support. Although she did not personally travel to Russia at that time, the American Red Cross was there with help from America. Gratitude came from Russians in all walks of life. A peasant sent a crude note and three colored Easter eggs. "North Americans!" he wrote. "May the Lord grant you a peaceful and long life, and prosperity to your land, and may your fields be filled with abundant harvest — Christ is risen!" The great novelist Leo Tolstoy offered his appreciation: "From what I have heard of Miss Barton, I feel she must be a very near relation. Please give her my love."

America was known as a rich, powerful nation; but thanks to Clara Barton and others like her, America became known as one of the most generous nations the world had ever seen.

77
Clara the Innovator

William E. Barton, a distant cousin of Clara, cited one of her most outstanding qualities: her almost complete disregard of precedent. "She always had faith in the possibility of something better," he said. "It irritated her to be told how things always had been done. She knew that a very large proportion of things that have been done since the Creation have been blunderingly done and . . . having once decided upon a course that defied the tyranny of precedent, she held true to her declaration of independence, and saw her experiment through."

78
Help in Need

In 1889 Clara Barton and her Red Cross were put to a most difficult task. An earthen dam above Johnstown, Pennsylvania, weakened by heavy rains, broke. Residents who witnessed what followed described it as a solid wall of water, thirty to forty feet high, rushing down the valley like a moving mountain. The gigantic wall of water was said to have been moving at a speed of twenty-two feet per second as it hit Johnstown, killing over two thousand persons — one of the worst single disasters in American history. Some forty-eight hours later, Clara Barton and a Red Cross team were in Johnstown, where they found but few houses standing. For five months the Red Cross team worked at Johnstown, helping the injured, building houses, burying the dead, and dispensing food and clothing to the many in need. The editor of the Johnstown *Daily Tribune* paid Clara Barton a tribute. "We cannot thank Miss Barton in words," he wrote. "Hunt the dictionaries of all languages through and you will not find the signs to express our appreciation of her and her work. Try to describe the sunshine.

Try to describe the starlight. Words fail, and . . . [in] silence to the idea which brought her here. God and humanity! Ne‍ they more closely linked than in stricken Johnstown."

Americans were beginning to see that a volunteer relief orga‍ was an essential body in peace as well as war.

79
Needed the Most Help

While extremely modest, Clara Barton was far from being a prude. She was never terrified by . . . gossip. . . . In 1884, when she was on her steamboat, *Josh V. Throop,* assisting in the Ohio River floods, the boat one night tied up at a landing, and a goodly number of people came on board. Among the rest were two women. One of the prominent ladies of the town found opportunity to whisper to her that these were young women whose social standing was not above question. "Then they will need help all the more," Clara said; and she gave those two girls an hour of her evening. Such warnings she often received, and . . . she invariably reacted in the other direction.

— William E. Barton

80
Forget the Hurts

Clara Barton never was known to hold resentment against anyone. One time a friend recalled to her a cruel thing that had happened to her some years previously, but Clara seemed not to remember the incident. "Don't you remember the wrong that was done to you?" the friend asked Clara. "No," Clara answered calmly, "I distinctly remember forgetting that."

81
Example and Fight Bring Victory

After the Civil War activities had ended for Clara Barton, she went to Europe for her health. But while there she became involved in the Franco-Prussian War that began in 1870. There she was once again giving her energies on the battlefields — first for the Germans and later helping the defeated French. Her humanitarian ideals knew no political barriers; she was there to bring comfort and aid to the wounded and distressed.

Not only did she become involved in the Franco-Prussian War, but Clara also became interested in the Red Cross and was anxious for the United States to become a member. In spite of sickness, Clara set out in her struggle for a Red Cross in America. Her attempts to convince President Hayes and his aides of the need only brought opposition. But when James A. Garfield was elected president and heard Clara's appeal, he endorsed her plans enthusiastically. Thus, on May 21, 1881, the American Red Cross was formed, with Clara Barton as president. One of the toughest and most frustrating battles of her life had ended — with victory.

82
Disagreeing Without Disagreeableness

Although not very popular today, the pseudoscience of phrenology was very popular in the nineteenth century. Phrenologists believed the character of a person could be determined by the shape of the head. Horace Mann, the famous educator, was a leading supporter of the theory. And Clara Barton firmly believed in it. Her friend Fannie Childs remembered a time when Clara argued the theory with an Episcopalian minister. The minister, who had no faith in the theory, told Clara of a man who had suffered an injury to the brain that had resulted in the removal of a considerable part of it. "He argued," Miss Childs said, "that if there was anything in phrenology, that man would have been deprived of a certain group of mental capabilities, but that he got on very well with only a part of a brain." Clara, either caught without a rebuttal or wishing to end the argument, quickly replied, "Then there's hope for me." The argument ended with a hearty laugh.

83
Specializing in Selfless Acts

The Sixth Massachusetts Regiment was called to Washington, D.C., at the outbreak of the Civil War in April 1861. As the regiment was changing trains in Baltimore, a mob of Southern sympathizers attacked them, killing four soldiers and wounding many more.

When the regiment finally arrived in Washington, Clara Barton was one of those waiting to greet them. One of the soldiers immediately recognized her and called to her. He lived on a farm next to Clara's brother. Then Clara learned the men were from Worcester, near her home town. Some, she discovered, had been her school pupils.

The soldiers had lost their baggage and clothes in the Baltimore attack, and Clara immediately dived in to remedy the situation. She took her own linens, tore them, and made handkerchiefs. Then she and her sister brought baskets of food to the men — food purchased with their own money.

Next Clara went to visit with the men and read aloud the one available copy of the *Worcester Spy* newspaper. She read to them the accounts of the Baltimore incident. They asked for a second reading, and then applauded at the end.

Marshall W. Fishwick, in *Illustrious Americans: Clara Barton,* says of the incident, "Clara Barton had performed the first of what would be a memorable sequence of selfless acts for human beings suddenly set adrift in a time of trouble and pain."

CLARA BARTON SAID IT

84
Discipline

Show me a child well disciplined, perfectly governed at home, and I will show you a child that never breaks the rule of school. A silken thread will bind that child.

85
Prejudice

Prejudice, if not altogether invincible, is perhaps the most difficult of all errors to be eradicated from the human mind; for by disguising itself under the respectable name of firmness it passes through the world without censure, whereas open vice would receive a severe reprimand.

86
Drunkenness

I regard drunkenness as the great father of crime, and the mother of prisons, almshouses, asylums, and workhouses — the parent of vice and want and the instigator of murder.

87
Death

I saw death as it is on the battlefield. . . . I saw the surgeons coming, too much needed by all to give special attention to any one. Once again I stood by them and witnessed those soldiers bearing their soldier pains, limbs being sawed off without opiates being taken, or even a bed to lie on. I crept around once more, trying to give them at least a drink of water to cool their parched lips, and I heard them at last speak of mothers and wives and sweethearts, but never a murmur or complaint.

— April 10, 1912, two days before her death

WILLIAM BOOTH
(1829–1912)

William Booth withdrew from the Methodist church in 1861 and dedicated his life to the poor of London. Later, his evangelism-social work was given the name The Salvation Army, *which today is a worldwide Christian organization operating in eighty-six countries. At first ridicule and severe persecution were the lot of Booth and his soldiers. But the organization later gained the highest respect everywhere. Booth was a tireless preacher and worker, never retiring from active duty as the army's general. His children followed him either into the Salvation Army or into similar Christian organizations.*

88

Dedication

As a boy of thirteen William was a social reformer, and longed to do something to alleviate the suffering of the poor. At an early age he deserted the Church of England and became a regular attendant at the Wesleyan Chapel. At the age of thirteen he yielded his heart and life to God. Describing this event, he says: "The Holy Spirit had continually shown me that my real welfare for time and eternity depended upon the surrender of myself to the services of God. After a long controversy I made this submission, cast myself on His mercy, received the assurance of His pardon, and gave myself up to His service with all my heart. The hour, the place, and many other particulars of this glorious transaction are recorded indelibly on my memory."

—James Gilchrist Lawson, *Deeper Experiences of Famous Christians*

89
Doctor's Advice Not Taken

Before William Booth became a minister, he conducted religious services in small country places as a lay preacher. And he had the poor in his heart and work, even as a teen-ager. At seventeen he was made a local preacher in the Methodist church. His superintendent wanted him to become a regular preacher at the age of nineteen. But his doctor advised him against the ministry, telling Booth that his health was so poor that he was totally unfit for the strain of the preacher's life. That doctor had no way of knowing that Booth would eventually take on strenuous work among London's poor, physical labor that would make the life of a Methodist minister seem like a vacation. Nor did the doctor have any way of knowing that Booth would launch an organization of worldwide proportions and that he would live to be eighty-three.

90
The Secret of Greatness

When J. Wilbur Chapman was in London, he had an opportunity to meet General Booth, who at that time was past eighty years of age. Dr. Chapman listened reverently as the old general spoke of the trials and the conflicts and the victories. Then the American evangelist asked the general if he would disclose his secret for success. "He hesitated a second," Dr. Chapman said, "and I saw the tears come into his eyes and steal down his cheeks, and then he said, 'I will tell you the secret. God has had all there was of me. There have been men with greater brains than I, men with greater opportunities; but from the day I got the poor of London on my heart, and a vision of what Jesus Christ could do with the poor of London, I made up my mind that God would have all of William Booth there was. And if there is anything of power in the Salvation Army today, it is because God has all the adoration of my heart, all the power of my will, and all the influence of my life.' "

Dr. Chapman said he went away from that meeting with General Booth knowing "that the greatness of a man's power is the measure of surrender."

91
Love for the Unlovely

The founder of the Salvation Army, William Booth, as a young pastor of a Methodist church on London's East Side, was not satisfied. He had

a comfortable job and security, but he saw the poor and nee
were untouched by the church. He tried to get his members int
in bringing them into the church. But the members refused to coo
with such a plan. "We have no place for them in our clean chu ͟ͅn,"
they would say. "Besides, they will never leave off their wicked ways.
It is a hopeless thing you ask of us, William Booth."

Finally, Booth knew he must leave the security of his church and help the poor on his own. He was not only interested in their finding Christ, but he was also interested in helping them socially. When he broke the news to his wife Catherine, she was in complete agreement with his decision. "We have trusted the Lord for our daily needs before," she declared, "and He hasn't failed us. We will just have to trust Him again."

And that is how the Salvation Army began — by faith in God and William Booth's motto: "A man may be down, but he is never out."

92
He Means Me!

Gen. William Booth was a dramatist in the pulpit. His sermons held his congregation spellbound and helped to bring results wherever he went. Once when he was preaching a sermon in Birmingham's town hall, his portrayal of a seducer on the Judgment Day brought unexpected results. "Here she comes," he shouted, "the woman he seduced! Her golden hair is falling over her shoulders — she is screaming, 'That is the man! That is the man!' " Suddenly, to the horror of all assembled in the hall, a man's voice from the gallery cried in torment, "My God — he means *me!*" Then with a crash he leaped over the balcony to the floor of the hall and stumbled up the aisle and fell to his knees at the altar.

93
A Different Perspective

In his last years, Booth seemed increasingly obsessed with the work still left undone. He drove himself to reach as many unsaved as possible. His aides worried over the way he continued the furious pace. One aide, who was excited about the response at the close of one the general's meetings, said, "Wonderful, general — did you see them? A hundred to the penitent-form [inquirers' room] in ten minutes!" Booth was sober, "I saw the hundreds going out, having rejected Christ."

94
People's Sins Kept Him Awake

Once late at night, Bramwell Booth saw a light burning in his aged father's room. Going in, Bramwell said, "Ought you not to be asleep?" His father shook his head. "No, I am thinking." After a pause, General Booth placed his hands on his son's shoulders and said sadly, "Bramwell, I am thinking about the people's sins. What will they do with their sins?"

95
Overlooking Criticism

One of the many antagonists of the early days of the Salvation Army was the brilliant Thomas H. Huxley, biologist and agnostic. Through the letter columns of the London *Times* Huxley launched an all-out attack on Booth and his organization. He saw Booth as a manipulator of the minds of his followers and termed it a "prostitution of the mind." He reasoned that Booth's sway over the soldiers was an evil worse than harlotry or intemperance. Others followed Huxley in his frequent blasts at Booth and the Salvation Army. Booth's enemies were most generous with invectives — a practice that angered Bramwell Booth, the general's son. The elder Booth reasoned with Bramwell that he couldn't waste time fighting his critics. He would not be diverted from what he felt God wanted him to do. "Bramwell," he said, "fifty years hence it will matter very little indeed how these people treated us. It will matter a great deal how we dealt with the work of God."

96
How the Infidel Evolved

William Booth ministered during the time that Darwin's theories on evolution were first being circulated. Once in a public address Booth took an opportunity to have a little fun with the evolutionists. Life began, the general explained, in a patch of mud. After a long time — "ages and ages and ages" — out of the mud came a fishy creature something akin to a shrimp. Then, the general continued, after "ages and ages and ages" the shrimp turned into a monkey. And then? Booth now had his audience eagerly waiting for the final explantion. "Ages and ages passed," he drawled, his eyes twinkling, "before the monkey turned into — *an infidel!*"

97
These Are Our People

William Booth knew that he alone would never be able to reach London's poor, its drunken, its criminals, the orphans, and the homeless. He needed to recruit preachers. And he set out to do it. His own teenager, Bramwell, was one of his recruits. Bramwell never forgot the first time his father took him into one of London's one hundred thousand pubs. There he saw the sight that had stirred his father: men with inflamed faces; drunken, disheveled women openly suckling tiny children; and the reek of gin and tobacco and acrid bodies. Most of the pubs kept a special set of steps to help even small children reach the counter where they could buy a penny glass of gin. Bramwell learned that children less than five years of age knew the raging agonies of delirium tremens. Some died from cirrhosis of the liver. Bramwell looked at the degradation inside the pub; then his father said quietly, "These are our people. These are the people I want you to live for and bring to Christ."

98
He Kept the Vow

Once when he was asked about the secret of his strength, General Booth revealed how, as a boy, he had knelt at a bare table in the schoolroom of Nottingham's Broad Street Chapel and vowed that "God should have all there was of William Booth." Years later his daughter added something to that answer: "That wasn't really his secret — his secret was that he never took it back."

99
Ambition

For over thirty years the Salvation Army and William Booth in particular were subject to some of the most vile persecution Christians suffered in modern times. But the general lived to see the day his army would be honored around the world. His own King Edward VII invited him to Buckingham Palace in 1904. All the persecution and trials of the previous decades must have seemed insignificant to Booth as he heard King Edward say, "You are doing a good work — a great work, General Booth." When the king asked Booth to write in his autograph album, the old man — now seventy-five — bent forward, took the pen, and summed up his life's work:

> Your Majesty,
> Some men's ambition is art,
> Some men's ambition is fame,
> Some men's ambition is gold,
> My ambition is the souls of men.

100
Family Training Pays

The training William and Catherine Booth gave their eight children paid big dividends for the kingdom of God. Their eldest son, William Bramwell, succeeded his father as second general of the Salvation Army. Ballington was founder and general of the Volunteers of America. Catherine married a Salvationist colonel, Arthur Sidney Clibborn. Emma married Frederick St. George De Latour Tucker, a former judge in India, who compiled the two-volume life of his mother-in-law, *Memoirs of Catherine Booth* (1895). Herbert Henry (Howard) pioneered the army in Canada. Marian was a staff captain in the Salvation Army. Evangeline served as the first and only woman general of the International Salvation Army (1934–1939). Lucy, their last daughter, married Emmanuel Hellberg, a Swedish Salvation Army worker.

Edith Deen in her book *Great Women of the Christian Faith* says, "No family in recent Christian history has served so diligently the poor and the outcast, the prisoner and the hoodlum, bringing to them the healing ministry of Christ."

101
Taking the Gospel to the People

England had never seen such a variety of methods to reach people with the gospel. William Booth used open-air meetings, factory and slum meetings, and worked with the many poor that the organized church ignored. He believed in taking the gospel to the people. He began to use many musical instruments, playing lively tunes. He found out that the music attracted the people. He taught that the sinner could be converted and live a victorious life. He believed in putting the Christian to work for the Lord; his soldiers testified, sang, prayed, and worked with the needy. It was all revolutionary.

What started out as William and Catherine Booth's humble efforts in London has expanded to eighty-six countries and colonies. There are over eight thousand centers in the United States alone. They are still carrying out Booth's original idea: take the gospel to the people.

WILLIAM BOOTH SAID IT

102
Helping Body and Soul

To get a man soundly saved, it is not enough to put on him a pair of new breeches, to give him regular work, or even to give him a university education. . . . To change the nature of the individual, to get at the heart, to save his soul is the only real, lasting method of doing him any good. In many modern schemes of social regeneration it is forgotten that "it takes a soul to move a body, e'en to a cleaner sty," and at the risk of being misunderstood and misrepresented, I must assert in the most unqualified way that it is primarily and mainly for the sake of saving the soul that I seek the salvation of the body.

103
Reservations

Our reservations are the damnation of our consecrations.

104
The Way to a Man's Heart

What is the use of preaching the gospel to men whose whole attention is concentrated upon a mad, desperate struggle to keep themselves alive? You might as well give a tract to a shipwrecked sailor who is battling with the surf which has drowned his comrades and threatens to drown him. He will not listen to you. Nay, he cannot hear you any more than a man whose head is under water can listen to a sermon. The first thing to do is to get him at least a footing on firm ground, and to give him room to live. Then you may have a chance. At present you have none. And you will have all the better opportunity to find a way to his heart, if he comes to know that it was you who pulled him out of the horrible pit and the miry clay in which he was sinking to perdition.

105
Determination

While women weep as they do now, I'll fight; while little children go hungry as they do now, I'll fight; while men go to prison, in and out, in and out, as they do now, I'll fight — I'll fight to the very end.

106
Women

The best men in the army are the women.

107
Emphasis on Souls

Go for souls, and go for the worst.

108
No Favoritism

The Salvation Army does not belong to the Booth family. It belongs to the Salvation Army. So long as the Booth family are good Salvationists, and worthy of commands, they shall have them, but only if they are. I am not the "general" of the family; I am the general of the Salvation Army.

109
Life Sentence

I sentence you all to hard labor for the rest of your natural lives.
— To his new officers

110
A Prophet Speaks

I am of the opinion that the chief dangers which confront the coming century [twentieth] will be religion without the Holy Spirit, Christianity without Christ, forgiveness without repentance, salvation without regeneration, politics without God, and heaven without hell.

JOHN BUNYAN
(1628–1688)

John Bunyan, an English preacher, is best known for his famous Pilgrim's Progress, *which was written in 1678.* He was born near Bedford and there followed his father's trade of tinker (maker and mender of utensils). It wasn't until he had served in the army for two years and after his marriage that he began to think seriously about religion. He later became a preacher but was arrested in 1660 for preaching without a license. Most of the next twelve years were spent in prison, where he wrote many religious articles. Released from jail in 1672 he became pastor of a church but was arrested and returned to jail three years later. He began to write *The Pilgrim's Progress during his second jail term. The book has been translated into over one hundred languages and read throughout the world.*

111
Word of God Planted

Although John Bunyan, the tinker of Bedford, as a youth was ungodly, beneath the facade of sin was a deep hunger for God. Three or four unnamed poor women are credited by Bunyan himself as bringing an awakening to his darkened heart. It happened one day while he was about his trade when he noticed the women sitting at a door. Bunyan heard their conversation and discovered they were talking about the things of God. He drew near to listen. "Their talk was about a *new birth*," Bunyan said, "the work of God in their hearts. . . . They talked how God had visited their souls with his love in the Lord Jesus. . . ." Bunyan had no idea what the women were talking about, but he said he was "greatly affected with their words."

Bunyan was later converted, the conversion a result of three or four poor women talking about spiritual things. The seed was unknowingly planted that day in the heart of a searching thinker that brought about one of the greatest spiritual returns recorded in the history of the church. "So shall my word be that goeth forth out of my mouth: It shall not return unto me void, but it shall accomplish that which I please, and it shall prosper in the thing whereto I sent it" (Isa. 55:11).

112
Righteousness of Christ

As a new Christian, John Bunyan had many questions about Bible teachings. He eagerly searched Scripture for the answers. One by one his questions were solved as he read the Word and prayed. He was concerned about his own righteousness being accepted by God. One day as he was walking in the fields he suddenly became aware of the righteousness of Christ. "Suddenly," he said, "this sentence fell upon my soul, 'Thy righteousness is in heaven.' And me thought, with awe, I saw, with the eyes of my soul, Jesus Christ at God's right hand; there, I saw, was my righteousness; so that wherever I was, or whatever I was doing, God could not say of me, He wants my righteousness, for that was just before Him. I also saw, moreover, that it was not my good frame of heart that made my righteousness better, nor yet my bad frame that made my righteousness worse; for my righteousness was Jesus Christ himself; 'the same yesterday, to day and forever,' Hebrews 13:8."

113
Power of the Printed Page

During a time when John Bunyan was struggling for spiritual certainty, and his mind was filled with doubts and fears, it happened that a translation of *Luther's Commentary on the Epistle to the Galatians* fell into his hands — an old book, so tattered and thumb-worn "that it was ready to fall piece from piece if he did but turn it over." Here, in the work of that compassionate and mighty mind, he saw his own soul reflected as in a glass.

"I had but a little way perused it," he said, "when I found my condition in his experience so largely and profoundly handled as if his book had been written out of my heart."

In later life he thought it his duty to declare that he preferred this book of Martin Luther before all the books he had ever seen (the Bible, only, excepted), as fittest for a wounded conscience.

— From *450 True Stories from Church History,* by J. Vernon Jacobs. Wm. B. Eerdmans Publishing Co. Used by permission.

114
Cloud with Silver Lining

John Bunyan, the tinker of Bedford, who felt called to preach, and had to spend twelve years in prison for being a non-conformist, found that God could overrule even a disaster like that, for during those years of enforced leisure, *Pilgrim's Progress* was written, which has had a larger sale than any other religious book aside from the Bible.

— J. Vernon Jacobs

115
Humility

Spiritual pride has overtaken many Christians, but according to one who knew John Bunyan it was not true of the "Shakespeare among divines." The friend wrote, "The grace of God was magnified in him and by him and a rich anointing of the Spirit was upon him; and yet this great saint was always in his own eyes the chiefest of sinners and the poorest of saints."

116
Freedom Denied

Back in seventeenth century England there was little religious freedom. Preachers who were not members of the Church of England were not allowed to preach. John Bunyan, however, felt called to preach regardless of the law. And he went to prison because of his preaching. His faithful wife stood before the judges to plead for John's release. She was told that they would release him immediately if he would promise not to preach. "He dares not leave preaching," she answered, "so long as he can speak." When John was given the chance to leave prison on the condition he would not preach, he replied, "If you free me today, tomorrow I'll speak in the streets that all men have a right to worship

God as conscience guides them, and that the state has no right to tell them how to worship."

117
A Transformed Cell

While on a trip to England I visited the little town of Bedford. I went into an old jail where they said a man had been shut up for twelve years. Then I remembered that with his imagination he had left that jail, had gone down by a beautiful river, had walked through the woods and into the celestial city; he had lived among angels and the great men and women of the past; then he came back and got down on his knees on the cold stones and wrote out the story that more people have read than any other book in the world except the Bible — Bunyan's *Pilgrim's Progress*. Bunyan, with his imagination, had transformed his prison cell, and had given to the world an inspiration for Christian living such as it had never had before, except in the Bible.

— J. W. Brougher, Sr.

118
The Mercy of God

John Bunyan in later years often looked back on his youthful years and marveled at the grace and mercy of God. He was an ungodly youth, but as in Paul's case, God had a ministry for him. Two times he barely escaped drowning; once he was nearly bitten by a poisonous adder; a man who took his place in the army was killed while on sentinel duty. He saw the mercy of God, yet he did not yield his life to God. "Here," he said, "were judgments and mercy, but neither of them did awaken my soul to righteousness; wherefore I sinned still, and grew more and more rebellious against God, and careless of mine own salvation."

As one reads *Pilgrim's Progress* he sees Bunyan's own struggles and triumphs in the person of Christian on his way to the Celestial City. After Christian is seized with conviction, he leaves the City of Destruction, struggles through the Slough of Despond, tries to find help at Mr. Legality's, and then enters Wicket Gate where the burden of sin rolls away at the foot of the cross.

> The mercy of God is an ocean divine,
> A boundless and fathomless flood.

119
John Bunyan's Death

John Bunyan's death was brought on by exposure when he was engaged in an act of charity. A quarrel had broken out in a family at Reading with which Bunyan had some acquaintance. A father had taken some offence at his son, and threatened to disinherit him. Bunyan undertook a journey on horseback from Bedford to Reading in the hope of reconciling them. He succeeded, but at the cost of his life. Returning by way of London, he was overtaken on the road by a storm of rain, and was drenched before he could find shelter. The chill, falling on a constitution already weakened by illness, brought on fever. In ten days he was dead. His last words were: "Take me, for I come to Thee!"

— F. W. Boreham, *A Bunch of Everlastings*

JOHN BUNYAN SAID IT

120
The Wicked

When wicked persons have gone on in a course of sin, and find they have reason to fear the just judgment of God for their sins, they begin at first to wish that there were no God to punish them; then by degrees they persuade themselves that there is none; and then they set themselves to study for arguments to back their opinion.

— From *Visions of Heaven and Hell*

121
Suicide

I took a resolution to destroy myself, and in order thereunto, went out one morning to a near-by wood, where I intended to act this bloody tragedy. But methought I heard a secret whisper saying, "O Epenetus, plunge not thyself in everlasting misery to gratify thy soul's worst enemy. That fatal stroke thou art about to give, seals up thine own damnation. For if there be a God, as surely there is, how can you hope for mercy from Him when you thus willfully destroy His image?"

— From *Visions of Heaven and Hell*

122
Prayer

The best prayers have often more groans than words.

123
Victory over Death

My sword I shall give to him that shall succeed me in my pilgrimage, and my courage and skill to him that can get it. My marks and scars I carry with me, to be a witness for me that I have fought his battles who now will be my regarder. When the day that he must go hence was come, many accompanied him to the riverside, into which as he went he said: "Death where is thy sting?" And as he went down deeper he said: "Grave where is thy victory?" So he passed over, and all the trumpets sounded for him on the other side.

— From *Pilgrim's Progress*

124
Inward Peace

If we have not quiet in our minds, outward comfort will do no more for us than a golden slipper on a gouty foot.

125
Following the Lord

I have loved to hear my Lord spoken of, and wherever I have seen the print of His shoe in the earth, there have I coveted to put mine also.

126
Trouble a Servant

I never had in all my life so great an inlet into the Word of God as now [in prison]: those Scriptures that I saw nothing in before are made in this place and state to shine before me; Jesus Christ also was never more real and apparent than now. . . .

    I never knew what it was for God to stand by me at all times, and at every offer of Satan to afflict me, as I have found since I came in hither; for, lo! as fears have presented themselves, so have supports and encouragements; yea, when I have started even as it were at nothing else but my shadow, yet God, as being very tender of me, hath not suffered me to be molested, but would with one Scripture or another strengthen me against all; insomuch that I have often said, were it lawful I could pray for greater trouble for greater comfort sake.

127
Prayer

In prayer it is better to have a heart without words, than words without a heart.

128
Religion

Religion is the best armor that a man can have, but it is the worst cloak.

129
Song from the Valley of Humiliation

The Shepherd Boy Sings in the Valley of Humiliation

He that is down needs fear no fall,
    He that is low, no pride;
He that is humble ever shall
    Have God to be his guide.

I am content with what I have,
    Little be it or much;
And, Lord, contentment still I crave,
    Because Thou savest such.

Fullness to such a burden is
    That go on pilgrimage:
Here little, and hereafter bliss,
    Is best from age to age.

ANDREW CARNEGIE
(1835–1919)

Andrew Carnegie was one of America's wealthiest men. As a boy of thirteen, he left Dunfermline, Scotland, with his parents and settled near Pittsburgh. They were poor, and what formal education Andrew received was in Scotland. But he soon proved himself as a hard worker, learning to operate telegraph equipment and becoming an operator at seventeen. He later worked for the Penn Central Railroad. He made his millions in steel, and it is estimated that his fortune was as high as half a billion dollars. At his retirement he began to give away his fortune to support education, churches, public libraries, and the world peace movement. Today, his foundations still operate his philanthropic interests.

130
Youthful Initiative

Shortly after the Carnegie family moved to America, Andrew got a job in a telegraph office in Pittsburgh as a messenger. But the industrious youth was not content to deliver telegrams the rest of his life. In his spare time he studied telegraphy and became acquainted with the equipment. One of the responsibilities of a messenger was to clean the office each morning. The other boys disliked the chore, but Andrew enjoyed every minute of it because it gave him opportunity to learn more about the operation. Early one morning while several of the messengers were cleaning the office, a message came on the wire; but there was no operator on duty. Andrew sat down at the telegraph key and tapped out a reply that he would receive the message if it was sent slowly. When Andrew's boss heard about his initiative, he was greatly pleased. And he rewarded Andrew with a promotion to be a regular operator — plus a raise in pay from $13.50 a month to $20.

131
A Carnegie Proverb

Andrew Carnegie's first thirteen years were spent in Scotland, where he was born in 1835. His father had separated from the Presbyterian faith and attended a Swedenborgian congregation in their city of Dunfermline. As a result, Carnegie's early training did not include much of the Bible. It was to bring embarrassment to him on his first day of school when the school teacher called on each child to stand up and say a proverb from the Bible. When it came time for Andrew to stand, he did so proudly and recited one of his mother's personal proverbs: "Take care of your pence; the pounds will take care of themselves." In telling of the experience years later, Carnegie could not forget the teacher's glare and his schoolmates' giggles.

132
Where There's a Will...

Some of the things Andrew Carnegie learned as a boy indicate his business sense. One experience came when his father brought home two rabbits as a gift for his son. Mrs. Carnegie wasn't so pleased, as she could foresee a family of rabbits with little to feed them. Finally, Andrew was given permission to keep the pets, provided he find food for them. It wasn't long before his business acumen was demonstrated to his parents. Andrew promised several boys in the neighborhood that he would give their names to the rabbits if they would provide food for them. The arrangement satisfied everyone — Mrs. Carnegie, Andrew, the boys, and, of course, the rabbits.

133
Money Can't Buy Health

Andrew Carnegie, the multimillionaire, sat in a dining room in a swanky hotel. Before him was untouched food. His health was failing and his appetite was gone. He chanced to look out of a window and saw a working man sitting on a curbstone, heartily enjoying his noonday lunch. Exclaimed Carnegie: "I'd give a million dollars to have an appetite like that man!"

—Walter B. Knight

134
Divine Guidance

In his book *The Wilson Era,* Josephus Daniels, secretary of the navy under Wilson, relates how he once asked Andrew Carnegie what was the secret of his remarkable success. Carnegie replied, "I owe it all to my flashes."

Mystified, Daniels said, "What do you mean by 'flashes'?"

"All my life," replied Carnegie, "I woke up early in the morning, and always there came into my mind with the waking a flash telling me what to do that day, and if I followed those matin flashes, I always succeeded."

"You mean," said Daniels, "that you have heavenly visions, and like the man in the Scriptures you were not disobedient to your visions?"

"Call it that if you like," answered Carnegie, "or call it flashes; but it was the following of those silent admonitions and directions which brought me the success you say I have achieved."

Whatever may be said about the flashes in the business world, there is no doubt about flashes of divine impulse in the moral and spiritual world. When they come, happy is the man who, like Paul, is not disobedient to the heavenly vision.

—From *Macartney's Illustrations,* by Clarence E. Macartney. Copyright 1945 by Whitmore and Stone.

135
Negroes in West Point and Heaven

It didn't take long for immigrant Andrew Carnegie to form an opinion on the slavery question that was such a hot issue in the 1850s. He was an abolitionist and would defend the position whenever the topic arose. A Mrs. Wilkins, whose husband had been in President Tyler's cabinet, complained about the Negroes in the North having freedom. "Is it not disgraceful," she said, "Negroes admitted to West Point." Carnegie replied, "Oh, Mrs. Wilkins, there is something even worse than that. I understand that some of them have been admitted to heaven!" There was silence, and then Mrs. Wilkins said gravely: "That is a different matter, Mr. Carnegie."

136
Envy

A tacit rebuke is hidden in Mark Twain's remark to a man who was envying the good fortune of Andrew Carnegie.

"But after all," said the man in a superior tone, "like all these great fortunes, Carnegie's money is tainted."

"Yes," agreed Twain, " 'taint yours, and 'taint mine."

137
Out of Context

Just after Andrew Carnegie had agreed to donate a large sum of money to universities in Scotland, he told a story of a Sunday school collection. "Each scholar had to quote an appropriate text," the wealthy man began. "Number one toddles forward, puts down his dime with 'Blessed is he that considereth the poor.' Number two, with 'The Lord loveth a cheerful giver.' Then comes up number three, puts his dime in, and solemnly quotes his text, 'A fool and his money's soon parted!' "

138
A Vote Against Football

Andrew Carnegie in his retirement years was being bombarded daily by people who wanted to help share his great wealth. He had given millions to schools and had established libraries in the United States and in the British Isles. Woodrow Wilson, as president of Princeton University, was bent on getting Carnegie's help in establishing libraries, laboratories, and law schools on his campus. The philanthropist was invited to Princeton and shown about the campus. When it came time to leave, he thanked Wilson for the tour and said, "I know exactly what Princeton needs and I intend to give it to her." Wilson's excitement was difficult for him to hide. "What?" he eagerly asked. "It's a lake. Princeton should have a rowing crew to compete with Harvard, Yale, and Columbia." Wilson then tried hard not to hide his disappointment as Carnegie added, "That will take young men's minds off football." Carnegie, who thought football should be banned from colleges, was true to his word. Lake Carnegie was built at a cost of $400,000 — quite a fortune in the early 1900s. It was hardly a gift that helped higher education, but it was the old philanthropist's way of voting against the "bloody" game.

139
Duty and a Little More

Andrew Carnegie, the great industrialist and philanthropist, once addressed a graduating class in New York. "There are several classes of young men," he said. "There are those who do not do all their duty, there are those who profess to do their duty, and there is a third class, far better than the other two, that do their duty and a little more.

"There are many great pianists, but Paderewski is at the head because he does a little more than the others. There are hundreds of race horses, but it is those who go a few seconds faster than the others that acquire renown. So it is in the sailing of yachts. It is the little more that wins. So it is with the young and old men who do a little more than their duty. Do your duty and a little more, and the future will take care of itself."

140
Wealth Not Without Problems

Andrew Carnegie became known as one of the great philanthropists of all time. Up to the time of his death, Carnegie had given nearly three thousand public libraries to cities and towns across the United States, in Scotland, and even in such faraway places as the island of Fiji. Some felt he was doing too much: "Better for a community to do for itself"; others thought he was not doing enough: "A building without books is not a library," they complained. In 1873 he donated an organ to a small church. By the time of his death in 1919 he had given 7,689 organs — at a cost of over six million dollars. It actually became a big business. It kept two men busy full time answering mail and deciding which churches should be granted the free organs. A British syrup concern even ran a contest on "How Mr. Carnegie Should Get Rid of His Wealth." Some forty-five thousand suggestions were submitted (about one in four was a personal request for part of the tremendous fortune). It isn't known just how the contest affected Carnegie's giving. But one thing he did find out: it isn't easy to systematically give away three hundred million dollars. He finally established a foundation to manage the business of philanthropy; it had gotten too big for him. He soon tired of giving away his wealth. He wrote one friend, "You have no idea the strain I have been under." And in Scotland where he was giving a speech, he departed from his prepared text to confess, "Millionaires who laugh are rare, very rare, indeed."

ANDREW CARNEGIE SAID IT

141
Youth and Opportunity

One evening early in 1850, when I returned home from work, I was told that Mr. David Brooks, manager of the telegraph office, had asked my Uncle Hogan if he knew where a good boy could be found to act as messenger. . . . My uncle mentioned my name and said he would see whether I would take the position. I remember so well the family council that was held. Of course I was wild with delight. No bird that ever was confined in a cage longed for freedom more than I. . . . And that is how in 1850 I got my first real start in life. From the dark cellar of the textile factory, I was lifted into paradise, yes, heaven, as it seemed to me, with newspapers, pens, pencils, and sunshine about me. There was scarcely a minute in which I could not learn or find out how much there was to learn and how little I knew. I felt that my foot was upon the ladder and that I was bound to climb.

— *The Autobiography of Andrew Carnegie*

142
Honor

No amount of ability is of the slightest avail without honor.

143
Prerequisite for Influence

The paper which obtains a reputation for publishing authentic news and only that which is fit to print . . . will steadily increase its influence.

144
Must Be Willing

There is no use whatever trying to help people who do not help themselves. You cannot push anyone up a ladder unless he be willing to climb himself.

145
Success

I believe the true road to preeminent success in any line is to make yourself master of that line.

146
Watch That Basket

Put all good eggs in one basket and then watch that basket.

147
Motto

Concentration is my motto — first honesty, then industry then concentration.

148
Courage of Convictions

The country is fortunate that boasts a class of men which rises on occasion superior to party. . . . To be popular is easy; to be right when right is unpopular is noble. . . . I repudiate with scorn the immoral doctrine, "Our country, right or wrong."

149
Wealth

Surplus wealth is a sacred trust which its possessor is bound to administer in his lifetime for the good of the community.

— From *Gospel of Wealth*

GEORGE WASHINGTON CARVER
(1859?–1943)

An American Negro and the son of a slave, George Washington Carver won international fame in agriculture research, developing products from such crops as peanuts, sweet potatoes, and pecans. He was born on a farm near Diamond Grove, Missouri (now a national mounment), and later through sheer industry and the help of friends, was able to study at Simpson College in Iowa. He graduated from Iowa State College in 1894, remaining at the school as an assistant botanist. Booker T. Washington invited him to join the faculty of Tuskegee Institute in 1896. He accepted the challenge and remained there for the rest of his life.

150
He Ain't Worth Nothin'

It is almost unbelievable that slavery was practiced in the United States up through the mid-nineteenth century. But it is a fact, a sad fact. Mary Carver was one of those caught in the web of slavery. She was the slave of Moses Carver in southwest Missouri.

A cruel gang rode into the Carver farm one winter evening and carried off Mary and two of her children. The next day Moses Carver hired a man to find and bring back Mary and the children. Six long days passed before the man returned. He related that he never did catch up with the gang. Then he pulled a bundle from under his coat. It was Mary's baby, more dead than alive. The man explained that the gang intended to sell Mary in Mississippi and didn't want to be bothered with the sick baby. "They just give him to some womenfolks down by Conway [Arkansas]," the man said. "He ain't worth nothin'."

The baby that "ain't worth nothin'" survived and grew up to be George Washington Carver, a man whose worth could never be measured by earth's standards.

151
God Had a Work for Him

From the day young George Carver learned there was such an institution as a school, he was determined to attend. Even when he found out it was limited to white children, he would not give up. He was determined to find a school that would accept him. He found it in Neosho, Missouri, a town about eight miles from the Carver farm. At about age fourteen he said good-bye to the Carvers and his brother Jim and walked toward Neosho. He had no place to stay, but providentially he met a colored lady, Mariah Watkins, a washerwoman and midwife. She and her husband had no children of their own but often took in the homeless to give them a chance in life. She thought the boy from Diamond Grove deserved a chance, so she took him in. It was a chapter in George's life that would influence all the others. George tried to express his gratitude in his stammering way: "I was mighty l-lucky, picking your yard to s-set in," he told Mariah. Mariah stopped what she was doing. "Luck had nothing to do with it, boy," she said. "God brought you to my yard. He has work for you, and He wants Andrew and me to lend a hand."

Mariah couldn't possibly realize at that moment to what extent her prophecy would be fulfilled.

152
He Had a Burning Zeal

When George Washington Carver was befriended by Dr. and Mrs. Milholland at Winterset, Iowa, it gave him an opportunity to enroll at Simpson College at Indianola. It was 1890 and George had roamed around the midwest for some ten years with no apparent direction to his life. Simpson College changed that.

In one sense, George had little when he enrolled at Simpson; but he had something more than the eye could see. A teacher summed it up: "He came to Indianola with a satchel full of poverty and a burning zeal to know everything." In 1894 he graduated near the top of his class, and he had the long sought Bachelor of Science degree. Little did those assembled on commencement day realize that George would go on to become the most famous alumnus in the school's history.

153
He Accepted the Challenge

George Washington Carver often looked back on his life to remind himself of God's leading. One of those times came after he had earned his master's degree and was on the faculty at what is now Iowa State University at Ames. He was determined to help his people, but didn't know how or where. In an Alabama town some eight hundred miles away, Booker T. Washington, the president of a struggling Negro college, sat down and wrote a letter to Carver, a letter that would weigh heavily on Carver's mind until he agreed to join Washington at Tuskegee. "I cannot offer you money, position, or fame," Washington confessed in the letter. "The first two you have. The last, from the place you now occupy, you will no doubt achieve. These things I now ask you to give up. I offer you in their place work — hard, hard work — the task of bringing a people from degradation, poverty, and waste to full manhood."

Carver accepted Washington's challenge. He moved to Tuskegee Institute, believing it was God's plan for his life.

154
Together We Got Down to Work

When George Washington Carver went to Tuskegee in 1896, he knew that the farmers of the South needed more than cotton. He convinced them that the peanut would be a good alternate crop. But soon it became evident that there was no market for the peanut. The farmers were indignant. Carver was beside himself; he needed a solution for the surplus. Later, he told in his own inimitable way of the help he received early one morning in the woods.

"Oh, Mr. Creator, why did You make this universe?" I cried. And the Creator answered me. "You want to know too much for that little mind of yours," He said. "Ask me something more your size." So I said, "Dear Mr. Creator, tell me what man was made for." Again He spoke to me, and He said, "Little man, you are still asking for more than you can handle. Cut down the extent of your request and improve the intent." And then I asked my last question. "Mr. Creator, why did You make the peanut?" "That's better!" the Lord said, and He gave me a handful of peanuts and went with me back to the laboratory and, together, we got down to work.

Before Carver died in 1943, there were well over three hundred products made from the little peanut — mayonnaise, instant coffee, cheese, chili sauce, shampoo, polish, plastics, and many, many more. "Together, we got down to work."

155
Money Isn't Everything

It seems hard to imagine that a son of a slave would be offered a job at one hundred thousand dollars a year. And it seems incredible that the same man would turn the offer down. But that is what happened to George Washington Carver. The offer was made by the famous inventor, Thomas Edison. And Henry Ford tried to persuade Carver to become a scientist for the Ford Motor Company. But Carver, unimpressed with the offers of money and prestige, chose to live in the South, living in relative poverty, wearing the same suit for forty years. He had already given up a promising position at Iowa State University to work with Booker T. Washington and his struggling Tuskegee Institute. When friends chided him for turning down the big salaries, Carver always had an answer for them. They argued that he could help his people if he had all that money. Carver invariably replied, "If I had all that money I might forget about my people."

And on his tombstone were carved fitting words: "He could have added fortune to fame, but caring for neither, he found happiness and honor in being helpful to the world."

156
They Couldn't Fool Carver

It was generally accepted that Professor Carver could identify any plant they [Tuskegee students] brought in, whether he had seen it before or not, but his entomology class once rashly tried to hoodwink him. They produced a bug neatly pinned to a piece of a cardboard and laid it on his desk.

"We just found this strange bug, professor. What is it?"

He looked long at the curious creature. It had the head of a large ant, the body of a beetle, the legs of a spider, the antennae of a moth, all ingeniously put togetheer. Finally he delivered his pronouncement, "Well, this, I think, is what we would call a humbug."

He liked pupils to do such things, and was delighted with the imagination that had fathered the hoax.

— Rackham Holt, *George Washington Carver*

157
Wisdom Came from the Book

Dr. Carver urged his people in the South to plant crops besides cotton, for if that crop failed all was lost. . . . He discovered how to make oils, varnishes, colorings, medicines, and hundreds of other things from peanuts. He was invited to testify before a Senate Committee, and there he was asked, "Dr. Carver, how did you learn all these things?" He replied, "From an old Book." The chairman asked, "What book?" He said, "The Bible." He was asked, "Does the Bible tell about peanuts?" He answered, "No, Mr. Senator, but it tells about the God who made the peanut. I asked Him to show me what to do with the peanut, and He did."

— Christian Life

158
Kindness Key to Race Relations

Although George Washington Carver received honors from presidents down, he nevertheless had to endure racial prejudice. It wasn't often that he spoke out on the subject. Once, however, a group of ministers asked him what they could do to improve race relations. That gave Carver a chance to say what he felt. "Your actions speak so loud I cannot hear what you are saying." The men, probably not expecting such frankness from Carver, knew, however, that Carver was speaking words that were too often the truth. "You have too much religion," he continued, "and not enough Christianity — too many creeds and not enough performance. This world is perishing for kindness."

159
A Perfect Blend

Tributes to George Washington Carver are almost unending. No doubt the peanut would speak in praise of the former slave if it could. One man who had the privilege of being close to Dr. Carver was Dr. Frederick D. Patterson, president of Tuskegee Institute during Carver's last years. Patterson was high in his praise. "His humility of spirit and simplicity of manner were as disarming as his keen intellect and wide ranging knowledge were a source of inspiration and challenge. These impressions were of a Dr. Carver, fully mature and renowned because of his discoveries and a life-long dedication of service to his fellowman through the practical applications of science. At this stage his life had become an almost perfect blend of the spiritual, the artistic, and the scientific."

Dr. Patterson told of the relationship between Booker T. Washington, the founder of Tuskegee, and Carver: "Though highly diverse in personality and talent, [they] found a common meeting ground in their dedication to the erasure of human want. Thus Carver's work became in the fullest sense the practical implementation of Booker Washington's philosophy."

> — From the book *George Washington Carver: The Man Who Overcame,* by Lawrence Elliott. © 1966 by Lawrence Elliott. Reprinted with permission of the publisher, Prentice-Hall, Inc., Englewood Cliffs, New Jersey.

160
Divine Direction

Said Dr. George Washington Carver, "There is no need for anyone to be without direction in the midst of the perplexities of this life. Are we not plainly told, 'In all thy ways acknowledge him, and he shall direct thy path'?" It was Dr. Carver's custom to arise every day at four a.m. and seek God's guidance for his life. In speaking of the blessings of those early morning hours, he said, "At no other time have I so sharp an understanding of what God means to do with me as in those hours when other folks are still asleep. Then I hear God best and learn His plan!"

— Walter B. Knight

GEORGE WASHINGTON CARVER SAID IT

161
Prayer

My prayers seem to be more of an attitude than anything else. I indulge in very little lip service, but ask the Great Creator silently, daily, and often many times a day, to permit me to speak to Him through the three great Kingdoms of the world which He has created — the animal, mineral, and vegetable Kingdoms — to understand their relations to each other, and our relations to them and to the Great God Who made all of us. I ask Him daily and often momently to give me wisdom, understanding, and bodily strength to do His will; hence I am asking and receiving all the time.

162
Only Two Ways

There are only two ways: one is right and the other is wrong. About is always wrong. Don't tell me it's *about* right. If it's only *about* right, then it's wrong. If you come to a stream five feet wide and jump four and a half feet you fall in and get drowned. You might just as well have tumbled in from the other side and saved yourself the exertion of the jump.

— To his students at Tuskegee

163
Excuses

Ninety-nine percent of the failures come from people who have the habit of making excuses.

164
Nature Speaks

I love to think of nature as an unlimited broadcasting station, through which God speaks to us every hour, if we only will tune in.

165
Sowing and Reaping

I feel most strongly that we have no right to ask God to change fixed laws of the universe. If we plant oats, we must expect to harvest oats and not corn or beans. If we sow hate and wrongdoing in our lives, we must expect to reap the awful results.

166
Secret of Success

The secret of my success? It is simple. It is found in the Bible, "In all thy ways acknowledge him, and he shall direct thy paths."

167
Testing Under Fire

A race that will not prove itself indispensable when the world is in a crisis does not deserve and need not look for recognition in times of peace and prosperity.

168
Discoverer's Trials

The discoverer must pass through three stages at least, each of which is important and quite natural. The first is the "knocking" stage. Any new article offered to the public must meet certain hostile critics who say, "This thing is not good. . . ." Then follows a stage of total apathy, when everybody apparently conspires to remain silent. . . . However, there always comes to a really valuable and significant discovery that interesting third stage — a stage in which many people, including the former critics and apathetic observers, tumble over each other trying to boost the discoverer, his discovery, and everything connected with the project.

169
Body a Temple

Your body is the Creator's dwelling place. Surely you would not want a landlord who represents everything good to be seated in an untidy house.

If God had intended the human nose to be used for a chimney, He would have turned our nostrils up.

170
Freedom

You must not let the haters of this world divert you from the path of your own duty. For the time will come when the haters will have been consumed by their own hatred and the ignorant will have learned the truth. And then, if you are prepared for it, you will walk the earth as free men, the equal of any other man.

— To students at Tuskegee

SIR WINSTON CHURCHILL
(1874–1965)

Twice the prime minister of Great Britain (1940-45, 1951-55), Sir Winston Churchill was one of the greatest statesmen in world history. The world remembers him primarily for his heroic service as prime minister during World War II. The odds against Britain in the early days of the war were high, but Churchill was an inspirational leader and brought his country back from almost certain defeat. Churchill also was a noted speaker, author, painter, soldier, and war reporter. He served in Parliament from 1901 to 1922, then from 1924 until his retirement in 1964. In 1963, Congress made Churchill an honorary citizen of the United States. (Note: Do not confuse his name with American writer Winston Churchill, 1871-1947, who wrote historical novels.)

171
Price Too Low

Winston Churchill achieved national prominence through his activities in the Boer War at the age of twenty-five. He was taken prisoner, but two weeks later he escaped. His enemies hunted him and even set a price on his head. Handbills were distributed that described the young soldier, journalist, and adventurer: "Englishman, 25 years old, about five feet eight inches tall, indifferent build, walks with a forward stoop, pale appearance, red-brownish hair, small and hardly noticeable mustache, talks through his nose and cannot pronounce the letter *s* properly."

Churchill didn't seem to mind the less than complimentary description, but he did resent the fact that the price on his head was only twenty-five pounds! Evidently the folks at home thought the assessment low, too, because his exploits became widely known and he was heralded as a national hero and later won a seat in Parliament.

172
He Would Drink the Poison

The battles between Winston Churchill and the American-born Lady Astor were long and often furious. Lady Astor, born Nannie Langhorn in Danville, Virginia, had a seat in the House of Commons. One day she was exceptionally furious at Winston and roared at him, "If I were your wife, I would put poison in your coffee." To which Churchill replied with dignity, "And if I were your husband, I would drink it."

173
A Phony Peace

It has often been said that Winston Churchill made history, wrote history, and at times even predicted history. His predictions of Hitler's ambition as far back as 1934 made him unpopular among his own countrymen. One writer during the period said, "Winston Churchill remains the most brilliant failure of political history — a man who could not pick a winner with only one horse in the race."

After Prime Minister Chamberlain capitulated to Hitler at Munich but calling it "peace in our time," a member of Parliament declared that Chamberlain would "go down to history as the greatest European statesman of this or any other time." Winston Churchill and time were to make it a poor prophecy. Through a storm of protests Churchill said, "I will begin by saying what everybody would like to ignore or forget but which must nevertheless be stated, namely, that we have sustained a total and unmitigated defeat, and that France has suffered even more than we have."

Britons later were to know the agony of the Chamberlain capitulation and be thankful that in the wings they had Winston Churchill, "the most brilliant failure of political history."

174
Winston Is Back

At sixty-five, Winston Churchill was asked to take over the British navy; and when he accepted, every unit of the British fleet received a welcome message, "Winston is back!" A few months later Prime Minister Chamberlain was compelled to step down and the king asked Churchill to form a coalition government. The rest is history.

175
You Look Healthy Enough

At the age of seventy-seven, in 1951, Winston Churchill was elected prime minister for the second time. Some of his enemies — and he had more than a few — were worried that he would live forever. Perhaps Churchill himself believed it. A news cameraman taking his picture called out, "I shall photograph you on your hundredth birthday, sir!" Winston barked back, "I see no reason why you shouldn't, young man. You look healthy enough."

176
He Gave It the Roar

Winston Churchill celebrated his eightieth birthday in November 1954. The prime minister was honored in Westminster Hall by lords and commons. Clement Attlee, himself a former deputy prime minister under Churchill during World War II and later prime minister, in his speech declared that his purpose on the occasion was "not to bury Caesar but to praise him." Geoffrey Bocca told how the great leader responded.

"Churchill rose, slowly now with his years, and his listeners were seized by that old tingling of the senses which they used to feel while waiting for him to speak during the dark days of the war. They were not disappointed. 'I have never accepted,' he said modestly, his S's slurring in the old way, 'what many people have kindly said, namely that I inspired the nation. Their will was resolute and remorseless, and, as it proved, unconquerable. It fell to me to express it and if I found the right words you must remember that I have always earned my living by my pen and by my tongue. It was the nation and the race dwelling all around the globe that had the lion's heart . . . ' — and now the great Churchillian boom was heard again with the resounding echo of 1940 — 'I had the luck to be called on to give the r-o-a-r.' "

— From *The Adventurous Life of Winston Churchill*

177
Shaw and Churchill Exchange Barbs

Bernard Shaw once sent Churchill two tickets for the opening of one of his plays with a note: "Come to the first night and bring a friend — if you have a friend." To which Churchill acidly replied: "Am too busy to come to the opening, but will be there the second night — if there is a second night."

178
Gratitude

The story is told of an ambassador who was in a conversation with Sir Winston Churchill. "You know, Sir Winston, I've never told you about my grandchildren." Whereupon Sir Winston clapped him on the shoulder and replied, "I realize it, my dear fellow, and I can't tell you how grateful I am!"

179
Never Defeated

When one thinks of great leaders of the twentieth century, he must of necessity include Sir Winston Churchill near the top, if not at the top of the list. President Richard Nixon, who was an unknown navy officer when Churchill was leading Britain during World War II, expressed great admiration for him. "Churchill, I suppose, is the world leader I most admire. He was never defeated; he was knocked down, and he came back, and it happened repeatedly, the last time at seventy-seven. And he was such a complete man — such an indomitable spirit."

WINSTON CHURCHILL SAID IT

180
Never Surrender

We shall go on to the end, we shall fight in France, we shall fight on the seas and oceans, we shall fight with growing confidence and growing strength in the air, we shall defend our Island whatever the cost may be, we shall fight on the landing grounds, we shall fight in the fields and in the streets, we shall fight in the hills; we shall never surrender, and even if, which I do not for a moment believe, this Island or a large part of it were subjugated and starving, then our Empire beyond the seas, armed and guarded by the British Fleet, would carry on the struggle, until, in God's good time, the New World, with all its power and might steps forth to the rescue and the liberation of the old.

— Speech, June 4, 1940

181
Finest Hour

Let us therefore brace ourselves to our duties, and so bear ourselves that, if the British Empire and its Commonwealth last for a thousand years, men will still say, "This was their finest hour."

— Speech, June 18, 1940

182
No Easy Road

I have nothing to offer but blood, toil, tears, and sweat.

— Speech, May 28, 1940

183
Debt to Air Force (RAF)

Never in the field of human conflict was so much owed by so many to so few.

184
Criticism

If the present criticizes the past, there is not much hope for the future.

185
Blessings and Misery

Capitalism is the unequal distribution of blessings. Socialism is the equal distribution of misery.

186
Eating Words

Eating words has never given me indigestion.

187
Courage

Courage is the first of human qualities because it is the quality which guarantees all the others.

188
A Call for Duty and Dedication

Long, dark months of trials and tribulations lie before us. Not only great dangers, but many more misfortunes, many shortcomings, many mistakes, many disappointments will surely be our lot. Death and sorrow will be the companions of our journey; hardship our garment; constancy and valor our only shield. We must be united, we must be undaunted, we must be inflexible. Our qualities and deeds must burn and glow through the gloom of Europe until they become the veritable beacon of its salvation.

—Speech, October 8, 1940

189
Fanatic

A fanatic is one who can't change his mind and won't change the subject.

190
Ready to Learn

Personally I am always ready to learn, although I do not always like being taught.

191
Plans Alone Not Enough

Any clever person can make plans for winning a war if he has no responsibility for carrying them out.

192
Best for the World

It is better to have a world united than a world divided; but it is also better to have a world divided than a world destroyed.

193
United to Defeat the Enemy

No one has been a more consistent opponent of Communism than I have been for the last twenty-five years. I will unsay no word that I have spoken about it. But all this fades away before the spectacle which is now unfolding. I see the Russian soldiers standing on the threshold of their native land, guarding the fields which their fathers have tilled from time immemorial. . . . Can you doubt what our policy will be? We are resolved to destroy Hitler and every vestige of the Nazi regime. . . . We will never parley, we will never negotiate with Hitler or any of his gang. We shall fight him by land, we shall fight him by sea, we shall fight him in the air, until, with God's help, we have rid the earth of his shadow and liberated its peoples from his yoke. Any man or state who fights on against Nazidom will have our aid.

—A broadcast the day after Germay attacked Russia

194
Gratitude Missing

At the outset of this mighty battle, I acquired the chief power in the State, which henceforth I wielded in ever-growing measure for five years and three months of world war, at the end of which, all our enemies having surrendered unconditionally or being about to do so, I was immediately dismissed by the British electorate from all further conduct of their affairs.

CHARLES DICKENS
(1812–1870)

Charles John Huffam Dickens was an English novelist of the nineteenth century — one of the greatest in history. His writings are still popular today, over a hundred years after his death. Dickens was a keen observer of life and had the ability to express his observations in his novels, which resulted in some of the most famous characters of literature. Many of the events of his own life are portrayed in his books. His career began as a newspaper reporter in the late 1820s. He was also a noted magazine editor as well as a successful writer. He is best remembered today for his books A Christmas Carol, David Copperfield, Oliver Twist, *and* A Tale of Two Cities.

195
Greed

Dickens' *A Christmas Carol,* the beloved story about stingy, crabby old Ebenezer Scrooge, who was reformed by three dream experiences, is the favorite of many at the Yuletide season. Scrooge, the surviving member of the firm of Scrooge and Marley, refused to celebrate Christmas, to give any donation to the poor, and in general was as disagreeable and ill-tempered as a man could be. After unwillingly granting Bob Cratchit, his poorly paid clerk, the Christmas holiday, he went to his lonely rooms to spend the night. There everything reminded him of his deceased miserly partner, Jacob Marley; and suddenly he saw Jacob's ghost, who told him of his own regret for the selfish life he had lived. Then in the night three spirits came one at a time to Scrooge. The first, the Spirit of Christmas Past, reminded him of his youth before he became miserly. The second, the Spirit of Christmas Present, among other scenes, showed him how bravely the Cratchits were keeping Christmas. The third was the Spirit of Christmas Yet to Come; he showed Scrooge his own death and burial, unmourned by anyone, Tiny Tim's absence from his family, and other gloomy eventualities. Then Scrooge awakened and found it was still Christmas morning. Joyfully he sent a turkey to the Cratchits, went to church and gave generously to the poor fund, and then went to dinner at his nephew's home. The next day he raised Bob's salary, and from then on looked after the Cratchits, and everybody agreed he knew how to keep Christmas if anybody did.

— Amy L. Person, in *Illustrations from Literature*

196
Pride and Money

Mr. Dombey, in Dickens's *Dombey and Son,* is a proud London merchant who looks forward to the day he will have a son who will come into partnership with him in his business. Little Paul, the long-awaited son, was born; but his mother died at his birth. Even as a small child Paul could see his father's pride in the business and his preoccupation with making money. Dickens portrays Mr. Dombey's main interest in life and Paul's insight.

"Papa, what's money?"
. . . Mr. Dombey was quite disconcerted.
"What is money, Paul?" he answered, "Money?"
"Yes," said the child laying his hands upon the elbows of his little chair, and turning the old face up towards Mr. Dombey's; "what is money?"
Mr. Dombey . . . would have liked to give him some explanation involving the terms circulating-medium, . . . bullion, rates of exchange, value of precious metals in the market and so forth; but looking down at the little chair and seeing what a long way down it was, he answered: "Gold, and silver, and copper. Guineas, shillings, half-pence. You know what they are?"
"Oh yes, I know what they are," said Paul. "I don't mean that, papa. I mean what's money after all? . . . What can it do?"
. . . "Money, Paul, can do anything." Mr. Dombey replied.

It is then that Paul counters with the unanswerable question, "Why didn't money save me my mamma?"

Money could not save little Paul either, as Mr. Dombey later found. In a scene filled with pathos, Paul dies; and in spite of a second marriage there is never another son to satisfy the desire of the materialistic and proud Mr. Dombey.

197
The Mercy of God

Before Charles Dickens was twelve years of age, his father was thrown into the debtors' prison, a prison of that day for those who could not pay their debts. Young Charles had ambitions to go to grammar school and a university, but he was forced to obtain employment at his young age. He was hired to stick labels on the jars of blacking, not a difficult job but a monotonous one. Mrs. Dickens found a room for him in a lodging house, and Charles started life on his own in a poor section of London. He was ill fed and poorly clothed and associated with rough companions.

As he later described in *Oliver Twist,* young boys were often dragged into the London underworld and trained to be pickpockets and thieves. Somehow he was spared that fate. "But for the mercy of God," he said, "I might easily have been, for any care that was taken of me, a little robber, a little vagabond."

Later, Charles's father was released from prison, the family was reunited, and Charles was delivered from the blacking warehouse and given the opportunity to resume his schooling.

But for the mercy of God all of us would have little to live for and little to offer humanity.

198
His Heart in the Right Place

Dickens (like Shelley) had a "passion for reforming the world." He attacked public wrongdoing and private sin. He wrote about the wretched lives led by the poor. He laughed at the pompousness of snobs and social climbers. He wrote often and with great compassion of the miserable existences of orphans and workhouse children. He cheered virtue wherever he found it. In all of his writings, Dickens' heart was in the right place. That is a great deal.

—Charles Haines, in *Charles Dickens*

199
A Blood-Thirsty Crowd

A terrified murderer named Francois Couvoisier was dragged to a hangman's noose in England. It was 1840 and the execution of criminals was still a public event in England and in other countries of the world. When the unfortunate Couvoisier appeared, spectators crowded as close as possible, shouting for the blood of the murderer. Couvoisier was dragged closer and closer to the rope and the trapdoor that would end his life. He was naturally terrified; he tried to pray. But the savage crowd shouted abuse and obscenities at him. When the rope broke Couvoisier's neck, a great bloodthirsty roar could be heard several blocks away.

In the crowd that day was a young writer, Charles Dickens. He was troubled greatly at what he saw. He had questions concerning capital punishment. But more than that, he knew making a circus of an execution was wrong. He saw a mob of spectators that gave no evidence of sorrow or fear or sympathy. They acted as if they were at their favorite sporting event and their team had just captured a championship.

Years later, because of public outrage, such executions were branded as savage and brutal spectacles. They were discontinued.

Charles Dickens and others had won a battle.

200
All That Glitters...

A Christmas Carol is one of the most popular writings of all time. Count Leo Tolstoy, the Russion novelist, considered it to be an example of the very highest of art — art "flowing from God and man." It made Charles Dickens even more famous — and he was already the most celebrated novelist alive. But all was not well.

Dickens's earnings were only half what he thought they would be. And to make matters worse, a small publishing company had printed *A Christmas Carol* illegally. Dickens applied for a court injunction to stop them from printing and selling the book. When the injunction was granted, Dickens sued for damages. But the small printing firm promptly filed bankruptcy. That left Dickens without recourse; and more than that, he had to pay all court costs, amounting to several hundreds of dollars.

Charles Dickens was learning the truth of Shakespeare's line in *Merchant of Venice,* "All that glitters is not gold."

201
He Died for Another

Charles Dickens's moving and powerful historical novel, <u>*A Tale of Two Cities,*</u> ends with Sydney Carton giving his life for the man who had won the love of the girl he hoped to marry. Few can read about Carton's death without being profoundly moved. Few can read it without being reminded of Christ who died for mankind.

The setting was during the French Revolution. Carton loved Lucie Manette, but she did not love him; she broke his heart and married Charles Darnay Evremonde. Darnay Evremonde was arrested and sentenced to death, although he was innocent of the charges. Carton, learning of the situation of his former rival, bribed his way into Darnay's cell. He drugged Darnay, changed clothes with him, and had him carried from the prison and safely back to Lucie.

The heroic acts in the plan to save Darnay from the guillotine are inspiring. But then Carton became Darnay's substitute and died in his place.

Before the mass execution that day a poor little seamstress, who was also scheduled to die, approached Carton. She knew Evremonde and realized Carton was in his place. "Are you dying for him?" she whispered. Carton confessed that he was. The novel ends with a line that has become one of the most famous in literature: "It is a far, far better thing that I do, than I have ever done; it is a far, far better rest that I go to, than I have ever known."

202
Pride

The characters in the novels of Charles Dickens are vivid and extremely lifelike. Dickens knew human nature and could portray it in a novel as nobody else could. He hated smugness, narrowmindedness, pompousness, and false pride. He seemed to sum up those characteristics in Mr. Podsnap in *Our Mutual Friend*, his last complete novel.

> Mr. Podsnap was well to do, and stood very high in Mr. Podsnap's opinion. Beginning with a good inheritance, he had married a good inheritance, and had thriven exceedingly in the Marine Insurance way, and was quite satisfied. He never could make out why everybody was not quite satisfied, and he felt conscious that he set a brilliant social example in being particularly well satisfied with most things, and, above all other things, with himself.

Some people think Dickens was portraying one of his associates in Mr. Podsnap. True or not, Dickens was portraying human pride of his day — and ours as well.

203
Forgiveness

William Makepeace Thackeray and Charles Dickens, toward the middle of the nineteenth century, became rivals and estranged. Just before Christmas, 1863, they met in London, and frigidly failed to recognize each other. Thackeray turned back, seized the hand of Dickens and said he could no longer bear the coldness that existed between them. Dickens was touched; they parted with smiles. The old jealousy was destroyed. Almost immediately afterward Thackeray suddenly died. Sir Thomas Martin later wrote, "The next time I saw Dickens he was looking down into the grave of his great rival. He must have rejoiced, I thought, that they had shaken hands so warmly a day or so before." Is it not always well to seek forgiveness now? Are we sure that another opportunity will be afforded?

—Jacob J. Braude, *The Speaker's Desk Book of Quips, Quotes, and Anecdotes*

CHARLES DICKENS SAID IT

204
Affection

Mature affection, homage, devotion, does not easily express itself. Its voice is low. It is modest and retiring, it lays in ambush and waits. Such is the mature fruit. Sometimes a life glides away, and finds it still ripening in the shade. The light inclinations of very young people are as dust compared to rocks.

205
Blessings

Reflect upon your present blessings, of which every man has many: not on your past misfortunes, of which all men have some.

206
Children

I love these little people; and it is not a slight thing, when they, who are so fresh from God, love us.

207
Cynics

It will generally be found that those who sneer habitually at human nature, and affect to despise it, are among its worst and least pleasant samples.

208
Dishonesty

I have known a vast quantity of nonsense talked about bad men not looking you in the face. Don't trust that idea. Dishonesty will stare honesty out of countenance any day in the week, if there is anything to be got by it.

209
Forgiveness

May I tell you why it seems to me a good thing for us to remember wrong that has been done us? That we may forgive it.

210
Charity and Justice

Charity begins at home, and justice begins next door.

211
Credit

Credit: A person who can't pay, gets another person who can't pay, to guarantee that he can pay.

212
Women Aging

She still aims at youth, though she shot beyond it years ago.

213
Books

There are books of which the backs and covers are by far the best parts.

214
Idleness

The first external revelations of the dry rot in men is a tendency to lurk and lounge; to be at street corners without intelligible reason; to be going anywhere when met; to be about many places rather than any; to do nothing tangible but to have an intention of performing a number of tangible duties tomorrow or the day after.

215
Immortality

The old, old fashion — death! Oh, thank God, all who see it, for that older fashion yet — of immortality!

216
Sunday Religion

There is a Sunday conscience, as well as a Sunday coat; and those who make religion a secondary concern put the coat and conscience carefully by to put on only once a week.

217
Mob Action

A mob is usually a creature of very mysterious existence, particularly in a large city. Where it comes from, or whither it goes, few men can tell. Assembling and dispersing with equal suddenness, it is as difficult to follow to its various sources as the sea itself; nor does the parallel stop here, for the ocean is not more fickle and uncertain, more terrible when roused, more unreasonable or more cruel.

218
The Quiet Life

Anything for a quiet life, as the man said when he took the situation at the lighthouse.

219
Accidents

Accidents will occur in the best regulated families.

220
Gentleman

Once a gentleman, always a gentleman.

221
Virtue

Virtue shows quite as well in rags and patches, as she does in purple and fine linen.

222
Better Than Gold

I would rather have the affectionate regard of my fellowmen than I would have heaps and mines of gold.

WALT DISNEY
(1901–1966)

For forty years Walt Disney entertained in comic books, cartoons, films, and television. Mickey Mouse and Donald Duck gave him his first fame. Disney was born in Chicago but grew up in Missouri. After serving with the Red Cross in France immediately following World War I, he became a commercial artist in Kansas City. His family films won many Academy Awards. Disneyland, a 180-acre amusement park in California, was opened in 1955; and Disney World, a similar park in Florida, was opened in 1971.

223
Hidden Dangers

Walt Disney was walking home from delivering papers one night in Kansas City. It was winter and he kicked aimlessly at chunks of ice along his path. On his feet he had a new pair of boots that his parents had given him for Christmas. He could send the chunks of ice skidding along the sidewalk with a hefty kick with his new boots. After one kick he tried to pull his foot away from a chunk of ice that didn't budge. It wouldn't come free. A nail frozen into the ice had gone through his new boot and was sticking into his big toe. It was painful, and every time he tried to pull the ice chunk free, the more painful it became. After twenty minutes in his painful situation, a man heard his calls for help. He ran to Walt's side, saw the problem, then broke the ice loose. He then dashed away for a doctor. The doctor ordered two people to sit on Walt's legs while he pulled the nail free with a pair of pliers. The pain was difficult to bear, but even worse for Walt was that his boot had to be sliced away from his foot. It took two weeks to recover from the freak accident, but it was a long time before Walt gave up thinking about the ruined boot.

224
How to Get an Informal Education

Walt Disney's formal education was only through the ninth grade. It was wartime, and he dropped out of school in order to join the navy. But he was turned down because he was too young. Then he joined the Red Cross ambulance corps, eventually going to France.

Walt didn't let the lack of a formal education keep him from learning and doing things. He used to say that he would find the person who knew something about the subject he was interested in and begin to ask questions. "I've never yet found anybody who knew a thing who wouldn't drop whatever he was doing and try to help me if I went to him and said, 'I know nothing about your specialty but I'd like to know about it.' People enjoy being helpful like that." Disney used to advise people not to pretend that they knew more than they did. "All you've got to do," he said, "is own up to your ignorance honestly, and you'll find people who are eager to fill your head with information."

225
Love for Mice Paid Off

Long before Walt Disney made a name for himself in Hollywood he was a poor, struggling artist in Kansas City. But something happened there that perhaps had something to do with his big break a few years later: the discovery of a friendly mouse. Mice would gather in Walt's wastebasket when he worked late at night. He would lift them out and keep them in little cages on his desk. One of the little mice was Walt's special friend. Before he left the hard times of Kansas City behind, Walt carefully carried his little mouse friend into a field and let him go.

No doubt when his mouse cartoon idea came, he thought back on those Kansas City friends. He first decided to call his mouse Mortimer, but his wife didn't like the name. "Too sissy," she argued. Finally, Walt suggested Mickey. Mrs. Disney liked it, but a movie exhibitor booking cartoons balked. "It's no use, Walt," he said. "Nobody has ever heard of Mickey Mouse." Walt, as optimistic as a wolf in a hen house, answered, "They will!"

226
Trying to Please

Everyone lives, as Samuel Johnson said, "in the hope of pleasing somebody." That isn't always possible — especially for one in the public limelight. Walt Disney knew that. He listened as some of his stockholders muttered that he was an artistic success and a commerical failure. Then his professional critics were heard to say that anything artistic about Disney's product was pure coincidence. Once when he and his associates were putting a story together, someone asked, "What will the critics say if we do this?" Walt looked at the man and replied, "We're not trying to entertain the critics. I'm taking my chances with the public."

The chances he took with the public were obviously the right ones.

227
He Put Us on the Map

As a boy in Oregon I used to get a thrill out of watching cartoonist Paul Murray in his home studio. Murray was a cartoonist for the Walt Disney studios. Each month he sent his comic strips to the studio and then, of course, all the kids in the neighborhood would watch the magazine racks for *Little Wolf* and other comic books to see the finished work. One *Little Wolf* book became special for us. Murray had a scene around a railroad station and took the liberty to label the station after a small town in our area, MARCOLA, and then placed a sign in the picture that read WENDLING 4. That was our hometown and it was in Walt Disney's comic book!

— Wayne Warner

228
She Didn't Know Her Daddy Was Famous

I didn't realize what my father did for a living until I was six. Then a playmate at school told me.

That night when Father came home he flopped down into his easy chair. I approached him with awe. He didn't look famous to me.

I asked, "Are you Walt Disney?"

"You know I am," he said.

"*The* Walt Disney?" I insisted.

He looked startled; then he grinned and nodded. Whereupon I said the five words he must have thought he was safe from in the bosom of his family: "Please give me your autograph."

— Diane Disney Miller, *The Story of Walt Disney*

229
We'll Get It Yet

Not long ago, at our Burbank, California, studio, a group of animators and writers were holding a story conference on a new Disney cartoon feature. They were having a tough time agreeing on a story line, and the atmosphere was as stormy as the weather outside. Suddenly, lightning scribbled a jagged streak over the San Fernando Valley and there was a rolling clap of thunder. "Don't worry, Walt," one of the animators quipped, glancing heavenward. "We'll get it yet."

— Roy Disney, "Unforgettable Walt Disney," *Reader's Digest,* February 1969.

230
Number One Businessman

He was reared in the small Missouri town of Marceline and then started a small animated cartoon company in Kansas City that went broke. Even after he went to Hollywood to establish a cartoon business, Walt Disney's immediate success was anything but spectacular. Through the depression the company struggled to meet the payroll. But when the University of Michigan's graduate school of administration conducted a poll in 1966 of three hundred businessmen to name the nation's top ten leaders in their field, the number one choice was former Missourian, Walt Disney. He had built an empire on good, clean, tasteful entertainment. A few months after the poll was taken, Disney died. A later poll asked respondents to select the ten greatest deceased businessmen in American history. Walt Disney was named second only to Henry Ford.

231
Work to Live On

The world has lost a genius in the truest sense of the word.... But in a larger sense, Walt Disney has not died because he will live for all time through his work.

— Sam Goldwyn's tribute at Disney's death

232
Dirty Jokes Didn't Go Over

It has been said that Walt Disney's ideals were so high that one of his studio chiefs once said of him, "I guess Walt is the only man in Hollywood to whom you don't tell a dirty joke. When you do, somehow it doesn't come out funny."

233
A Moral in His Success

It must be reassuring to many that in the sea of filth engulfing the film capital and turning Hollywood into an economic disaster area, Disney's simple tales that are fit for the whole family have flourished. . . . The wonderful worlds of Walt Disney live on. And there must be a moral in that.

—Norma Lee Browning
Chicago Tribune

234
More Exciting When Walt Told It

Once when young Roy Disney, Walt's nephew, had the measles, Walt came to visit and told him the story of *Pinocchio,* which he was making into a film at the time. The boy was so absorbed in the story — especially with Walt's graphic descriptions — that he forgot all about his illness. Later, when the boy saw the film, he was disappointed. "It didn't seem as exciting as when Uncle Walt told it," he said.

235
X-rated Films Second Rate

In an article for the *Chicago Tribune,* Norma Lee Browning asked, "Can a Clean Movie Succeed?" She answered the question by comparing a Walt Disney film, "The Love Bug," with X-rated films such as "Myra Breckinridge" and "Beyond the Valley of the Dolls." The Disney film, a whimsical adventure comedy about a Volkswagen named Herbie, had grossed twenty million dollars at the time of the author's story. The other two in the same period had grossed but eight million dollars combined. Although Disney didn't live to see "The Love Bug," it was made in the family entertainment tradition he established in 1928. He no doubt would be proud that his family films remain more popular than the X films.

WALT DISNEY SAID IT

236
A Box Office Gauge

Every time other films get dirtier, our box office goes up.

237
Importance of Family

We have never lost our faith in family entertainment. The one important thing to me is to keep the family together. That's been the backbone of our whole business, catering to the families.

238
Two Kinds of People

There are two kinds of people: the first kind are licked if they can't get a job. The second kind are sure that even if jobs are scarce they can always do *something*.

BENJAMIN DISRAELI
(1804–1881)

He was the only man born a Jew to become prime minister of Great Britain. He served about ten months in 1868, and then from 1874 to 1880. Although born a Jew, Disraeli became a member of the Church of England in 1817. A political opponent of William E. Gladstone, he described himself as "a conservative to preserve all that is good in our constitution, and a radical to remove all that is bad." He was named Earl of Beaconsfield.

239
A Good Listener

Bruce Larson, in his book *Dare to Live Now!* underlines the importance of being a good listener. "To care about a person enough to hear what he is saying may do more initially to introduce him to Christ than to tell him all kinds of things about God or yourself." Then Larson tells about the young British woman who had the privilege of having dinner in the same week with two of England's most famous prime ministers, Gladstone and Disraeli. A friend asked her what the two men were like. "When I was with Mr. Gladstone," she replied, "I thought I was with the smartest man in the whole world. But with Mr. Disraeli, I thought I must be the smartest person in the world."

240
Great Men Fail

Scarcely a great man can be named who has not failed the first time. In such defeat no shame lies; the shame consists in one's not retrieving it. Lord Beaconsfield (Benjamin Disraeli) made, as everybody knows, a signal failure in his maiden speech in the House of Commons. But he was not cowed by the derisive laughter which greeted him. With astonishing self-control, and no less astonishing self-knowledge, he exclaimed, "I have begun several times many things, and have succeeded in them at last. I shall sit down now; but the time will come when you will hear me." The command of temper, the mastery over self, which these words displayed, is almost sublime.

— Lucas

241
Gratitude

In her own self-evaluation, Disraeli's wife, Mary Anne, labeled herself a "dunce." Some of her contemporaries would agree with her after hearing her talk when she should have remained silent. Mary Anne was often a source of embarrassment to her husband, whom she regarded as a genius. One day a friend of Disraeli's asked if his wife's conversation bothered him. "Oh, no, I'm never put out by that." With that, the friend remarked that he "must be a man of extraordinary qualities." "Not at all," Disraeli answered, "I only possess one quality in which most men are deficient — gratitude." He went on to say that his wife believed in him when men despised him. Her belief in him was enough to cause him to overlook her most obvious fault.

242
A Vote for Equality

Disraeli was a member of the Church of England and a professing Christian, but his enemies would often assail him for no other reason than his Hebrew ancestry. It was politically dangerous for him to do it, but he spoke out one day in the House of Commons against a law which kept a Jew from assuming a seat in Parliament. What Christian would not have his conscience pricked by Disraeli's logic? "Is it not the first business of the Christian Church to make the population whose minds she attempts to form, acquainted with the history of the Jews? . . . On every sacred day you read to the people the exploits of Jewish heroes, the proofs of Jewish devotion, the brilliant annals of past Jewish magnificence. . . . Every Sunday, if you wish to find expression of solace in grief, you find both in the words of the Jewish poets."

Disraeli concluded his speech to make his position clear: "I cannot sit in this House with any misconception of my opinion on this subject. Whatever may be the consequences on the seat I hold, I cannot, for one, give a vote which is not in deference to what I believe to be the true principles of religion. Yes, it is as a Christian that I will not take upon me the awful responsibility of excluding from the legislature those who are of the religion in the bosom of which my Lord and Saviour was born."

243
Misfortune and Calamity

Benjamin Disraeli and William Gladstone were long the heads of the two leading political parties in England. Both were great men, but there was never any doubt which was the greater wit.

Once, someone asked Disraeli to define the difference between a misfortune and a calamity. The reply, delivered with the utmost suavity, was typical of the man.

"Well, if Gladstone fell into the Thames, it would be a misfortune. But if anybody dragged him out, ah! *that* would be a calamity!"

BENJAMIN DISRAELI SAID IT

244
Proud to Be a Jew

Yes, I am a Jew, and when the ancestors of the right honourable gentleman were brutal savages in an unknown island, mine were priests in the temple of Solomon.

— Reply to Daniel O'Connell, who had called Disraeli "a damned Jew"

245
Pride

Talk to a man about himself and he will listen for hours.

246
Opportunity and Advantage

Next to knowing when to seize an opportunity, the most important thing in life is to know when to forego an advantage.

247
Patience

We cannot eat the fruit while the tree is in blossom.

248
Life

Youth is a blunder; manhood a struggle; old age a regret.

249
Pride

The author who speaks about his own books is almost as bad as a mother who talks about her own children.

250
Christianity

Christianity is completed Judaism, or it is nothing.

251
Circumstances

Man is not the creature of circumstances; circumstances are the creatures of men.

252
Critics

Critics are the men who have failed in literature and art.

253
Marks of a Gentleman

Propriety of manners and consideration for others are the two main characteristics of a gentleman.

254
Patience

Everything comes if a man will only wait.

255
Putting Up with Inconveniences

Demagogues and agitators are very unpleasant, but they are incidents to a free and constitutional country, and you must put up with these inconveniences or do without many important advantages.

256
Step to Knowledge

To be conscious that you are ignorant is a great step to knowledge.

257
Love

We are all born for love. . . . It is the principle of existence and its only end.

258
Adversity a Teacher

There is no education like adversity.

259
Tact

Without tact you can learn nothing.

260
Secure Government

No government can be long secure without formidable opposition.

261
Patience

Patience is a necessary ingredient of genius.

262
Truth

Time is precious, but truth is more precious than time.

263
A Different Perspective

What is crime amongst the multitude is only vice among the few.

THOMAS A. EDISON
(1847–1931)

Considered the world's greatest inventor, Thomas Edison had but three months of formal education. He patented more than one thousand inventions in sixty years, including the electric light bulb and the phonograph. He helped to perfect motion pictures, the telephone, the typewriter, and the electric generator, to name a few. As a boy, Thomas had a great curiosity; and if nobody could answer his questions, he would begin to experiment to get the answer. He never quit experimenting for the rest of his life. In 1928, Congress awarded Edison a gold medal for "development and application of inventions that have revolutionized civilization in the last century." The Edison National Historic Site at West Orange, New Jersey, is managed by the National Park Service.

264
Edison's Value

How can one put a cash value on the brain? Someone did it for Thomas Edison and came up with the highest value ever. At the time of his death, it was estimated by a *New York Times* analyst that the business interests based on or largely due to Edison's inventions amounted to no less than twenty-five billion dollars. Some brain!

265
Home Education

Young Tom Edison's formal education lasted just three months. When he was seven, his parents moved to Port Huron, Michigan, where he was enrolled in school. His mother expected great things from her youngest child. However, she was greatly disappointed and indignant when the teacher complained that Tom paid little attention in the class. The teacher even told Mrs. Edison that she thought her young son was slightly "addled." With that, Mrs. Edison withdrew Tom from school and taught him herself at home. Nobody can say that he didn't apply himself at home. By the time he was twelve, he had read such scholarly works as Gibbon's *Decline and Fall of the Roman Empire* and Burton's *Anatomy of Melancholy* and the *Dictionary of Sciences*.

266
Using His Head

Even as a fifteen-year-old newsboy, Thomas Edison was a shrewd businessman. During the Civil War the demand for news of the action made newspapers extremely valuable. The day that the Battle of Shiloh was reported in the paper, Edison dashed into the office of the *Detroit Free Press* and talked them into letting him have a thousand papers. He then sent word ahead to telegrapher friends along his train route, asking them to post notices that he would be along with the latest news of the battle. The rail stations were jammed. And when Edison saw that people were eager to get the papers, he raised the price from a nickel to ten cents, then to fifteen, and then to a quarter. He finally sold the remaining copies for thirty-five cents each. At the end of the day, Edison pocketed a profit of about one hundred dollars. Later, he said concerning that day that he "had a chance to learn that money can be made out of a little careful thought."

267
Unique Marriage Proposal

As a boy Thomas Edison learned telegraphy. Later, after he had become a successful inventor, he used his ability at the telegraph key to send a proposal of marriage to his sweetheart, Mina Miller. Edison's first wife died when he was thirty-seven. Later, he met Mina, a young and lovely lady. Edison taught Mina the Morse code, and after she had learned it, he tested her with a message tapped out with a coin. Mina decoded the "message," which was really a marriage proposal, and tapped out her acceptance.

Not the most romantic proposal in history, but certainly as effective as any on record.

268
Hard Work

To say Thomas Edison was a hard worker is an understatement. The United States Patent Office granted him 1,098 patents — 122 of them before he was thirty years of age. "Work heals and ennobles," he said on his seventy-fifth birthday. "Work brings out the secrets of nature and applies them for the happiness of men."

Once when asked why a certain workman was no longer with him, Edison replied, "He was so slow that it would take him half an hour to get out of the field of a microscope."

269
Clock Watching Foiled

Shortly after he opened his first plant, Thomas Edison noticed that his employees were in the habit of watching the lone factory clock. To the inventor, who was an indefatigable worker, this was incomprehensible. He did not indicate his disapproval verbally; instead, he had dozens of clocks placed around the plant, no two keeping the same time.

From then on, clock watching led to so much confusion that nobody cared what time it was.

270
Results

Thomas A. Edison, inventor of the incandescent light, made experiment after experiment in a search for a new source of natural rubber in plant matter. After the 50,000th failure, a discouraged assistant said to him, "Mr. Edison, we have made 50,000 experiments and have had no results."

"Results!" exclaimed the great inventor with enthusiasm. "We have wonderful results. We now know 50,000 things which won't work."

—Edward L. Friedman, *The Speechmaker's Complete Handbook*

271
A Tribute to Thomas Edison
And Yet Fools Say

He captured light and caged it in a glass,
Then harnessed it forever to a wire;

He gave men robots with no backs to tire
In bearing burdens for the toiling mass.

He freed the tongue in wood and wax and brass,
Imbued dull images with motion's fire,
Transmuted metal into human choir —
These man-made miracles he brought to pass.

Bulbs banish night along the Great White Way,
Thin threads of copper throb with might unseen;
On silver curtains shadow actors play
That walk and talk from magic mouth machine.

While continents converse through skies o'erhead —
And yet fools say that Edison is dead!

— George S. Holmes

272
Money Used for New Experiments

Any one of Edison's major achievements — the incandescent bulb, the phonograph, the motion picture — would have been a creditable life's work for an inventor. Edison's restless mind, though, turned from one enterprise to another in an endless quest for mastery in a dozen fields. If he had chosen to retain and exploit all his patents, he could have built a personal fortune to dwarf that of John D. Rockefeller. Money for Edison, however, was merely the means to finance new experiments; he sold his interest in one company to pay for the research expenses of the next. Although he died a wealthy man, he forfeited his chance to be a billionaire in order to carry on continued investigation.

— Robert Silverberg, *Light for World*

273
Introducing the Phonograph

After Edison invented the phonograph — crude as it was then — he took it to the skeptical but influential F. C. Beach, editor of the *Scientific American*. Beach later wrote of the meeting in New York.

I had not been at my desk very long that morning when Mr. Edison was announced. He came in, and set his parcel, which he appeared to handle somewhat carefully, on my desk. As he was removing the cover, I asked him what it was.

"Just a minute!" replied young Edison.

Presently with a "here you are," he pushed the quaint-looking little instrument toward me. As there was a long shaft having a heavy wheel at one end and a small handle at the other, naturally I gave the handle a twist, and, to my astonishment, the unmistakable words, emitted from a kind of telephone mouthpiece, broke out, "Good Morning! What do you think of the phonograph?"

Edison was later summoned to Washington, D.C., to demonstrate his invention. While demonstrating it in the home of a senator, a White House messenger arrived to say that President Hayes wished a demonstration. The president and several guests were captivated by the sounds the phonograph reproduced — until three-thirty in the morning.

274
The Stereo's Father

One day Edison wrapped a sheet of tinfoil around a small cylinder that was connected to a crank. Then he placed a metal point against the tinfoil and turned the crank. While an associate watched in wonder, Edison began reciting a nursery rhyme into another part of the strange machine. When he completed the rhyme, Edison stopped the cylinder, readjusted the needle, and began turning the crank once more. Out of the machine came a squeaky but distinguishable sound: "Mary had a little lamb; its fleece was white as snow. . . ." The world had its first phonograph. Nobody would want to compare its quality that day in 1877 to today's stereos, but it was a beginning.

THOMAS A. EDISON SAID IT

275
Debt to Others

Through all the years of experimenting and research, I never once made a discovery. I start where the last man left off. . . . All my work was deductive, and the results I achieved were those of invention pure and simple.

276
Thrift

Waste is worse than loss. The time is coming when every person who lays claim to ability will keep the question of waste before him constantly. The scope of thrift is limitless.

277
Genius

Genius is one percent inspiration and ninety-nine percent perspiration.

278
Work

I never did anything worth doing by accident, nor did any of my inventions come by accident; they came by work.

279
Ingredients for Progress

Restlessness and discontent are the first necessities of progress.

280
Mother

I did not have my mother long, but she cast over me an influence which has lasted all my life. The good effects of her early training I can never lose. If it had not been for her appreciation and her faith in me at a critical time in my experience, I should never likely have become an inventor. I was always a careless boy, and with a mother of different mental calibre, I should have turned out badly. But her firmness, her sweetness, her goodness, were potent powers to keep me in the right path. My mother was the making of me. The memory of her will always be a blessing to me.

281
Electric Lights

We will make electric light so cheap that only the rich will be able to burn candles.

282
Discovery and Invention

Discovery is not invention, and I dislike to see the two words confounded. A discovery is more or less in the nature of an accident. A man walks along the road intending to catch the train. On the way his foot kicks against something and . . . he sees a gold bracelet imbedded in the dust. He has discovered that — certainly not invented it. He did not set out to find a bracelet, yet the value is just as great.

283
Art Appreciation

To my mind the old masters are not art; their value is in their scarcity.

284
Invented No Weapons to Kill

I'm proud of the fact that I never invented weapons to kill.

DWIGHT D. EISENHOWER
(1890–1969)

Dwight D. Eisenhower was the thirty-fourth president of the United States (1953–1961). He had distinguished himself as a military leader, especially during World War II when he became supreme commander of the Allied armies in Europe. He was born in Denison, Texas, but his parents moved to Kansas when he was nearly two years old. He graduated from West Point in 1915. He defeated Gov. Adlai E. Stevenson of Illinois in the 1952 and 1956 presidential races. Although he suffered several serious illnesses while he was president, he lived to be, at age seventy, the oldest president in history. He is buried at Abilene, Kansas, where his Presidential Library and Museum are located.

285
Ike Follows Washington

As a boy in Abilene, Dwight Eisenhower was an avid reader. History was his first love, and his favorite American hero was George Washington, a man he never tired reading about. Later, he said, "The qualities that excited my admiration were Washington's stamina and patience in adversity, first, and then his indomitable courage, daring, and capacity for self-sacrifice."

Who in Abilene would have thought they had another famous general-president growing up in their town?

286
Hope for a Peaceful World

At his final news conference as president, a reporter asked Dwight Eisenhower to sum up his idea of what kind of a United States he would like his grandchildren to live in. The outgoing president answered by saying he hoped they could live "in a peaceful world . . . enjoying all of the privileges and carrying forward all the responsibilities envisioned for the good citizen of the United States, and this means among other things the effort always to raise the standards of our people in their spiritual, intellectual, and economic strength. That's what I would like to see them have."

287
Patriotism

Dwight Eisenhower remembered June 14, 1911, as a very rough day. It was his first day at West Point, and he was one of 285 who were kept busy doing all sorts of ridiculous chores on the double. At the end of the day they were weary and resentful.

Before nightfall the new class was assembled outdoors to be sworn in as cadets of the United States Military Academy. Eisenhower recalled it as being an impressive ceremony. He said he looked up at the American flag floating majestically above them and then he swore his allegiance to that flag. He said he realized humbly that he then belonged to the flag.

Later, Eisenhower became color sergeant of the class and in his final year at West Point carried the flag at all official parades and ceremonies.

In the March 1969 *Reader's Digest* Eisenhower called on Americans for a new commitment to the basic principles that he said made our nation great and which the flag represents. "Our flag is the symbol of these principles," he said, "and I would hope that all of us might find some way to display it, not merely on patriotic holidays but every day in the year." He reasoned that the display would do much to "help bring about a new national solidarity, a renewed pride and faith in America."

The appeal from the old general was one of his last. On March 28, 1969, he died of heart failure.

288
Duty

President Eisenhower inherited several major foreign problems when he assumed office in January 1953. The Korean War was still being fought, tensions were mounting in the Middle East, and relations with

Russia were strained. At home the new president was receiving pressure to commute the death sentences of Julius and Ethel Rosenberg, convicted of supplying atomic secrets to Russia. He refused to commute the sentence, stating rather that justice must be carried out. "By their act these two individuals have in fact betrayed the cause of freedom for which free men are fighting and dying at this very hour. . . . I have determined that it is my duty, in the interest of the people of the United States, not to set aside the verdict."

The Rosenbergs were executed on June 19, 1953.

289
Differences Forgotten

General Eisenhower's chief Republican rival for the 1952 nomination was Sen. Robert A. Taft, the respected majority leader of the Senate. Before and after the Republican convention their views sharply differed. In addition, it was Taft's last chance to be nominated for the position held by his father, William Howard Taft; and he was specially disappointed. But because of the kindness and consideration President Eisenhower showed the senator, they became warm friends. Taft died July 31, 1953, just a few months after Eisenhower took office. Soon after the news reached the White House, President and Mrs. Eisenhower drove to the Taft home to console Mrs. Taft. William S. White said the president took Mrs. Taft's hand in both of his and said, "I don't know what I'll do without him — I don't know what I'll do without him."

Those who were intimately acquainted with the president knew the words were genuine.

290
Value of Human Life

President Eisenhower recalled how in a conversation with a Russian general at the close of World War II it was impressed on him how the value of human life differed between the two.

The Soviet general told how the Russians had a practice in the Red Army of clearing the way for tanks by marching troops over minefields. The story shocked Eisenhower. The same general expressed surprise that Americans should have taken the trouble they did in treating German prisoners humanely. Eisenhower said that he explained to the Russian that ill treatment of German prisoners would have brought retaliation against American prisoners in German hands. With that the Russian reasoned that the Americans shouldn't have been concerned with their soldiers in German prisons since these men no longer were of any military value.

The value of human life differs considerably, depending on which side of the Iron Curtain the measure is being made.

291
From the Heart of America

The flags in Washington and around the nation were at half-mast on March 30, 1969. Two days earlier, the man whom millions loved had died in Walter Reed Hospital. Pres. Richard Nixon, who had served as Dwight D. Eisenhower's vice-president for eight years, paid tribute to the old soldier.

It was in 1945, shortly after VE Day at a ceremony in London's historic Guildhall. The triumphant Supreme Commander of the Allied forces in Europe was officially given the freedom of the city of London.

In an eloquent address that day, Dwight Eisenhower said, "I come from the heart of America."

Perhaps no one sentence could better sum up what Dwight Eisenhower meant to a whole generation of Americans. He did come from the heart of America, not only from its geographical heart but from its spiritual heart. He exemplified what millions of parents hoped their sons would be — strong and courageous and honest and compassionate. And with his own great qualities of heart, he personified the best in America.

292
Authentic Hero

Dwight Eisenhower was the rarest of men — an authentic hero. Wars bring the names of many men into the headlines, and of those some few become national or even international heroes. But as the years pass, their fame goes down.

Not so with Dwight Eisenhower. As the years passed, his stature grew. Commander of the mightiest expeditionary force ever assembled, receiver of the surrender of the German armies in World War II, president of Columbia University, Supreme Commander of NATO, 34th President of the United States — the honors, the offices, were there in abundance. Every trust that the American people had it in their power to bestow, he was given.

And, yet, he always retained a saving humility.

His was the humility, not of fear, but of confidence. He walked with the great of the world and he knew that the great are human. His was the humility of a man too proud to be arrogant.

— President Nixon's eulogy in Washington, March 30, 1969

293
A Lift to the Spirit

There is growing conviction that the measure of the man [Eisenhower] himself may be more of a factor in the national life than anyone has been willing to admit. The eight years of relative world calm under Ike, achieved without losing any territory or much prestige, have taken on new importance. There are even those who dare suggest that this soothing spirit and innate goodness did more to lift up the hearts of Americans and hold them together in a reasonable state of public happiness than many of the social reforms that have been propounded since.

— Hugh Sidey in *Life*

DWIGHT D. EISENHOWER SAID IT

294
Controlling Temper

The year when I was ten, my mother gave permission to Arthur and Edgar, the two older Eisenhower boys, to go out with a group for Halloween "trick or treating." It was upsetting when my father and mother said I was too young to go along. I argued and pleaded until the last minute. Finally, the two boys took off.

I have no exact memory of what happened immediately afterward, but soon I was completely beside myself. Suddenly my father grabbed my shoulders to shock me back into consciousness. What I had been doing was standing by an old apple tree trunk and pounding it with my bleeding fists, expressing resentment in rage. My father legislated the matter with the traditional hickory switch and sent me off to bed.

Perhaps an hour later, my mother came into the room. . . . She began to talk about temper and controlling it. Eventually, as she often did, she drew on the Bible, paraphrasing it, I suppose. This time she said, "He that conquereth his own soul is greater than he who taketh a city."

Hatred was a futile sort of thing, she said, because hating anyone or anything meant that there was little to be gained. The person who had incurred my displeasure probably didn't care, possibly didn't even know, and the only person injured was myself.

In the meantime, she had set about putting salve on my injured hands and then bandaging the worst places. I have always looked back on that conversation as one of the most valuable moments of my life.

— From *In Review*

295
Censorship

Don't join the book burners. Don't think you are going to conceal faults by concealing evidence that they ever existed. Don't be afraid to go in your library and read every book, as long as that document does not offend your own ideas of decency. That should be the only censorship.

— Speech at Dartmouth College in refence to Sen. Joseph McCarthy, 1953

296
Gratitude and Prayer

I should like to feel that, in every American family, some place is made for an expression of our gratitude to Almighty God, and for a frank acknowledgment of our faith that He can supply that additional strength which, for these trying times, is so sorely needed.

297
America, the Greatest Force

America is the greatest force that God has ever allowed to exist on His footstool.

298
Sacrifice

We must be willing, individually and as a nation, to accept whatever sacrifices may be required of us. A people that values its privileges above its principles soon loses both.

299
America's Need

There is nothing wrong with America that the faith, love of freedom, intelligence, and energy of her citizens cannot cure.

300
Our Deepest Prayers

Before all else, we seek, upon our common labor as a nation, the favor of Almighty God. And the hopes in our hearts fashion the deepest prayers of our people.

May we pursue the right — without self-righteousness.
May we know unity — without conformity.
May we grow in strength — without pride of self.
May we, in our dealings with all people of the earth, ever speak the truth and serve justice.
May the light of freedom, coming to all darkened lands, flame brightly — until at last the darkness is no more.
May the turbulence of our age yield to a true time of peace, when men and nations shall share a life that honors the dignity of earth, the brotherhood of all.

301
Solving Problems

I for one refuse to become pessimistic about America's future. Granted that storm signals are up, I believe nevertheless that we as a people have the good sense to place patriotism and human understanding above the arrogance of personal prejudice — and that we can and will solve peacefully the problems that beset us. I believe that we will do so through our traditional reliance upon the philosophy of moderation — or Government by Common Sense.

302
Decency

Decency is one of the main pillars of a sound civilization. An immoral nation invites its own ruin.

303
Didn't Know They Were Poor

I have found out in later years we were very poor [as a boy in Abilene], but the glory of America is that we didn't know it then.

304
Leadership

Leadership is the art of getting someone else to do something that you want done because he wants to do it.

305
Inaugural Prayer

Almighty God, as we stand here at this moment, my future associates in the executive branch of the government join me in beseeching that Thou wilt make full and complete our dedication to the service of the people in this throng, and their fellow citizens everywhere.

Give us, we pray, the power to discern clearly right from wrong, and allow all our words and actions to be governed thereby, and by the laws of this land.

Especially we pray that our concern shall be for all the people, regardless of their station, race, or calling. May cooperation be permitted and the mutual aim of those who, under the concepts of our Constitution hold to differing political faiths; so that all may work for the good of our beloved country and Thy glory. . . . Amen.

—First inaugural prayer

BENJAMIN FRANKLIN
(1706–1790)

Statesman, scientist, public leader — Franklin did all of them well. The fifteenth child of a family of seventeen, Benjamin Franklin never went to school after age ten; but he never stopped learning. He read every book he could get his hands on and taught himself such subjects as algebra, geometry, navigation, and learned to write well. He became one of the best-educated men of the eighteenth century. He was the only man who signed all four of America's key documents during the eighteenth century: the Declaration of Independence, the Treaty of Alliance with France, the Treaty of Peace with Great Britain, and the Constitution of the United States. His famous kite experiment took place at Philadelphia in 1752.

306
Washington, the Joshua

Following the American Revolution, Benjamin Franklin attended a dinner at which were present the British and French ministers. Toasts were drunk. The British minister exclaimed: "To England — the Sun, whose beams enlighten and fructify the remotest corners of the earth."

Thereupon the French minister arose and toasted, "France — the Moon, whose mild, steady, cheering rays delight all nations and penetrate the darkness."

Last, Benjamin Franklin stood up and gave a toast. "George Washington, the Joshua who commanded the sun and the moon to stand still, and they obeyed him."

307
Advice Not Heeded

Thomas Paine wrote a manuscript and then showed it to his friend Benjamin Franklin. Franklin read the manuscript, which Paine titled

The Age of Reason, and then advised him not to have it published. "The world," Franklin told him, "is bad enough *with* the Bible; what would it be without it?"

Paine, of course, did not take Franklin's advice and published one of the sharpest attacks on the Bible in its history.

308
Consider the New Birth

Benjamin Franklin went often to hear the English evangelist George Whitefield preach. Shortly after he conducted his famous electrical experiment with a homemade kite during a thunderstorm, he received a letter from Whitefield. It was dated August 17, 1752. "I find you grow more and more famous in the learned world. As you have made a pretty considerable progress in the mysteries of electricity, I would now humbly recommend to your diligent, unprejudiced pursuit and study, the mystery of the new birth. It is a most important, interesting study; and, when mastered, will richly answer and repay you for all your pains. One, at whose bar we are shortly to appear, hath solemnly declared, without it we cannot enter the kingdom of heaven."

It isn't known whether Franklin ever took Whitefield's recommendation.

309
Revised Edition

Few men in American history could approach Benjamin Franklin's skill in so many fields. He was an inventor, scientist, writer, publisher, statesman, and wit. He has been quoted for over two hundred years and will no doubt be quoted for many years to come. Named after him have been streets, schools, children, cars, and his picture has been on money and postage stamps. One of the most unusual epitaphs ever written — but never used — is one Franklin wrote for his own tombstone:

REVISED EDITION

The Body
of
Benjamin Franklin, Printer
(Like the cover of an old book,

Its contents torn out,
And stripped of its lettering and gilding,)
Lies here food for worms.
Yet the work itself shall not be lost,
For it will (as he believes) appear once more
In a new
And beautiful Edition
Corrected and Amended
By
The Author

310
Can't Be Replaced

When Thomas Jefferson presented his credentials as United States minister to France, the French premier remarked, "I see that you have come to replace Benjamin Franklin."

"I have come to succeed him," corrected Jefferson. "No one can replace him."

311
Idle Silence

Most of us fail all too often to express appreciation or consolation to those about us. Benjamin Franklin put his finger on it when he said, "As we must account for every idle word, so we must for every idle silence."

— George W. Crane

312
Master of Many Fields

Although Benjamin Franklin was not a graduate of any medical school, still he was elected to membership in several medical societies. . . . Physicians dedicated their works to him, translated his writings into French, invited him to their meetings. . . . Many patients consulted him; many doctors wrote to him for advice.

Franklin invented the first American instrument for showing the circulation of the blood; started research in the use of electricity for treat-g paralysis; studied causes of lead poisoning, infection from impure water, the contagious nature of colds and influenza, and mental diseases.

— Dr. William Pepper, *The Medical Side of Benjamin Franklin*

313
Spreading the Light

When Benjamin Franklin wished to interest the people of Philadelphia in street lighting, he didn't try to persuade them by talking about it — instead, he hung a beautiful lantern on a long bracket before his own door. Then he kept the glass brightly polished, and carefully and religiously lit the wick every evening at the approach of dusk.

People wandering about on the dark street saw Franklin's light a long way off and came under the influence of its friendly glow with grateful hearts. To each one it seemed to say: "Come along, my friend! Here is a safe place to walk. See that cobblestone sticking up? Don't stumble over it! Good-bye! I shall be here to help you again tomorrow night, if you should come this way."

It wasn't long before Franklin's neighbors began placing lights in brackets before their homes and soon the entire city awoke to the value of street lighting and took up the matter with interest and enthusiasm.

— Cole D. Robinson, *World Horizons*

314
Interest Adds Up

Benjamin Franklin left a fund of $5,000 to the City of Boston in 1791. His will provided that interest from this fund be allowed to accumulate for 100 years. By 1891 the $5,000 had grown to almost $400,000. A school was established with part of the accumulated fund and the balance, $92,000, was invested for a second century. It was reported that by 1950 the $92,000 had increased to almost a million. Apparently Ben knew what he was talking about when he said, "Money begets money and its offspring begets more."

— Jacob M. Braude

BENJAMIN FRANKLIN SAID IT

315
Laws

Laws too gentle are seldom obeyed; too severe, seldom executed.

316
Liberty

Those who would give up essential liberty to purchase a little temporary safety deserve neither liberty nor safety.

317
God and Doctors

God heals and the doctor takes the fee.

318
Value of Money

If you would know the value of money, go and try to borrow some.

319
Patience

He that can have patience can have what he will.

320
No Rivals

He that falls in love with himself will have no rivals.

321
War and Peace

There never was a good war or a bad peace.

322
Holidays Easier to Keep Than Commandments

How many observe Christ's birthday; how few His precepts! Oh! 'tis easier to keep holidays than commandments.

323
Imitating and Counterfeiting

There is much difference between imitating a good man, and counterfeiting him.

324
Money

The use of money is all the advantage there is in having money.

325
Money

He that is of the opinion money will do everything may well be suspected of doing everything for money.

326
Anger

Anger is never without reason, but seldom with a good one.

327
Christian Principles

He who shall introduce into public affairs the principles of primitive Christianity will revolutionize the world.

328
Duty

Would you live with ease,
Do what you ought,
Not what you please.

329
Two Opposites

The same man cannot be both friend and flatterer.

330
To Be Remembered

If you would not be forgotten as soon as you are dead, either write things worth reading or do things worth writing.

331
Becoming Mature

At twenty years of age the will reigns; at thirty the wit; at forty the judgment.

332
Essentials

A Bible and a newspaper in every house, a good school in every district — all studied and appreciated as they merit — are the principal support of virtue, morality, and civil liberty.

333
For Want of a Nail

For want of a nail the shoe was lost; for want of a shoe the horse was lost; and for want of a horse the rider was lost; being overtaken and slain by the enemy, all for the want of care about a horseshoe nail.

334
Keep Quiet

Teach your child to hold his tongue. He'll learn fast enough to speak.

335
Jesus Christ

As to Jesus of Nazareth, my opinion of whom you particularly desire, I think the system of morals and His religion, as He left them to us, is the best the world ever saw, or is likely to see.

336
Complaining

Constant complaint is the poorest sort of pay for all the comforts we enjoy.

337
Memory

Creditors have better memories than debtors.

338
Temptation

It is easier to suppress the first desire than to satisfy all that follow it.

339
Justice

Pity and forbearance should characterize all acts of justice.

340
No Offense, No News

If all printers were determined not to print anything till they were sure that it would offend nobody, there would be very little printed.

341
Justice

Justice is as strictly due between neighbor nations as between neighbor citizens. A highwayman is as much a robber when he plunders in a gang, as when single; and a nation that makes an unjust war is only a great gang.

342
Wealth

He does not possess wealth that allows it to possess him.

343
Recipe for Life

Work as if you were to live one hundred years. Pray as if you were to die tomorrow.

BILLY GRAHAM
(1918-   )

Since 1949, Billy Graham has conducted large-scale evangelistic crusades in the United States, Europe, South America, the Middle East, the Far East, and Africa. It has been estimated that at least fifty million people have seen him in person. Millions of others have seen him on television and heard him on radio. He has been a friend of four United States presidents and has had audiences with royalty and other political leaders around the world. He has written several books: Peace with God (*1954*), Secret of Happiness (*1955*), My Answer (*1960*), World Aflame *(1965), and* The Jesus Generation *(1971).*

344
His First Sermon in Jail

Billy Graham preached his first sermon — an unplanned one at that — in a jail. He had just graduated from high school, and he and Grady Wilson were spending the summer as Fuller Brush salesmen. When Jimmie Johnson, an evangelist friend, told the youths he was going to hold a service in a nearby jail, they wanted to go along. It was the first time inside a jail for Billy and Grady. Jimmie Johnson conducted the brief service and calmly announced that Billy would give his testimony. Billy was taken by surprise but rose to the occasion. Neither the Fuller Brush people nor the occupants of the jail on that hot summer afternoon had any idea that the tall youth was launching a preaching ministry that would take him around the world to preach to millions of people.

345
Something to Believe In

Many parents have not given their children anything to believe in, according to Billy Graham. He told of a friend's son who came to the father and suddenly declared, "I'm dropping out of school, dad." Asked why, the son replied, "Well, dad, the truth is, I hate you." The father was stunned and demanded, "But *why,* son? I've given you everything!" Graham said the son turned on his father and replied, "That's just it. You've given me everything — everything except something to believe in."

346
Procrastination

Everyone gets too busy at times and puts off things that should be done. Billy Graham put off talking to a celebrity — and he was later to regret it. Jerry Beavan, a former Graham aide, remembers the incident.

>We had a luncheon in 1957 in New York City and were riding down the street in a friend's car. When we paused at a corner we heard a newsboy shouting, "EXTRA — JIMMY DORSEY A SUICIDE." Billy slumped back.
>
>He said, "Two days ago I had a call from Jimmy Dorsey. He wanted me to come and talk to him. I told him I couldn't make it this week but I'd get in touch with him next week. I might have been able to do something for him."

— "The Billy Graham I Know," *Christian Herald,* Sept. 1966

347
Too Late

One night in 1962 in a hotel in Seattle, Billy Graham was sound asleep. Suddenly he awoke with what he later described as "a burden to pray for Marilyn Monroe," the movie actress. When the feeling continued the next day, one of Graham's associates tried to reach the actress through one of her agents. The agent offered no hope for a meeting immediately. "Not now. Maybe two weeks from now," he said.

Two weeks later Marilyn Monroe's suicide shocked the world. Two weeks was too late.

348
Conversion Made the Difference

One of the remarkable things about the ministry of the evangelist Billy Graham is his association with the world's leaders. The associations give Graham an opportunity of expressing his own personal faith — possibly the only personal testimony some of them will ever have. While conducting meetings in India, Graham was invited to meet with the late Prime Minister Jawaharlal Nehru. The prime minister was touched by Graham's confession of faith.

"Mr. Nehru," he said, "when I decided to live for Christ, He changed me. He gave me peace and joy! Before this decision, I didn't care anything about God, the Bible, or people. I was filled with intolerance, but the simple act changed my nature. I began to worship God and I loved people no matter what color their skin might be. Christ can do that for everyone!"

349
Patient and Psychiatrist Find Christ

A humanly hopeless alcoholic was placed under the care of a psychiatrist. He received little help. During the Billy Graham meetings in London, the alcoholic was induced to attend. He listened in wonderment to the gospel messages. "Possibly there is some hope for me," he thought. One night, when the invitation was given, he, with several others, went forward. Christ saved him. A new power came into his life. That night, before going to sleep, he reached for the nearby bottle of liquor. Something, or rather, *Someone,* held back his hand. Getting out of bed, he took the bottle of liquor and emptied it down the drain. When he awoke in the morning, through force of habit, he reached for the usual morning "bracer." It was not there. There was no feeling of disappointment, however. He phoned the psychiatrist and said, "You have lost a patient! Christ has saved me from drink. I am a new man!" The psychiatrist said, "That sounds fine. Maybe I can find help where you found it." He began to attend the meetings, and he too accepted Christ as his Saviour. Some days thereafter, in a lobby of a fashionable London hotel, the psychiatrist and the former alcoholic testified along with some fifty others of the saving power of Christ.

—Hubert Mitchell, in *Knight's Treasury of Illustrations*

350
Rejection Notice

It is a mistake to think that great people have always been successful in everything they attempt. The first article Billy Graham ever wrote for publication was submitted to *Moody Monthly* — and rejected. No doubt if that Moody editor could have seen the future he would have accepted the article and signed the young Wheaton student as a magazine column writer.

351
He Refused to Pray

Would Billy Graham refuse to pray for a sinner if he were asked? He did in the case of Stuart Hamblen in 1949.

Hamblen was a tough Texas cowboy who had a daily radio program in Los Angeles. He sang, composed songs, led a dance band, was a successful race horse owner and gambler, and he was a heavy drinker. Graham moved into Los Angeles with a tent in the fall of 1949 for three weeks. It was the largest meeting Graham had ever conducted. Hamblen attended some of the meetings but then became convicted and began to hate Graham. One night he drifted from one bar to another but couldn't shake the conviction of the Holy Spirit. Finally, in desperation he called Graham at 2 A.M. Graham invited Hamblen to his apartment. Hamblen strode through the door and roared as he met Graham, "I want you to pray for me." Graham's reply shocked the cowboy singer: "No, I'm not going to do it."

Graham was sure Hamblen was like the rich young ruler who had approached Jesus, and he wanted to make sure Hamblen sincerely wanted Jesus Christ to be Lord of his life. At last, about 5 A.M., Hamblen bowed in prayer and asked the Lord to take complete control of his life.

Graham's refusal to pray for Hamblen was just what Hamblen needed.

352
Preconceived Opinions

John Pollock, the Billy Graham biographer, admitted that the more he researched for his book, *Billy Graham,* the more he realized that he had held many misconceptions of the man. Pollock believed it was also true with others who didn't know Graham intimately. One such individual Pollock cites is Helmut Thielicke, professor of systematic theology and social ethics at Hamburg University. Dr. Thielicke wrote Graham after attending the Los Angeles crusade in August 1963: "How different it is when men encounter each other face to face, rather than just hearing about each other! I am ashamed that we Christians — including myself — are always susceptible to preconceived opinions. . . . The evening beneath your pulpit was a profound 'penance' experience for me in this respect."

353
Maturity and Discipline

After a typical amount of youthful searching, Billy Graham seemed to find his place in the summer of 1938 at the small Florida Bible Training Institute in Tampa (now Trinity College, Clearwater). A clipping from those days recorded a service where Graham was the speaker.

> Old timers say that last night's meeting in East Palatka was the greatest meeting of the history of the church. Rev. Cecil Underwood and his Peniel Fellowship Club Choir gave a song service with choruses and guitar duets. Billy Graham, the young 19-year-old student evangelist of the Florida Bible Institute . . . is causing quite a sensation, according to Cecil Underwood. Young Graham does not mince words when he tells church members that they are headed for the same hell as the bootlegger and racketeer unless that they get right and live right, Underwood said.

According to John Pollock, Graham stated that he had found his purpose: "I now had a purpose, an objective, a call. That was when the growing up began, and the discipline to study."

354
A Friend of Presidents

Four presidents of the United States have claimed friendship with evangelist Billy Graham. Graham has been both friend and spiritual counselor to Presidents Eisenhower, Kennedy, Johnson, and Nixon.

Before Eisenhower's inauguration, the general told Graham he wanted to do something spiritual at the ceremony. Four or five verses of Scripture were suggested by Graham. Eisenhower took the suggestions and then led in prayer — the general's own idea, according to Graham.

It was no secret that Graham supported Richard Nixon in the 1960 presidential race, but when John F. Kennedy was elected, he invited Graham to play golf and their friendship grew.

Lyndon B. Johnson's coming to the White House brought no change in Graham's visits; the two became close friends. Graham and his wife had the distinction of being out-going President Johnson's last guests at the White House and the new President Nixon's first White House guests. The Grahams bade farewell to the Johnsons and then stayed at the White House to welcome the Nixons.

BILLY GRAHAM SAID IT

355
Race Solution

The race question will not be solved by demonstrations in the streets, but in the hearts of both Negro and white. There must be genuine love to replace prejudice and hate. This love can be supplied by Christ and only by Christ.

356
Universal Need

Whether the story of Christ is told in a huge stadium, across the desk of some powerful leader, or shared with a golfing companion, it satisfies a common hunger. All over the world, whenever I meet people face to face, I am made aware of this personal need among the famous and successful as well as the lonely and obscure.

357
America the Blessed

The ethical and moral concepts of Christianity are found all the way through the Declaration of Independence. It was on July 4, 1776, that fifty men gathered in Independence Hall in Philadelphia to declare this nation free from Great Britain and they affixed their signatures and then the Liberty Bell rang out. It was the birthday of a small nation that was to become the mightiest and greatest nation the world has ever known. Down through the years God has mightily blessed America.

358
A Real Christian

A real Christian is a person who can give his pet parrot to the town gossip.

359
Permissive Thinking Dangerous

In many churches, one can attend services for a full year without once hearing the word "sin" mentioned. Not a few ministers and teachers of religion have fallen prey to this permissive thinking, which holds that there are no absolutes, that the right or wrong of an act depends upon the circumstances of time and place. As for such acts of premarital or extramarital sex, these are said to be justified "if the relationship is meaningful" and "if it hurts nobody else." With even religious leaders talking this way, it is small wonder that youth is bewildered, and that the church's moral authority is eroding almost to the vanishing point.

— From "What the Bible Says about Sex," *Reader's Digest,* May 1970

360
Hope for the World

Some years ago, I was invited to No. 10 Downing Street in London by Sir Winson Churchill. It was a dark hour in Britain's history, and the prime minister was deeply discouraged. He had hardly greeted me before he asked, "Young man, do you have any hope for the world?" I took a New Testament from my pocket, saying, "Mr. Prime Minister, this book is full of hope." Quickly, he replied, "Would you read me some passages?" For the next thirty minutes I read selections that I thought would fit this mood. As I left, he said warmly, 'I thank you. You have given an old man a renewal of faith for the future." I hadn't. But the Bible had.

361
Prayer

The Christian should have an appetite for prayer. He should want to pray. One does not have to force food upon a healthy child. Exercise, good circulation, health, and labor demand food for sustenance. So it is with those who are spiritually healthy. They have an appetite for the Word of God and for prayer.

Sin breaks fellowship with God. A little girl committed a certain offense, and when her mother discovered it she began to question her daughter. Immediately the child lost her smile and a cloud darkened her face as she said, "Mother, I don't feel like talking." So it is with us when our fellowship with God is broken by sin in our lives. We do not feel like talking to Him. If you do not feel like praying, it is probably a good indication that you should start praying immediately.

362
Personal Faith

In Augustine's personal experience with God, I am convinced, lies the basic explanation for youthful restlessness today. In it also, I firmly believe, lies the prime solution to youth's worldwide rebellion. Youth needs a personal faith that is challenging and life changing. This is what Christ can give.

363
The Home

If civilization is to survive, the home and the institution of marriage must survive.

364
Premarital Sex

Indiscriminate passionate lovemaking can be dangerous, psychologically and physically. The sex urge is never stronger than in the teen years, and requires great restraint. Competent youth advisers are quick to point out that deep trouble often follows promiscuous petting. To put the matter bluntly, kissing and intimate embracing are natural preludes to more serious intimacies. Happy marriages are built upon mutual respect for each other before marriage, and the wise and prudent couple will not forfeit their future happiness for a few moments of sensual pleasure.

— Decision

365
Blow the Trumpet

God has handed the Gospel trumpet to His church, and in our day we have blown it like a Boy Scout practicing with his first bugle. The noise of our solemn assemblies seems to be one uncertain sound after another. One might think that Christians were following some pseudo-Messiah like Napoleon or Lenin or Hitler, so eager are we to apologize for all our shortcomings.

— Decision

HORACE GREELEY
(1811–1872)

One of the most influential newspaper editors in American history, Horace Greeley founded and edited the New York Tribune. *He took an antislavery position that helped form public opinion prior to the Civil War. He was a vigorous fighter who created many enemies with his editorials. He helped Abraham Lincoln win the presidency, although he differed later with him about the way the war should be conducted. Later, he supported Ulysses S. Grant but then broke with him. He was nominated to run for president in 1872 against Grant but was beaten badly. He died less than a month later. Greeley popularized the phrase, "Go west, young man," originally attributed to an Indiana newspaperman, John Soule, as advice to New York's unemployed.*

366
Emancipation Proclamation

It took a year of defeat and disappointment to bring the government to a state of mind where it was ready to proclaim the emancipation of the slave. Horace Greeley — the great editor of the *Tribune,* who ran in the masthead of his paper the slogan "On to Richmond!" — was fiercely critical of what seemed to be the blundering failures of the government. But when he came to write his reminiscences, after the war was over and slavery had been destroyed and the Union preserved, Greeley saw clearly the hand of God in that early history of the war. "Had Napoleon or Jackson," he wrote, "been in Scott's place in 1861, the rebellion would have been stamped out ere the close of that year. But slavery would have remained to scourge us still. Thus disaster is overruled to subserve the ends of beneficence. Thus the evil of the moment contains the germ of good that is enduring."

That was a great sentence by Greeley: "Thus the evil of the moment contains the germ of good that is enduring."

—From *Macartney's Illustrations,* by Clarence E. Macartney. Copyright 1945 by Whitmore and Stone.

367
A Sermon for Beecher

Horace Greeley was once on his way to lunch with the famous minister, Henry Ward Beecher. Greeley was always a soft touch for those who asked him for a handout or a loan. On this particular day a begging child approached him. Greeley scowled at the boy but shoved a bill into his hand. "Don't you know it's shameful to beg?" he snapped.

"Horace," Beecher smiled as they went on their way, "you're a shrewd man. But you forever let yourself be imposed upon by beggars, even though you know most of them are base and undeserving. Why?"

"I would have thought a man of God understood why," Greeley replied dryly. "Can you think of a heavier curse of heaven, Henry, than being born with a burden of lazy shiftlessness, or a mean cunning? Those of us who come into life better equipped *owe* these incurables our help!"

368
Rule of Lecture Success

Some of Horace Greeley's contemporaries described the famous editor's wardrobe as resembling that of a Quaker farmer in the West. And his speech was described as being squeaky, screechy, singsong, and shrill. Yet he became an attraction on the lecture circuit because of what he had to say, not how he appeared nor how he delivered his speech. Once he admitted to an audience that he was probably the worst public speaker in America. Henry Ward Beecher, one of the greatest orators of the day, asked him how he could tell when any lecture he gave was a success. Greeley scratched his head a moment, then said, "Well, Henry, I guess it's when more folks stay in than go out."

369
Concentration

It is told of Horace Greeley that once while walking down the street a thought occurred to him that was good material for an editorial. He at once sat down on the curb, took a piece of paper and a pencil out of his pocket, and began to write. About that time a circus parade came along. When it had passed, a friend approached Mr. Greeley and asked him how he liked the parade. "What parade?" asked Greeley. "Why, the circus parade that has just passed by," replied the friend. "Beg your pardon," answered Greeley, "I did not see it."

370
No Handouts Expected

As editor of the *New York Tribune*, Horace Greeley was instrumental in helping elect Abraham Lincoln in 1860. Unlike others in a similar position, Greeley was too proud to ask the president for a single favor. One day his brother Barnes visited the editor at his office.

"Horace," he said, "I'm sick of farming. I'm applying for a job as mail agent. I bid to do it for a thousand dollars a year."

"Anyone else after it?" Horace inquired.

"Yes, that's the trouble," Barnes replied. "Another feller is offering to do it for only five hundred dollars." Barnes then asked his brother to use his political influence with the president to get him the job.

"I can't, Barnes," Horace said with regret. "It would be wrong." And then he went further to remind his brother that the government would be losing five hundred dollars a year if he got the job. But then he put his hand in his pocket and pulled out all the bills in it. "I'm doing right well these days," he said, "and I wouldn't miss this a bit!" Barnes accepted the bills and left.

It isn't known whether Barnes ever found out that Horace had to borrow money for lunches for the next two weeks.

371
Pride

A pompous, inflated congressman once remarked to Horace Greeley, "I am a self-made man." To which Greeley replied, "Well, sir, that relieves the Almighty of a great responsibility."

372
Pride

Mrs. Horace Greeley was a very independent if somewhat eccentric woman. At one time she bought three goats for the children to play with, and all this livestock was installed in the Greeley's New York house.

Once a friend called on Sunday morning and found the family preparing for church. Mr. and Mrs. Greeley, the children, and the goats were all milling around in the front hall.

"The question is," said Mr. Greeley to the friend, "whether the goats shall go up Broadway with us. Mrs. Greeley insists that I shan't go to church unless at the head of a procession of children and goats."

Several days later Mr. Greeley met the friend. "Well," he remarked, "we got off at last without the goats, though Mrs. Greeley said to me, 'It's only your miserable pride!'"

HORACE GREELEY SAID IT

373
Bible

It is impossible to mentally or socially enslave a Bible-reading people. The principles of the Bible are the groundwork of human freedom.

374
Good Old Days

The illusion that times that were are better than those that are, has probably pervaded all ages.

375
Principles

If, on a full and final review, my life and practice shall be found unworthy my principles, let due infamy be heaped on my memory; but let none be thereby led to distrust the principles to which I proved recreant, nor yet the ability of some to adorn them by a suitable life and conversation. To unerring time be all this committed.

376
Alcohol

Abstaining is favorable both to the head and pocket.

377
Apathy

Apathy is a sort of living oblivion.

378
Common Sense

Common sense is very uncommon.

379
Alcohol

No man has a moral, and none should have a legal right to sell that debasing and maddening poison, alcohol, to his neighbors.

380
Spiritualism

I find it dull sitting for two dreary hours in a darkened room in mixed company, waiting for somebody's disembodied grandfather or aunt to tip a table or rap on a door. I have little time for poking and peering into life beyond the grave. . . . We would all do better to attend to each world in its proper order!

—Comment after attending Fox sisters' spiritualist séances

381
Truth

What people say is none of my affair. My job is to print the truth.

382
Oblivion Certain

Fame is a vapor; popularity an accident; riches take wings; the only earthly certainty is oblivion; no man can foresee what a day may bring forth; while those who cheer today will often curse tomorrow; and yet I cherish the hope that the journal I projected and established will live and flourish long after I shall have mouldered into forgotten dust . . . and that the stone which covers my ashes may bear to future eyes the still intelligible inscription, "Founder of the *New York Tribune.*"

383
Woe to Selfish

Authorship is a royal priesthood; but woe to him who rashly lays unhallowed hands on the ark or altar, professing a zeal for the welfare of the race, only to secure his own selfish ends.

JEROME HINES
(1921–   )

For a fellow who couldn't carry a tune in junior high, Metropolitan Opera singer Jerome Hines has come a long way. As a youth, Hines had his eye on a career in chemistry. When his singing potential became evident, he took opera lessons and began singing in the famous Metropolitan Opera at age twenty-five. In his youth Hines had no place for God. But after what he called a thirty-year search for reality, he found it in the person of the Lord Jesus Christ. Whenever possible he goes to the skid rows of major cities, singing and giving his testimony in missions. He tells his story in the book This Is My Story, This Is My Song. *He also composed an opera about the life of Jesus,* I Am the Way.

384
God's Guidance

If Metropolitan Opera performer Jerome Hines had fulfilled his youthful ambition, he would today be a chemist. Singing was as foreign to him as Chinese. There were no musicians in his family, and for a time it appeared there never would be; for Jerome had been kicked out of the junior high glee club because he couldn't carry a tune. Chemistry became his idol.

His singing career began because, of all things, he was an introvert. Mrs. Hines was concerned about her son's quiet, withdrawn nature. A neighbor suggested the singing lessons with the idea that it would help Jerome get away from his shyness. The teacher discovered that Jerome had an excellent voice, and his singing career was soon launched. Even though he was not serving the Lord at the time, Jerome could look back on those early days in singing and see God's hand leading him. It wasn't until several years later that he realized he needed the God who was quietly watching him in his climb for the world's fame and fortune. After his fruitless search, he finally knew what he was looking for: "One day," he said, "I found Jesus Christ through the Holy Spirit."

385
One Letter Makes a Difference

Leaving out just one letter of the alphabet in a wedding ceremony can give it an entirely different meaning, Jerome Hines found out. His bride, Lucia Evangelista, was from Italy and didn't speak English too well. Everything went well in the ceremony until the justice of the peace asked Lucia to repeat after him, "I, Lucia Evangelista, take thee, Jerome Hines, to be my lawful wedded husband. . . . "

Lucia followed, "I, Lucia Evangelista, take dee, Jerome Hines, to be my *awful* wedded husband. . . . "

Fortunately, the intent of the heart was sincere, the wedding ceremony went on, and the Hineses have had a happy and *lawful* marriage.

386
A Humbling Experience

Although Jerome Hines had worldwide fame as an opera singer, he had never sung in a church service as a believer until he had a chance to sing at a Salvation Army meeting in London. He was bothered when the meeting leader asked a woman to sing just before he was to be introduced. "Why," he wondered, "do they let her sing? What a terrible sound. It's strange that they'd let *her* sing, knowing there's a Metropolitan Opera singer on the program." He was disturbed.

Then Hines was struck by the radiant, beautiful look on the woman's face. The impact of the words of the song struck him. He soon forgot the unpleasant scratch of her voice. He was impressed by the glow that shone from her face. When she finished the number, Hines rose to sing. To his complete consternation his voice was so scratchy and hoarse that he had to stop in the middle of the hymn, make an apology for an unexpected laryngitis attack, and then sat down. He was confused; here he was trying to sing for the Lord for the first time and it was a complete failure. He questioned God and seemed to hear Him reply, "I am not interested in your beautiful voice, but in your message."

It was a humbling but a valuable experience for Jerome Hines. Since then the "message" has been the motivation for his singing.

387
Not Ashamed

One evening several years ago my wife and daughter Gwen joined Jerome Hines at the Italian Village restaurant, Chicago haunt of show people, after a performance. We had been delayed. But the producer of the opera in which Hines was playing the leading role had reserved seats for us at the table where a party of a dozen or more were already eating. We were engrossed in conversation when our food finally was served.

"We are going to thank the Lord for this food. We will appreciate it if you will be quiet while we pray," Hines said. Then, in a voice that could be heard for fifty feet in every direction above the clink of glasses and the murmur of voices, Hines prayed.

When he finished, the conversation had been turned to spiritual subjects and Hines recounted his experiences in seeing how God transformed lives in skid row missions where he had sung and witnessed to others what Jesus Christ had meant to him.

> — By Robert Walker. Reprinted by permission from *Christian Life* magazine, Copyright 1964, Christian Life Publications, Inc., Gundersen Drive and Schmale Road, Wheaton, Illinois 60187.

388
God No Respecter of Persons

Shortly after President Kennedy's inauguration, Jerome Hines was invited to sing at the annual prayer breakfast attended by the president and many government leaders. Hines was excited; he would be the first person to give a testimony to America's first Catholic president. He paced the streets of Washington for an hour before the breakfast, seeking the mind of the Lord about his testimony. He made up several gimmicks of speech to impress the president, but finally discarded them all and asked for the Lord's help. The help came, but not the way Hines thought. He was suddenly impressed that God was just as much interested in reaching a busboy waiting on tables as He was the president or other political leaders. The Lord continued to impress him that he was to just tell the audience what the Lord meant to him — nothing fancy, just a simple personal testimony. And that is what he gave. Later he was invited back to Washington to sing several times, and at each performance remembered what the Lord wanted from him.

389
Healed of Cancer

A former newspaperman, Hugh Redwood, was a guest speaker in a London Salvation Army meeting that Jerome Hines was attending. Hines told how Redwood chided his hearers about the lack of prayer in the average Christian's life and then told a story of a miracle in answer to prayer. A former newspaper colleague of Redwood was dying of cancer, and his wife asked Redwood to visit him in the hospital. The man asked Redwood if he believed God could cure him. Redwood answered in the affirmative, but admitted he was panicky until he heard God's voice assuring him that He was in the room and He would heal the man. They bowed in prayer for an hour and were convinced God indeed would bring healing.

As Redwood told the story, he took out a letter that he had recently received from the man. Two years had passed since that hospital experience; the man was still living and praising God for the miracle. Redwood began to read the letter:

> I know you'll be happy to hear that my first book has just been accepted by the publisher and at last a life-long dream of mine will be accomplished. How impossible all this would have seemed two years ago as you sat at my bedside in the cancer clinic. But now by the grace of God I have been spared to have a full and fruitful life.

Jerome Hines, a new Christian at the time, left London reflecting on that testimony. He vowed to pray more and believe God for the seemingly impossible things he faced in his own life.

390
Not Too Big to Serve

Not too many big stars would offer their time and talent in skid row missions and the Salvation Army. Could there be any who would? Yes, and his name is Jerome Hines, Metropolitan Opera's leading basso. Hines frequently finds his way down to New York's skid row or similar areas in other cities where he might be performing. He seeks out a rescue mission and offers his help with songs and testimony. Derelict drunks, who have never been near the Met and know nothing of Jerome Hines's fame, listen carefully as Hines gives his testimony and sings old favorites such as "The Old Rugged Cross" and "Are You Washed in the Blood?"

Why does Hines do it? He believes God loves every man — and that love includes the Bowery drunks — and wants them to hear the gospel message. Some of the panhandlers on the street know Hines as a "soft touch." "I used to avoid them," he says; "now I welcome a chance to talk to them. If a man needs money for a meal, I find a restaurant and take him in. Sometimes these men are so hungry they will promise to do almost anything to get food. So, I give them a Gospel of John and make them promise to read it."

Jerome Hines is a Metropolitan Opera star, but he doesn't feel he is too big to minister to the less fortunate on skid row.

391
A Circle of Protection

Jerome Hines had never faced such a schedule. It was 1962 and he was headed for Argentina and Russia. The performances lined up for him were so heavy his friends feared his health would suffer. On top of that, Argentina was faced with a revolution and later it was discovered the Russians were trying to install missile bases in Cuba. He was urged to cancel the trip. It was too dangerous and strenuous.

The tall Metropolitan Opera star went for a walk so he could be alone and talk with the Lord about the trip. Later he said he had never had such an experience. "It was just like the heavens themselves opening up," he said. He sensed the Lord speaking to him: "For the next two months I am going to put a circle of protection around you. The devil cannot touch you. Go with my protection."

The day after the Hines family boarded their plane in Argentina for Russia, the airport was closed and fighter planes bombed the runways. In Russia he faced Khrushchev and the Russians during the Cuban crisis. But the Lord used him and then brought him home safely. "I am going to put a circle of protection around you." Jerome Hines will never forget that personal promise from his Lord.

392
Prayer Answered

October 1962 will be long remembered as the month of the Cuban crisis. For two months the Russians had been shipping technicians and equipment to Castro's Cuba. High-flying United States planes were able to photograph offensive missile sites. President Kennedy revealed the photographs to the world and demanded that Premier Khrushchev remove them. The United States set up a naval blockade to prevent Cuba-bound Russian ships from delivering more missile cargo. It was an extremely touchy international situation.

In Moscow during one of those long, long days, an American opera star, Jerome Hines, was scheduled to perform. To make matters more sticky for the American, the Russian people had just been told of the blockade, and Khrushchev was scheduled to attend Hines's performance! Hines was naturally edgy. Before the performance, Bill Jones, an American businessman who was in Russia at the time, went backstage and joined Hines in prayer. And of course Christians around the world were praying.

After a nervous but brilliant performance, Hines was given a standing ovation — led by Khrushchev. Then Hines was told that Khrushchev waited to see him backstage. Who wouldn't be nervous!

The meeting that followed no doubt had something to do with Khrushchev's softening in the Cuban crisis. The Russian leader proposed toasts to peace and friendship between the Soviet Union and the United States. Then after thirty minutes, Khrushchev and his party prepared to leave. Hines used his best Russian in a farewell, "Blagaslavi Vas Bog" (God bless you).

A few days later the Russian leader announced that the ships had turned back. God had answered prayer.

393
Encouragement

Everyone has moments of discouragement. But one does not have to keep in that mood. He can turn to the personal Lord who is able to change defeat into victory.

One morning Jerome Hines was sitting in his dressing room at the Met waiting for the moment he would sing a part in a radio opera. He was in a gloomy mood and his voice was giving him problems. "I wanted to turn to the Lord in the trouble with my voice, but that seemed a selfish sort of act," he reasoned. He said he was feeling about as low as he could and asked God how anyone could possibly love him. Hines was startled to sense the uplifting presence of God, who seemed to impress him that He loved him enough to die for him. "The truth of God's love burst upon me like warm sunshine. . . . I sang *Tannhauser* as I never had before."

Later, a friend wrote: "I have seen you many times on stage but on the Saturday broadcast of *Tannhauser* your whole being radiated the peace and love of God. It was a memorable experience."

Hines accepted the incident as another essential lesson in his Christian life.

JEROME HINES SAID IT

394
The Jerome Hines Testimony

I wandered about for 30 years with an inner fire burning in my soul, an inner fire that relentlessly drove me here and drove me there. What was this fire? Some men call it ambition; in some, it is a sense of unfulfilled destiny. Other men can find no name for it. But something was missing in my life. What was it? Where was it?

First I sought the answer in science. I spent six years getting degrees in chemistry and mathematics. I studied psychology, psychiatry, philosophy and many other subjects. None of these gave the answer or satisfied that internal fire. . . . I became a successful opera singer, joined the Metropolitan Opera, and sang in concerts and on television. Still no satisfaction to a restless soul.

Then one day I found Jesus Christ through the Holy Spirit and I discovered it was He that I had been seeking all my life: How wonderful to find that burning fire quieted within me — to find my life complete.

I have become a servant of the Lord. I am His tool to use as He sees fit, and I try to live according to His will.

> — Reprinted by permission from *Christian Life* magazine, Copyright 1964, Christian Life Publications, Inc., Gundersen Drive and Schmale Road, Wheaton, Illinois 60187.

395
The Devil's Work

As soon as God makes a promise, the devil tries to make it seem a lie.

396
Pride

I had a voice and talent and was driven by worldly ambitions. I was going places fast, and the whole world lay before me. I had no family responsibilities, and I surely felt I was master of my own fate. . . . I had no need of a personal God or answered prayer. I felt I was sufficient unto myself, and instead of thinking of what God needed to do for me, I was thinking of what I was going to do for Him.

> — Personal philosophy as college student

397
His Tool

I have become a servant of the Lord. I am His tool to use as He sees fit since I found Jesus Christ and discovered it was He I had been seeking.

398
Religion

I doubt if there is a man who can remove himself from the religious picture. I particularly like to do operas that have a deeply religious significance for everyone.

399
Knows God

I don't believe in God — I know Him.

400
Dead Ends

Everyone has his dead ends in one way or another. . . . Dead ends — big ones and little ones — pop up unexpectedly in everyone's life all the time. If we back up, learn by our mistakes and try again in a new direction, our dead ends can be profitable experiences. But sometimes we are too stubborn or too lazy to back up and try again. We rationalize, claiming the dead end is not an error at all, but our intended goal. Many times a bright future has been ruined by the claim that life is empty, without meaning or purpose.

—From *This Is My Story, This Is My Song*

J. EDGAR HOOVER
(1895–1972)

Named director of the Federal Bureau of Investigation (FBI) in 1924, J. Edgar Hoover held the position through the administrations of eight presidents. He developed the FBI into one of the most efficient law enforcement agencies in the world. Hoover worked as a messenger in the Library of Congress after he completed high school. He became a member of the Department of Justice in 1917. He led dramatic campaigns against public enemies, such as George "Machine Gun" Kelly and John Dillinger. He wrote many articles and several books on communism and the methods of fighting it.

401
Youthful Guidance

Radio Evangelist C. M. Ward in an interview with J. Edgar Hoover asked the FBI chief about those who contributed to his spiritual development as a child. Hoover credited his parents and a pastor.

> Both Father and Mother provided spiritual training in the home. They took me to church and Sunday school. I recall vividly the Sunday evenings when we sat in a family circle listening to the Word of God. Ours was a family whose strength rested in the Christian faith.

Hoover said many others contributed to his spiritual development, but he would always remember Donald MacLeod.

> He was a young Presbyterian preacher who served my boyhood church. He believed in boys like myself. His concern and compassion for young people made Dr. MacLeod my hero. He found

time for us. He didn't think it "unsaintly" to play a little softball with the teen-age boys in the neighborhood. I remember him with gratitude for his example as a true Christian.

402
Youth and Communism

The *Sunday Times* magazine interviewed J. Edgar Hoover on the topic of youth and communist influence. The reporter asked Hoover if the young people of America were a prime target of communist influence.

> Yes. This is the natural result of looking to the future. In order to exist, every organization is dependent upon a continuous supply of new blood. If it does not get an infusion in time it will disintegrate and die.... In addition to the compulsion to survive, and, of course to expand, the Communist Party, USA, is motivated by the assessment of Lenin that: "The youth will determine the whole struggle, the student youth and still more the working class youth."

J. EDGAR HOOVER SAID IT

403
The Role of the FBI

We are a fact-gathering organization only. We don't clear anybody. We don't condemn anybody. Just the minute the FBI begins making recommendations on what should be done with its information, it becomes a gestapo.

404
Terrorism

The voices of temperance, logic, and decency must speak out. Terrorism cannot be tolerated in a free society. Hate, terror, and lawlessness are not the American way.

405
Discipline

Either you will teach your children discipline or the world will teach them discipline in ways that will be destructive to their individual happiness.

406
Anti-Communism Serum

We in America have anti-communism serum, the answer to the Communist challenge. It lies in the strength of our Judaic-Christian tradition, the power of the Holy Spirit working in men. Too frequently, both clergy and laymen do not realize the full resources at their command in the Christian tradition — the tremendous power of God to turn men toward good, to make personalities bloom with the living courage of sainted men. The job of . . . clergymen is to help channel this divine power into the hearts, minds, and souls of men. Literally, the Gospel has the power to turn the world upside down. That should be your [clergy's] mission.

— *Christianity Today,* Oct. 24, 1960

407
American Qualities

These strong qualities — faith, individualism, courage, integrity, discipline, and vision — are the keys to freedom. Let us protect and defend the real meaning of America. This is the debt we owe to the brave legions of the past who laid down their lives to safeguard the great truths which guide our destiny today.

— Congressional Record, September 16, 1964

408
Nation under God

This nation was conceived under God and its progress has been under God. There could be no greater disaster for our nation than that it should deny in any respect, to even the smallest degree, the presence, the power, the guidance, the protection, the instruction of almighty God.

—Congressional Record, December 5, 1963

409
Three of a Kind

I place the fiery cross of the vicious Ku Klux Klan in the same category as the swastika of the Nazis and the godless hammer and sickle of atheistic communism. All ignore the rights of everyone to life, liberty, and the pursuit of happiness.

All right-thinking citizens know that there is no place in America for vigilantes, rabble rousers, the "lunatic fringe," and those who make a profit — political or material — out of merchandising prejudice.

410
Children and Sunday School

Shall I make my child go to Sunday school and church? Yes! And with no further discussion about the matter. Startled? Why? How do you answer Junior when he comes to breakfast on Monday morning and announces to you that he is not going to school any more? You know! Junior goes. How do you answer when Junior comes in very much besmudged and says, "I'm not going to take a bath." Junior bathes, doesn't he?

Why all this timidity then, in the realm of his spiritual guidance and growth? Going to let him wait and decide what church he'll go to when he's old enough? Quit your kidding! You didn't wait until you were old enough! You don't wait until he's old enough to decide whether he wants to go to school or not — to start his education. You don't wait until he's old enough to decide whether he wishes to be clean or dirty do you? Do you wait until he's old enough to decide if he wants to take his medicine when he is sick? Do you?

What shall we say when Junior announces he doesn't like to go to

Sunday school and church? That's an easy one to answer. Just be consistent. Tell him, "Junior, in our house we all go to church and Sunday school, and that includes you." Your firmness and example will furnish a bridge over which youthful rebellion may travel into rich and satisfying experience in personal religious living.

The parents of America can strike a telling blow against the forces which contribute to our juvenile delinquency, if our fathers and mothers will take their children to Sunday school and church regularly.

—*Knight's Treasury of Illustrations*

411
The Family Circle

The picture of the family circle, the father, mother, and children sitting together reading the Bible, is a scene of inspiring beauty. There the Word of God is at work — molding character, lighting the path of good, inspiring deeds of service. Religion has a vital meaning, touching every aspect of life. God is there in the home, working through purposeful lives to create His kingdom.

412
The Home

There is no synthetic replacement for a decent home life. Our high crime rate, particularly among juveniles, is directly traceable to a breakdown in moral fiber — to the disintegration of home and family life. Religion and home life are supplementary. Each strengthens the other. It is seldom that a solid and wholesome home life can be found in the absence of religious inspiration.

413
Shocking Comparisons

For every one dollar contributed to religious organizations, crime costs the citizens of our nation nine.

414
Prayer

The spectacle of a nation praying is more awe-inspiring than the explosion of an atomic bomb. The force of prayer is greater than any possible combination of man-controlled powers, because prayer is man's greatest means of tapping the infinite resources of God.

415
Religious Training

The bulwark of religious training is vital if the line is to be held against the forces of corruption, crime, and disloyalty. I believe that men imbued with spiritual values do not betray their country. I believe that children reared in homes in which morality is taught and lived rarely become delinquents.

416
Good Advice for Parents

Surround your child with a loving and stable atmosphere in the home. Teach him the Word of God. Set for him an example of honesty, self-respect, and self-discipline. Give him responsibilities. Help him to set high personal standards for himself and his friends, and to take pride in his rich inheritance of freedom. Make sure that he knows the living stories of those great Americans who march like magnificent giants through the pages of this nation's brief history.

417
Importance of Church and Sunday School

Children imbued with true spiritual values are not likely to accept a philosophy which is atheistic, materialistic, and totalitarian. It is the responsibility of the home, the church, and the Sunday school to cultivate those values which undergird our free way of life through the development of responsible, conscientious citizens. The church and the Sunday school can be effective forces both in educating young people to understand the threat which atheistic communism poses to our way of life, and in teaching your youth to oppose it through legal, orderly means.

LYNDON B. JOHNSON

(1908–1973)

Texan Lyndon B. Johnson was the fourth vice-president to become president of the United States upon the assassination of the president. He was sworn in as the thirty-sixth president, November 22, 1963, a short time after President Kennedy was shot. In 1964 he was elected with a landslide victory over Sen. Barry M. Goldwater. Johnson went to Washington, D.C., in 1931 as a congressional secretary. He was elected to the House of Representatives in 1937 and then became a senator in 1948. He was the Senate majority leader from 1955 to 1960. The Johnson Presidential Library is located in Austin, Texas. His presidential memoirs are recorded in his book The Vantage Point: Perspective of the Presidency 1963–1969 *(1971).*

418
I Want to Hear Your Prayer

Bill Moyers, former President Johnson's press secretary, is an ordained minister and on a few occasions conducted devotions at the White House or at the LBJ ranch when the family did not attend church services. Sometimes the president would ask him to say grace at White House meals. At one such meal at the White House, Moyers's prayer was in such a low voice that the president asked him to pray louder. Moyers replied, "I wasn't talking to you, Mr. President." Later, when the president invited some reporters to have lunch with him at the ranch, he asked Moyers to lead in prayer and said, "And this time I don't care who you're talking to. I want to hear you."

419
Search for Spiritual Help

Sam Houston Johnson in his book *My Brother Lyndon* took issue with some of the critics of President Johnson who declared that the president was "courting the church vote" by attending church services of various denominations — Episcopalian, Baptist, Methodist, Catholic, and Quaker.

> They were dead wrong. I am personally convinced that the Presidency, with all its terrible and awesome burdens, made him feel a desperate need for greater spiritual comfort. In going from one church to another, I think he was unconsciously searching for some special type of solace, a kind of spiritual ease that no president can hope to have.

420
Loyal to the Baptists

Lyndon Johnson's father was a state legislator in Texas. In one governor's election, he was campaigning hard in his district for Joe Bailey. The opponent was Pat Neff (the eventual winner), who generally received strong support from the Baptists. The senior Johnson had his volunteer staff methodically check every precinct to get a preelection count for his man Bailey. In his home district of Johnson City, much to his consternation, his preelection prediction was off one vote. He was certain that someone in his district had lied to him, and he was anxious to find out who it was. Finally, Lyndon's mother spoke up in an effort to calm her husband. "That's sheer nonsense, Sam," she said. "No one lied to you. And you *didn't* talk to everyone. You never asked *me* how I was going to vote. You took it for granted that I'd vote for your man. Well, I might as well tell you that I voted for Neff." Mr. Johnson was flabbergasted at what he termed disloyalty in his own household and let his wife know what he thought of Neff. But Mrs. Johnson, who had a long line of Baptist preachers in her family background, wasn't about to vote against a Baptist. "He's a good, decent Baptist; and that's why I voted for him. You won't catch me voting against my own people."

421
Smooth Takeover

There is no word less than superb to describe the performance of Lyndon Baines Johnson as he became President of the United States.

All the accounts of his behavior through the week of tragedy — his calm, his command-presence, his doings, his unlimited energies — endow him with superlative grace. Yet such stories limit the tale only to his positive deeds. To measure the true quality of his takeover, one must consider not only these positive acts, but what did *not* happen. So much *might* have gone wrong — yet did not.

— Theodore H. White, in *The Making of the President, 1964*

422
Waxing Eloquent

One of former President Johnson's favorite stories is about the late Senator Tom Connally of Texas. As the former chief tells it, Connally, in a speech "down home," started talking about the beautiful piney woods of east Texas, moved on through the bluebonnets and out to the plains, then through the hill country to the gulf, and started again on the piney woods of east Texas. While he was thus making the rounds of the state for about the third time, an old man stood up in the back of the room and shouted to Connally, "When you pass Lubbock the next time, will you kindly let me off?"

423
Nothing on His Mind

Lyndon B. Johnson told about Al Smith, a presidential candidate in 1928, who was making a speech when a heckler yelled, "Tell 'em what's on your mind, Al. It won't take long." Smith grinned, pointed at the man and shouted, "Stand up, pardner, and I'll tell 'em what's on both our minds. It won't take any longer."

424
Donation Assured

Former President Johnson tells a story he borrowed from Brooks Hays, the former congressman who at one time served as president of the Southern Baptist Convention.

An Internal Revenue Bureau agent telephoned a Baptist minister and said, "I'm going over the tax return of one of your church members, a Mr. _____. He lists a donation of $260 to the church. Can you tell me if he made this contribution?"

The minister replied, "Well, I haven't got my records before me — but if he didn't, he will!"

LYNDON B. JOHNSON SAID IT

425
Danger of War

The world has changed and so has the method of dealing with disruptions of the peace. There may have been a time when a commander in chief would order soldiers to march the very moment a disturbance occurred. Once upon a time large-scale war could be waged without risking the end of civilization; today, such war is unthinkable. In a matter of moments, we could wipe out a hundred million of our adversaries. They could, in the same amount of time, wipe out a hundred million of our people, taking half of our land in a matter of an hour.

426
Bible

If you will just go back to the Good Book and practice some of the teachings of the Lord, if we will just follow the golden rule and do unto others what we would have them do unto us, if we just engage in a little introspection and look where we were and where we are, we won't be unhappy very long. We won't feel sorry for ourselves very long.

— From campaign speech, 1964

427
Government

It was here [Austin, Texas] as a barefoot boy around my Daddy's desk in that great hall of the House of Representatives, where he served for six terms and where my grandfather served ahead of him, that I first learned that government is not an enemy of the people. It is the people. The only attacks that I have resented in this campaign are the charges which are based on the idea that the presidency is something apart from the people, opposed to them, against them. I learned here, when I was the NYA administrator, that poverty and ignorance are the only basic weaknesses of a free society, and that both of them are only bad habits and can be stopped.

— Election eve speech, 1964

428
Power Can Do Only So Much

Neither our nuclear power nor our great wealth can force events into a mold of our making. Our nuclear power can deter massive aggression. Our resources can help other nations develop their own self-defenses. Our diplomats, guided by our commitments to order in the relations among states, can help to forge agreements that reduce the threat of war. But our power cannot change men who are determined to satisfy old hatreds or new ambitions. It can help to limit the scope of a conflict that has already begun. But it cannot prevent conflict from breaking out.

— *In Quest of Peace,* Britannica Book of the Year, 1969

429
America Young

In the long view of history, these years are the early summer of America. Our land is young. Our strength is great. Our course is far from run.

430
Voluntary

If there is one word that describes our form of society in America, it may be the word *voluntary.*

431
World Neighborhood

We live in a world that has narrowed into a neighborhood before it has broadened into a brotherhood.

432
Weapons Human Folly

We often say how impressive power is. But I do not find it impressive at all. The guns and the bombs, the rockets and the warships, are all symbols of human failure. They are necessary symbols. They protect what we cherish. But they are witness to human folly.

433
Solving Problems

There are no problems we cannot solve together, and very few that we can solve by ourselves.

434
Fellow Passengers

We are all fellow passengers on a dot of earth. And each of us, in the span of time, has really only a moment among our companions.

435
For All the People

A tragic twist of fateful sorrow made me president. From that awful day on November 22, when President Kennedy was assassinated, I have had but one thought, but one conviction, but one objective: To be the president of all the people, not just the rich, not just the well fed, not just the fortunate, but president of all America.

436
Aim of Communists

Communists, using force and intrigue, seek to bring about a communist dominated world. Our convictions, our interests, our life as a nation demand that we resolutely oppose, with all of our might, that effort to dominate the world.

437
Divided World

The world cannot remain divided between rich nations and poor nations, or white nations and colored nations. In such division are the seeds of terrible discord and danger in decades to come. For the wall between rich and poor is a wall of glass through which all can see.

438
Hand in Hand

As man increases his knowledge of the heavens, why should he fear the unknown on earth?

As man draws nearer to the stars, why should he not also draw nearer to his neighbor?

As we push ever more deeply into the universe, probing its secrets, discovering its way, we must also constantly try to learn to cooperate across the frontiers that really divide earth's surface.

439
Solving World Problems

I know that vast problems remain, conflicts between great powers, conflicts between small neighbors, disagreements over disarmament, persistence of ancient wrongs in the area of human rights, residual problems of colonialism, and all the rest. But men and nations, working apart, created these problems; and men and nations working together must solve them.

440
Prayer

Today — in our times — the responsibilities and burdens imposed upon us all are great and destined to grow. On us, on our decisions, rest the hopes of mankind for a world not left to chance, to war, or conquest.

We could find no more appropriate way to begin our days and our duties than to pray — for as we are taught, "except the Lord build this house, they labor in vain that build it."

In these times more than any other, the public life is a lonely life. The burden of every vote, every decision, every act, and even of every utterance, is too great to be shared and much too great to be borne alone. I find for myself, as I know men and women throughout the government also find, a sustaining strength from moments of prayer.

— From speech at annual presidential prayer breakfast

441

Civil Rights

No memorial oration or eulogy could more eloquently honor President Kennedy's memory than the earliest possible passage of the Civil Rights Bill for which he fought so long. We have talked long enough in the country about equal rights. . . . It is time now to write the next chapter — and to write it in the books of law.

— Speech to Congress, Nov. 27, 1963, five days after death of Kennedy

442

Ancient Enemies

I don't know what will be written about my administration. Nothing really seems to go right from early in the morning till late at night. And if they do . . . someone approves . . . almost accidentally. . . . But I would hope that it would be said of this decade, if not of this administration, so far as the ancient enemies of mankind are concerned . . . [we coped with] those ancient enemies . . . ignorance, illiteracy, ill health, and disease.

— Speaking for education bill, March 1965

SAMUEL JOHNSON
(1709–1784)

Samuel Johnson, the son of a poor bookseller, was an English critic and writer. He attended Oxford University but had to drop out after two years because he ran out of money. In 1755 Johnson's famous Dictionary of the English Language *was published. Four years later he wrote a novel,* Rasselas, Prince of Abyssinia. *He wrote other books, including the ten volumes of* The Lives of the Poets. *His wise sayings are still quoted today, some two hundred years after his major writings were first published. He is featured in one of the most famous biographies ever written,* The Life of Samuel Johnson *(1791), by his friend James Boswell.*

443
Horseback Not for Him

Samuel Johnson was once taken by his friend James Boswell to see the Giant Causeway in Ireland. He arrived at the site in a disagreeable mood, having been brought there on horseback, a method of conveyance he thoroughly despised. He shrugged his shoulders contemptuously as he gazed at the columnar basalt rock, which is considered one of the wonders of the world.

"Isn't this worth seeing?" Boswell asked him.

"Yes," replied Johnson, "worth seeing. But not worth going to see."

444
It's All in the Mind

One evening, an amateur philosopher professed himself convinced of the truth of Bishop Berkeley's theory that nothing exists but that which is perceived by some mind. Samuel Johnson listened to this theorizing for a while, and then said, "Pray sir, never leave us. For we may very likely forget to think of you, and then you will cease to exist."

445
Second Marriage

When Samuel Johnson heard of the second marriage of a friend, he said, "Alas! another instance of the triumph of hope over experience."

SAMUEL JOHNSON SAID IT

446
Friendship

We cannot tell the precise moment when friendship is formed. As in filling a vessel drop by drop, there is at last a drop which makes it run over; so in a series of kindnesses there is at last one which makes the heart run over.

447
Life

Life is surely given us for higher purposes than to gather what our ancestors have wisely thrown away.

448
Praise

Praise, like gold and diamonds, owes its value only to its scarcity.

449
Friendship

If a man does not make new acquaintances as he advances through life, he will soon find himself left alone. A man, sir, should keep his friendship in constant repair.

450
Suffer and Trust

It is better to suffer wrong than to do it, and happier to be sometimes cheated than not to trust.

451
Opportunity

To improve the golden moment of opportunity, and catch the good that is within our reach, is the great art of life.

452
Youth and Old Age

The first years of man must make provision for the last.

453
Enjoyment

A man who both spends and saves money is the happiest man, because he has both enjoyments.

454
Words and Things

I am not yet so lost in lexicography, as to forget that words are the daughters of earth, and that things are the sons of heaven.

455
Never Satisfied

Our desires always increase with our possessions. The knowledge that something remains yet unenjoyed impairs our enjoyment of the good before us.

456
Eating

For a man seldom thinks with more earnestness of anything than he does of his dinner.

457
Ignorance

Ignorance, when voluntary, is criminal.

458
Knowledge

Knowledge is of two kinds. We know a subject ourselves, or we know where we can find information upon it.

459
Labor Necessary

Labor, if it were not necessary for the existence, would be indispensable for the happiness of man.

460
Avarice

Avarice is generally the last passion of those lives of which the first part has been squandered in pleasure, and the second devoted to ambition.

461
Doing Good

He who waits to do a great deal of good at once, will never do anything.

462
Minister's Life

I do not envy a clergyman's life as an easy life, nor do I envy clergyman who makes it an easy life.

463
Curiosity

Curiosity is one of the permanent and certain characteristics of a vigorous intellect.

464
Calamity

When any calamity has been suffered, the first thing to be remembered is, how much has been escaped.

465
Finding Real Character

More knowledge may be gained of a man's real character by a short conversation with one of his servants than from a formal and studied narrative, begun with his pedigree and ended with his funeral.

466
Self-Love

Self-love is often rather arrogant than blind; it does not hide our faults from ourselves, but persuades us that they escape the notice of others.

HELEN KELLER
(1880–1968)

If asked to name an American who triumphed over handicaps, many would name Helen Keller first. Born a normal child, she contracted a brain fever that destroyed her sight and hearing before she was two years old. Because of the condition, she could not speak. By the time she was sixteen she had learned to speak well enough to enroll in a preparatory school. In spite of her disabilities, she rose to international fame for her help to other handicapped people. Two women who helped Helen throughout her lifetime were Anne Sullivan and Mary Agnes "Polly" Thompson. Her books have had wide circulation with translations in more than fifty languages. The stage play and motion picture, The Miracle Worker, *tells how Anne Sullivan taught Helen through the sense of touch.*

467
Overriding Objections

Helen Keller graduated from Radcliffe College in 1904, a tough assignment even for a normal person. She finished with excellent reading knowledge of Greek, Latin, German, and French — all in braille, of course. Some years later Woodrow Wilson asked her why she had chosen Radcliffe when she could have selected an easier college. "Because they didn't want me at Radcliffe," she answered; "and, being stubborn, I chose to override their objections."

468
Spiritual Sight

Shortly before her sixtieth birthday, Helen Keller expressed pity for the real unseeing, for those who have eyes yet do not see. Her long years of physical blindness had given her a spiritual insight which enabled her to enjoy life in all its fulness. She said: "If the blind put their hand in God's they find their way more surely than those who see but have not faith or purpose."

— *Western Recorder*

469
Approach to Old Age

Helen Keller was once asked, "How do you hope to approach old age?" Characteristic of her, the following classic answer was given:

> You are the first person who asked me point-blank how I intend to approach old age. I cannot help smiling — I who have these many years declared that there is no age in the spirit! Age seems to me only another physical handicap, and it excites no dread in me.
>
> Once I had a dear friend of eighty who impressed upon me the fact that he enjoyed life more than he had done at twenty-five. "Never count how many years you have, as the French say," he would insist, "but how many interests you have. Do not stale your days by taking for granted the people about you, or the things which make up your environment, and you will ever abide in a realm of fadeless beauty."
>
> Then and there I resolved, vestal-like to cherish an inextinguishable flame of youth. I have tried to avoid ruts — doing things just because my ancestors did them before me — leaning on the crutches of vicarious opinion — losing my childhood sense of wonderment. I am glad I still have a vivid curiosity about the world I live in.

— *Gospel Herald*

HELEN KELLER SAID IT

470
Faith

Faith, the spiritual strong searchlight, illumines the way, and although sinister doubts lurk in the shadow, I walk unafraid toward the Enchanted Wood where the foliage is always green, where joy abides, where nightingales nest and sing, and where life and death are one in the Presence of the Lord.

— From *The Open Door*

471
Four Things to Learn

I have four things to learn in life:
To think clearly without hurry or confusion;
To love everybody sincerely;
To act in everything with the highest motives;
To trust in God unhesitatingly.

472
Communication Through Hands

The hands of those I meet are dumbly eloquent to me. I have met people so empty of joy that when I clasped their frosty fingertips it seemed as if I were shaking hands with a northeast storm. Others there are whose hands have sunbeams in them, so that their grasp warms my heart. It may be only the clinging touch of a child's hand, but there is as much potential sunshine in it for me as there is in a living glance for others.

473
Knowledge

Knowledge is happiness, because to have knowledge — broad, deep knowledge — is to know true ends from false, and lofty things from low. To know the thoughts and deeds that have marked man's progress is to feel the great heartthrobs of humanity through the centuries; and if one does not feel in these pulsations a heavenward striving, one must indeed be deaf to the harmonies of life.

474
Bible

Unless we form the habit of going to the Bible in bright moments as well as in trouble, we cannot fully respond to its consolations because we lack equilibrium between light and darkness.

475
Love Overcomes

Once I knew the depth where no hope was and darkness lay on the face of all things. Then love came and set my soul free. Once I fretted and beat myself against the wall that shut me in. My life was without a past or future, and death a consummation devoutly to be wished. But a little word from the fingers of another fell into my hands that clutched at emptiness, and my heart leaped up with the rapture of living. I do not know the meaning of the darkness, but I have learned the overcoming of it.

476
Every Person Important

I long to accomplish a great and noble task, but it is my chief duty to accomplish tasks as though they were great and noble. The world is moved along, not only by the mighty shoves of its heroes, but also by the aggregate of the tiny pushes of each honest worker.

477
Kings and Slaves

There is no king who has not had a slave among his ancestors, and no slave who has not had a king among his.

478
Reading

Literature is my utopia. Here I am not disfranchised. No barrier of the senses shuts me out from the sweet, gracious discourse of my book friends. They talk to me without embarrassment or awkwardness.

479
Reading

Truly, each book is as a ship that bears us away from the fixity of our limitations into the movement and splendor of life's infinite ocean.

480
Tolerance

The highest result of education is tolerance. Long ago men fought and died for their faith; but it took ages to teach them the other kind of courage — the courage to recognize the faiths of their brethren and their rights of conscience. Tolerance is the first principle of community; it is the spirit which conserves the best that all men think. No loss by flood and lightning, no destruction of cities and temples by the hostile forces of nature has deprived man of so many noble lives and impulses as those which his intolerances has destroyed.

— The Open Door

481
Religious Beliefs

I believe that we can live on earth according to the teachings of Jesus, and that the greatest happiness will come to the world when man obeys His commandment "Love ye one another."

I believe that every question between man and man is a religious question, and that every social wrong is a moral wrong.

I believe that we can live on earth according to the fulfilment of God's will, and that when the will of God is done on earth as it is in heaven, every man will love his fellow men and act towards them as he desires they should act towards him. I believe that the welfare of each is bound up in the welfare of all.

I believe that life is given us so we may grow in love, and I believe that God is in me as the sun is in the colour and fragrance of a flower — the Light in my darkness, the Voice in my silence.

— From Midstream: My Later Life

482
Heartfelt Things

The best and most beautiful things in the world cannot be seen or even touched. They must be felt with the heart.

483
Appreciate Senses

I who am blind can only give one hint to you who can see. Use your eyes as if tomorrow you would go blind. Do the same with all your senses. Hear the song of a bird as if tomorrow you would go deaf. Touch everything as if tomorrow you would never be able to touch anything again. Smell flowers, taste every bit of food as if tomorrow you would never smell or taste again.

484
Life

Life is an adventure, or it is nothing.

485
Optimism

Keep your face to the sunshine and you cannot see the shadows.

486
Handicaps

I thank God for my handicaps, for through them I have found myself, my work, and my God.

487
In Debt to One Another

The world is so full of care and sorrow that it is a gracious debt we owe to one another to discover the bright crystals of delight hidden in somber circumstances and irksome tasks.

JOHN F. KENNEDY
(1917–1963)

The thirty-fifth president of the United States, John F. Kennedy was the youngest man ever elected president and the youngest ever to die in office. He was also the first Roman Catholic to hold the office and the first president born in the 1900s. Some of the highlights of his administration include the Cuban crisis, the increased freedoms enjoyed by Negroes, and the first manned space flights in preparation for moon flight. After winning fame in the navy during World War II, Kennedy was elected to the Senate. In 1960 he defeated Richard Nixon in a close race for the presidency. His book Profiles in Courage *won for him the Pulitzer Prize for biography in 1957. He is buried in Arlington National Cemetery.*

488
Tight Security – In or Out

Soon after John F. Kennedy became president, he invited some old friends over for dinner. The friends found out that guards at the White House gate took their responsibilities seriously. There was considerable delay and telephone calls before the friends were finally allowed to enter. As the visit was drawing to a close, one of the friends commented to the president about the experience at the gate. "Mr President, now that we are about to leave I can assure you you don't have to worry about strangers getting in here. The way that guard at the gate interrogated us, you better not let your children outside or they might never get back in." President Kennedy saw the security from another point of view: "Here you are worried about getting in here while I'm worried about trying to get out. If I want to walk across the street, Secret Service men appear from all sides to watch my every move."

489
It Only Hurts When You Laugh

President Kennedy's sense of humor was demonstrated often in public as well as private life. Once when the navy staged maneuvers off the West Coast, the president and Gov. Pat Brown of California were honored guests aboard a ship. While the maneuvers were taking place, stewards on the ship served coffee. Governor Brown, while paying attention to President Kennedy, upset the cream pitcher in his lap. Startled, he jumped to his feet. Then he realized he was the center of attention for the correspondents and photographers. He sat down, but shot to his feet again when he realized the chair had a pool of cream on it. The president held off laughing at first, but then he burst into laughter. He leaned over to the governor. "Pat," he whispered, "with that phalanx of photographers in front of me, that steward could have poured boiling oil onto my lap and I still would have smiled." Later, the newspapers printed pictures of the incident, showing the president trying to hold his laughter. The president got a copy of the photograph and signed it for Governor Brown: "It only hurts when you laugh."

490
Whispered Tribute

On Good Friday afternoon 1963, President Kennedy attended services in a Roman Catholic church in Palm Beach. Following the service the priest greeted him outside and then called him aside to whisper something in his ear. Later, when the president and his party drove away from the church, he revealed to the others the priest's whispered conversation. "He whispered in my ear, 'Mr. President, you're doing a wonderful job.' I told him, 'Father, you don't have to whisper that kind of news,' but that cagey old Irishman wasn't about to broadcast a statement like that in this Republican stronghold."

491
Wrong Number

Early one morning in 1961, President Kennedy was in his bedroom when a special, top-secret telephone began to ring. A direct line between the president and the strategic air force bomber and missile commands, the phone was to be used only in the event of impending attack. Kennedy, expecting the worst, picked up the receiver.

"This is the president," he said. There was a pause.

"I must have the wrong number," came the startled voice at the other end. "I'm trying to reach a French laundry."

White House communications experts swarmed over the equipment for several weeks, but could never discover where the call had come from, or how it had wound up on that vital telephone line.

— *Life* magazine quoting Pierre Salinger

492
Couldn't Waste Time on Rumors

Paul B. Fay, Jr., served with John F. Kennedy in the navy and was one of his closest friends following the war and during Kennedy's administration. He served as undersecretary of the navy from 1961-65. As a close friend and adviser, Fay was alert to anything that would hurt Kennedy — in his private or political life. Once he heard a rumor at a party that Kennedy had had a secret marriage before he was married to Jacqueline. After he heard similar stories, Fay went to the president and advised him to make a statement to the press denying the rumor. The president was less concerned about the rumor than Fay.

"If I make a statement to the public on everything I have been accused of," the president told Fay, "I'd spend all my time on radio and television trying to keep the record straight. If people want to believe such tales, no denial on my part is going to convince them differently."

493
Sad Tradition

Lee Harvey Oswald, accused assassin of President Kennedy, probably didn't know it, but Kennedy's death continued the sad tradition that, since William H. Harrison, every American president elected in a year ending in "0" had died while in office. They included Harrison (1840), Lincoln (1860), Garfield (1880), McKinley (1900), Harding (1920), Roosevelt (1940), and Kennedy (1960). Four of these — Lincoln, Garfield, McKinley, and Kennedy — were assassinated. The deaths are coincidental, of course; but there might be some superstitious candidates unwilling to be elected in 1980.

494
Presidential Leadership

A Washington correspondent asked President Kennedy to offer advice and guidance to a high school or college student who would someday be sitting in his chair. President Kennedy cited, among other ideals, some of the great qualities of two early presidents, Lincoln and Adams.

> The most important human qualities of leadership are best embodied in that most towering of American Presidents, Lincoln: a combination of humility and self-confidence, inner resolution and energy, which gives a President the capacity to listen to others, to be aware of his own limitations, but also to follow the command of John Adams that "In all great and essential measures the President is bound by honor and his conscience . . . to act his own mature and unbiased judgment." I can advise you to be aware of the importance of these qualities, but no one can tell you how to develop them. I only hope, for the welfare of our country, that you will possess them when you come to office.
> — *Parade*

JOHN F. KENNEDY SAID IT

495
Duty

My fellow Americans: ask not what your country can do for you; ask what you can do for your country.

My fellow citizens of the world: ask not what America will do for you, but what together we can do for the freedom of man.

— From inauguration speech

496
Inequity

There is always inequity in life. Some men are killed in a war, and some are wounded, and some men are stationed in the Antarctic and some are stationed in San Francisco. It's very hard in military or personal life to assure complete equality. Life is unfair.

497
Seeking Power

In the past, those who foolishly sought power by riding on the back of the tiger ended up inside.

498
Freedom

The irresistible tide that began five hundred years before the birth of Christ in ancient Greece is for freedom, and against tyranny. And that is the wave of the future — and the iron hand of totalitarianism can ultimately neither seize it nor turn it back. In the words of Macaulay: "A single breaker may recede, but the tide is coming in."

499
Security Endangered

The free world's security can be endangered not only by a nuclear attack, but also by being nibbled away at the periphery . . . by forces of subversion, infiltration, intimidation, indirect or nonovert aggression, internal revolution, diplomatic blackmail, guerilla warfare, or a series of limited wars.

500
War

Mankind must put an end to war or war will put an end to mankind.

501
Church and State

I believe in an America where the separation of church and state is absolute — where no Catholic prelate would tell the president (should he be Catholic) how to act, and no Protestant minister would tell his parishioners for whom to vote.

502
Politics Astonishing

Politics is an astonishing profession — it has permitted me to go from being an obscure lieutenant serving under General MacArthur to commander in chief in fourteen years, without any technical competence whatsoever.

503
Courage

During the Korean War a young American was called out of the ranks by his Chinese captors and asked, "What do you think of Gen. George C. Marshall?" He said, "I think General Marshall is a great American." He was hit by the butt of a rifle and sent to the ground. They picked him up and said, "What do you think of General Marshall now?" He said, "I think General Marshall is a great American." This time there was no rifle butt because in their own hard way they had classified him and determined upon his courage. I think in the next decade as individuals and as citizens of the United States, we, too, are going to be called out of the ranks.

504
Wouldn't Trade Places

I do not believe that any of us would exchange places with any other people or any other generation. The energy, the faith, the devotion which we bring to this endeavor will light our country and all who serve it — and the glow from that fire can truly light the world.

505
God's Work Ours

With a good conscience our only sure reward, with history the final judge of our deeds, let us go forth to lead the land we love, asking His blessing and His help, but knowing that here on earth God's work must truly be our own.

506
System Must Succeed

I am determined upon our system's survival and success, regardless of the cost and regardless of the peril.

507
The World

It is a very dangerous, untidy world. But we have to live with it.

508
Liberty

Let every nation know, whether it wishes us well or ill, that we shall pay any price, bear any burden, meet any hardship, support any friend, oppose any foe to assure the survival and the success of liberty.

ABRAHAM LINCOLN
(1809–1865)

The sixteenth president of the United States was born February 12, 1809, in a log cabin on a farm in Kentucky. They later moved to Indiana, and when Abe was twenty-one the Lincoln family moved to Illinois. He was elected to the Illinois General Assembly in 1834 and admitted to the state bar in 1837. From 1846 to 1849 he was a member of the House of Representatives. In 1858 he won much fame by debating slavery with Stephen A. Douglas. He was elected president in 1860, and the Civil War followed his inauguration. He was reelected in 1864. General Lee surrendered April 9, 1865; five days later Lincoln was shot by John Wilkes Booth in Ford's Theater, Washington. He died early the next morning; he is buried in Springfield, Illinois.

509
Lincoln a Healer

Some of the frontiersmen who knew Abraham Lincoln liked to exaggerate when they recounted the story-telling ability of the circuit lawyer. One even credited Lincoln with healing the sick with his stories.

> In the role of story teller, I never knew his equal. His power of mimicry was very great. He could perfectly mimic a Dutchman, Irishman, or Negro. . . . I have heard men say that they had laughed at his stories until they had almost shaken their ribs loose. I heard cases where men had been suffering for years from some bodily ailment and could get no relief but who have gone a couple of evenings and listened to Lincoln and laughed their ailments away, and become hale and hearty men, giving Lincoln credit of being their healer.

510
Pardon

An elderly man came to President Lincoln with a tale of sorrow. His boy had been convicted for some offense and sentenced to death. Lincoln wrote a few lines on a sheet of paper and handed it to the weeping father. It read, "Job Smith is not to be shot until further orders from me. — Abraham Lincoln."

The old gentleman received it with a look of surprise and disappointment. "I thought it was a pardon. You may order him to be shot next week."

"My friend," replied the President, "I see you are not well acquainted with me. If your son never dies till orders come from me to shoot him, he will live to be a great deal older than Methuselah."

— C. L. Paddock

511
Freedom Comes from God

Abraham Lincoln is not to be credited with the freedom of the Negroes. A political enemy could have made that statement, but it was Lincoln himself who said it. When Richmond was captured, Lincoln went to get a firsthand look. When he landed, a Negro yelled, "Glory, hallelujah!" The Negro and several others dropped to their knees as the president approached.

"Don't kneel to me," Lincoln said. "You must kneel to God only and thank Him for your freedom."

512
Humility at Gettysburg

When the National Cemetery at Gettysburg was dedicated, the chosen orator of the day was Edward Everett. He prepared an oration which was scholarly and eloquent enough to satisfy all the conventions of such an occasion. President Lincoln was deeply affected by it, and humbly expressed his own sense of unworthiness in the contrast which he felt his brief address offered to Everett's eloquence. But we all know how needless were Lincoln's regrets. His wonderful words have become one of the gems of permanent literature.

— W. S. Stranahan

513
More Light and Less Noise

To people who kept criticizing his administration, President Lincoln once told the following story:

> A traveler on the frontier found himself, as night came on, in a wild region. A terrible thunderstorm added to his trouble. He floundered along until his horse gave out and then had to get out to lead him. Occasional flashes of lightning afforded the only clue to the path, and the crashes of thunder were frightful. One bolt, which seemed to crush the earth beneath him, made him stagger and brought him to his knees. Being by no means a praying man, his petition was short and to the point: "O Lord! If it's all the same to you, give us a little more light and a little less noise!"

514
True Friendship

An old druggist from Springfield, Illinois, made the journey to Washington on one occasion for no other purpose than to see Abraham Lincoln and "tell him a few yarns." It had been Mr. Lincoln's habit to stop in at the drug store from time to time to exchange stories with the quaint old man, and one day the druggist discovered that he usually did it when he was on the eve of a difficult law case, or when he had some special load on his mind.

The old apothecary was under no delusions as to his own skill as a politician, and he had no requests to make of the president nor suggestions as to how the war was to be conducted. But he did have some good stories that were designed to relieve anxiety, and armed with a mind full of fun and good cheer he presented himself at the White House and was given a cordial welcome.

Late that night, when the dinner was done and all the guests were gone, Mr. Lincoln and Uncle Billy found themselves alone in a quiet place. It was then that the president said, "Billy, what did you come to Washington for?"

"Just to see you, Mr. Lincoln," the old druggist replied. "Just to see you and tell you some yarns."

"Didn't you want a post office, or anything?" the president persisted.

"No sir. I just wanted to be with you for a little while."

And with that the president bowed his head for a moment, and lifting his eyes, infinitely sad, he began to unload his heart. For an hour he poured out into the ear of the man he could trust all the pain and grief of his soul. No one knows what the Union may owe to the humble man who assumed a stewardship over another man's grief in the hour of his testing.

— Roy L. Smith

515
More Than He Bargained For

One of Lincoln's generals had succeeded in having his pet strategical maneuver put into operation. But the plan backfired. Now he found that he needed many more men and much more material than he had counted on. When he explained the situation to Lincoln, the latter told him a story.

"In early days," he said "a party of men went out hunting for a wild boar. But the game came upon them unawares, and they, scampering away, climbed trees, all save one, who seizing the animal by the ears, undertook to hold him. After holding him for some time and finding his strength giving way, he cried out to his companions in the trees: 'Boys, come down and help me let go!' "

The general got the message.

ABRAHAM LINCOLN SAID IT

516
Freedom

That on the 1st day of January, A.D. 1863, all persons held as slaves within a State or designated part of a State the people whereof shall then be in rebellion against the United States shall be then, thenceforward, and forever free; and the executive government of the United States, including the military and naval authority thereof, will recognize and maintain the freedom of such persons and will do no act or acts to repress such persons, or any of them, in any efforts they may make for their actual freedom.

— From The Emancipation Proclamation

517
Honesty

There is a vague, popular belief that lawyers are necessarily dishonest. I say vague, because when we consider to what extent confidence and honors are reposed in and conferred upon lawyers by the people, it appears improbable that their impression of dishonesty is very distinct and vivid. Yet the impression is common, almost universal. Let no young man choosing the law for a calling for a moment yield to the popular belief — resolve to be honest at all events; and if in your own judgment you cannot be an honest lawyer, resolve to be honest without being a lawyer. Choose some other occupation, rather than one in the choosing of which you do, in advance, consent to be a knave.

518
Character and Reputation

Character is like a tree and reputation like its shadow. The shadow is what we think of it; the tree is the real thing.

519
Counterfeit

If it is a crime to make a counterfeit dollar, it is ten thousand times worse to make a counterfeit man.

520
Example

There is just one way to bring up a child in the way he should go and that is to travel that way yourself.

521
How to Be Remembered

Die when I may, I want it said of me by those who knew me best, that I always plucked a thistle and planted a flower where I thought a flower would grow.

522
Force

Force is all-conquering, but its victories are short lived.

523
Freedom

Those who deny freedom to others deserve it not for themselves and under a just God cannot long retain it.

524
Consent

No man is good enough to govern another man without that other's consent.

525
Private Property

Property is desirable, is a positive good in the world. Let not him who is houseless pull down the house of another; but let him work diligently and build one for himself, thus by example assuring that his own shall be safe from violence when built.

526
Come Back

If you have been taught doctrines conflicting with the great landmarks of the Declaration of Independence; if you have listened to suggestions which would take away from its grandeur and mutilate the fair symmetry of its proportions; if you have been inclined to believe that all men are not created equal in those inalienable rights enumerated by our chart of liberty, let me entreat you to come back.

527
Happiness

Most people are about as happy as they make up their minds to be.

528
Right Makes Might

Let us have faith that right makes might; and in that faith, let us, to the end, dare to do our duty as we understand it.

529
Liberty

Our defense is in the spirit which prized liberty as the heritage of all men, in all lands everywhere.

530
Freedom

Those who deny freedom to others deserve it not for themselves.

CHARLES A. LINDBERGH
(1902–1974)

This American was just another airmail pilot until he made the first solo flight across the Atlantic Ocean. Then he became an international hero. The historic event took place in a single-engine airplane, the Spirit of St. Louis. Lindbergh was twenty-five years old when he took off from Roosevelt Field, New York, at 7:52 A.M. on May 20, 1927. After more than 3,600 miles and 33½ hours, he landed at LeBourget Field near Paris. Lindbergh was the son of a United States congressman from Minnesota. His wife's father was Dwight W. Morrow, who was United States ambassador to Mexico from 1927 to 1930. Many of the decorations and trophies given to Lindbergh for his historic trip are housed in the Jefferson Memorial, Saint Louis. In later years, Lindbergh has been active in conservation efforts.

531
Wouldn't Take Money He Didn't Earn

Few international celebrities have been so baffling as Charles Lindbergh. It was unreasonable to many — yet remarkable to others — why he did not capitalize more on his flight across the Atlantic in 1927. But commercializing the flight was the last thing he wanted. One friend estimated that Lindbergh could have made five million dollars in one week if he would have accepted the hundreds of offers to sign testimonials, write books, or go into the movies. William Randolph Hearst offered Lindbergh five hundred thousand dollars if he would star in a film about aviation. He declined a vaudeville contract to which was attached a one million dollar guarantee. A movie company made him another million dollar offer; it was turned down. Another movie company upped its offer to five million. Money came to him as gifts, but it was always returned. An associate summed it up: "Lindbergh won't take money he hasn't earned."

532
More Remarkable for a Committee

The college professor was in his bathroom shaving when Lindbergh landed in Paris on the occasion of his historic solo flight across the Atlantic Ocean. His wife, anxious to break the news to him, shouted through the closed door: "Lindbergh has flown the ocean alone!" And to make sure that he heard it she repeated: "Lindbergh has flown the ocean alone!" She was, however, somewhat disappointed that the professor did not share her enthusiasm when he shouted back: "It would have been much more remarkable if a committee had done it."

— Jacob M. Braude

533
Practicing Staying Awake

They called him "Lucky Lindy" when he made his history-making flight across the Atlantic, but Charles A. Lindbergh was no carefree daredevil trusting to chance. The late Frank Samuels told me an anecdote to prove it.

When Lindbergh was flying air mail in St. Louis in 1926 and 1927 he occasionally found time to hop out to San Diego, where his plane, the "Spirit of St. Louis," was being built at the little Ryan aircraft factory. Samuels would go along with him to inspect progress on the craft.

After a long day crowded with drawingboard and shop problems the two would put up at the small sidestreet hotel. One night Samuels woke shortly after midnight and noticed Lindbergh's bed was unoccupied.

He finally made out Lindbergh sitting by the window, studying the stars. "For goodness' sake, boy," he asked, "what are you sitting there for?"

"Just practicing."

"Practicing *what?*"

"Staying awake all night," was the answer.

— Russell S. Johns, in *Chicago Tribune Magazine*

534
Saved by a Trick

When Charles Lindbergh landed at LeBourget Field in Paris after his successful flight, he was not prepared for the reception — neither were the French police. As the wheels touched the field, thousands of Frenchmen swarmed past barriers and to the *Spirit of St. Louis*. Hands reached in and pulled him from the plane. Then he was carried through the huge crowd — all the while people reaching out to touch him or pound him on the back. He became fearful that he would be crushed. But he was helpless. All at once his soft leather helmet was snatched from his head. Unknown to Lindbergh, help was on the way. Two French pilots, Detroyat and Delage, placed the helmet on the head of another American as a decoy. Then the two pilots hustled Lindbergh into a small car and dashed away from the cheering, milling crowd and into a hangar across the field. Later he was taken to the safety of the American embassy.

535
Life or Death Decisions

Charles Lindbergh carefully prepared a flight pattern from Roosevelt Field on Long Island to Paris — a nonstop flight. Time was a factor. Others were preparing to make the trip to claim the twenty-five thousand dollar prize and the certain fame for a successful flight. There were some critical decisions that only Lindbergh himself could make. He knew at three of these checkpoints his decision could mean life or death. He had to make the right decision each time. His first checkpoint was halfway down the soggy runway at Roosevelt Field. There as he roared the *Spirit of St. Louis* toward takeoff, he had to decide whether or not he should try to lift the overloaded plane into the air or turn back. He lifted the nose skyward and cleared wires at the end of the runway by only twenty feet. His second checkpoint was at Nova Scotia. There, if the fog was too heavy or if he found he could not fly by compass, he was going to return to Long Island. He passed the second checkpoint. The third and probably the most critical checkpoint was halfway across the Atlantic — the point of no return. The decision had to be made by Lindbergh — he had no radio help as the radio was removed to eliminate weight. At the point of no return his decision was made. He gunned the little plane and pushed toward his goal at LeBourget Field in Paris.

536
A New Hero

For years the American people had been spiritually starved. . . . Romance, chivalry and self-dedication had been debunked; the heroes of history had been shown to have feet of clay, and the saints of history had been revealed as people with queer complexes. . . . Something that people needed, if they were to live at peace with themselves and with the world, was missing from their lives. And all at once Lindbergh provided it. Romance, chivalry, self-dedication — here they were, embodied in a modern Galahad for a generation which had forsworn Galahads.

— Frederick Lewis Allen, in *Only Yesterday*

537
Hard to Be an Agnostic

When his trusted plane, *Spirit of St. Louis,* was midway on its transatlantic flight between New York and Paris, Colonel Charles A. Lindbergh began to think of the smallness of man and the deficiency of his devices, and the greatness and marvels of God's universe. He mused, "It's hard to be an agnostic here in the *Spirit of St. Louis* when so aware of the frailty of man's devices. If one dies, all God's creation goes on existing in a plan so perfectly balanced, so wondrously simple and yet so incredibly complex that it is beyond our comprehension. There's the infinite magnitude of the universe, the infinite detail, and man's consciousness of it all — a world audience to what, if not to God."

— Walter B. Knight

538
Encouragement

Charles Lindbergh's name is immediately associated with airplanes — more specifically, a flight across the Atlantic in 1927 — and in later years, conservation and ecology. In addition, at least some of the credit for the pioneering in space travel belongs to Lindbergh.

It all started when Lindbergh became interested in the rocket experiments of Robert H. Goddard, a physics professor. Goddard had been experimenting with rockets since 1909 and in 1919 proposed reaching the moon by rocket — fifty years before it was actually accomplished. But Goddard was ridiculed. He was laughingly called the "moon man"; others said he was dreaming. In 1929, he fired a liquid-powered rocket nearly one hundred feet into the air. Still he wasn't taken seriously and there was more ridicule. Later, in 1929, Lindbergh paid a visit to Goddard and for the next fifteen years, until Goddard's death, he quietly encouraged him and talked the Guggenheim Foundation into supporting Goddard's experiments. The two became close friends. When Goddard had disappointments in his experiments, Lindbergh encouraged him to continue; when Goddard needed more money, Lindbergh would go back to the Guggenheims for help.

Today, Goddard is referred to as "the father of modern rocketry and space flight." Wernher von Braun said, "Every liquid-fuel rocket that flies is a Goddard rocket."

Lindbergh's part in the Goddard story wasn't generally known until 1963; publicity-shy Lindbergh wanted it that way.

539
A Famous Daddy

When one of Charles Lindbergh's children was in the first grade, another pupil approached him and said, "I hear your father discovered America." The Lindbergh child accepted the statement as historical fact and added, "Yes, and he flew across the ocean, too."

540
Became God-fearing

Today, Lindbergh has lost his scientist's arrogance. And, as for God — God may be dead for some theologians, but not for Lindbergh. He has become a God-fearing man. "To me in youth," he wrote, "science was more important than either man or God. The one I took for granted; the other was too intangible for me to understand."

—Walter S. Ross, in *The Last Hero*

541
He'd Rather Have the Birds

"I've had enough publicity for fifteen lives," said Charles A. Lindbergh, 67. But even as the Lone Eagle was explaining his reluctance to grant an interview, he was granting one — his first in more than 30 years. The journalistic coup was chalked up by New York *Times* reporter Alden Whitman, 55, after six months of not taking no for an answer. Finally, to help further his favorite cause, Lindbergh agreed to let Whitman and a *Times* photographer accompany him on the latest trip in his far-ranging conservation campaign. The men toured the Philippines for more than a week, traveling by plane, helicopter, jeep and on foot, sleeping in jungles and remote villages. Wherever he went, assisted by guides and translators, Lindy tirelessly gathered data on birds, animals and aborigines and delivered pep talks in behalf of preserving wildlife. "If I had to choose," proclaimed history's most famous flier, "I would rather have birds than airplanes."

— *Newsweek,* July 7, 1969

CHARLES A. LINDBERGH SAID IT

542
Spiritual Truths

In my youth science was more important to me than either man or God. I worshiped science. Its advance had surpassed man's wildest dreams. It took many years for me to discover that science, with all its brilliance, lights only a middle chapter of creation.

I saw the aircraft I love destroying the civilization I expected it to save. Now I understand that spiritual truth is more essential to a nation than the mortar in its cities' walls. For when the actions of a people are undergirded by spiritual truths, there is safety. When spiritual truths are rejected, it is only a matter of time before civilization will collapse. We must understand spiritual truths and apply them to our modern life. We must draw strength from the almost forgotten virtues of simplicity, humility, contemplation and prayer. It requires a dedication beyond science, beyond self, but the rewards are great and it is our *only* hope.

543
Which Way to Ireland?

I saw a fleet of fishing boats. . . . I flew down almost touching the craft and yelled at them, asking if I was on the right road to Ireland. They just stared. Maybe they didn't hear me. Maybe I didn't hear them. Or maybe they thought I was just a crazy fool. An hour later I saw land.

— On flight to Paris, May 21, 1927

544
Improvement

The improvement of our way of life is more important than the spreading of it. If we make it satisfactory enough, it will spread automatically. If we do not, no strength of arms can permanently impose it.

545
Lives On

It was not the outer grandeur of the Roman but the inner simplicity of the Christian that lived on through the ages.

546
Balance Needed

The quality of a civilization depends on a balance of body, mind, and spirit in its people measured on a scale less human than divine. . . . To survive, we must keep this balance. To progress, we must improve it. Science is upsetting it with an overemphasis of mind and a neglect of spirit and body.

547
Man's Own Weapons Used Against Him

The tragedy of scientific man is that he has found no way to guide his own discoveries to a constructive end. He has devised no weapon so terrible that he has not used it. He has guarded none so carefully that his enemies have not eventually obtained it and turned it against him. . . . His security today and tomorrow seems to depend on building weapons which will destroy him tomorrow.

548
The Right Combination

Our salvation, and our only salvation, lies in controlling the arm of Western science by the mind of a Western philosophy, guided by God's eternal truths.

549
Dreams and Reality

One is constantly aware of the fact that we live in a world where dreams and reality interchange.

550
Moral Force Needed

I must confess to you that I am fearful of the use of power. . . . History is full of its misuses. There is no better example than Nazi Germany. Power without a moral force to guide it invariably ends in the destruction of the people who wield it. We need integrity, humility, and compassion. . . . Without them, we simply sow the wind with our aircraft and our bombs.

551
Spiritual Truths

In Germany (after World War II), I learned that if his civilization is to continue, modern man must direct the material power of his science by the spiritual truths of his God.

DAVID LIVINGSTONE
(1813–1873)

Few missionary names are as well known as that of David Livingstone. He went to Africa in 1841 and — except for furloughs — remained there the rest of his life. No other white man had ever explored Africa as Livingstone did. He was a dedicated fighter of the slave trade and believed that converting the African to Christianity would help end it. After a period of years when Livingstone was out of touch with the world, Sir Henry Morton Stanley, a newspaper reporter, led an expedition in 1871 and found him. Livingstone chose to remain in Africa, however, and died in 1873. He was later buried in Westminster Abbey in London.

552
Very Big Man

No one paid much attention the day the little Scotsman was born, but when he was buried . . . well, that was a different story.

David Livingstone was born in Blantyre, Scotland, and was reared in a tenement which allowed the seven Livingstones one ten-by-sixteen-foot room. It was said that when they went to sleep at night, one couldn't step anywhere without stepping on someone. David, as other children of his day, arose at 5:30 A.M. and worked all day until 8 P.M. in a cotton mill. Just an ordinary youth, but sixty years after his birth they brought his body back from Africa and buried him with the greats in Westminster Abbey.

The devoted Africans who carried his body those fifteen hundred miles through the jungle couldn't dream what England was like, but they knew his body should not be buried there in the remote bush.

All along the trail they were told it was too dangerous to make the trip with Livingstone's body and were urged to bury it there. "No, no," they said, "very big man, cannot bury here."

553
Everyone Flubs Occasionally

The London Missionary Society almost lost the most prominent missionary of the nineteenth century when they were considering him because the candidate forgot his sermon. Had it not been for one member of the society's board, they probably would have rejected the young man. The candidate was David Livingstone.

James I. McNair, in *Livingstone the Liberator,* told about Livingstone's embarrassing inaugural: "He took his text, read it very deliberately and then — then — then his sermon fled. . . . 'Friends,' said the flunking missionary, 'I have forgotten all I had to say,' and hurrying out of the pulpit, he left the chapel."

A poor launching doesn't always mean poor sailing. A poor beginning doesn't always dictate a poor ending.

554
A Smile

One Sunday evening, a youthful David Livingstone sat in the Aberdeen Music Hall listening to a service rendered by a deputation from the London Missionary Society. When the service was over, Livingstone looked wistfully after the team as they filed out the door. The look on his face so attracted the attention of a Congregational minister who was standing nearby, that he stepped quietly to the boy's side and with a smile asked, "My boy, would you like to be a missionary?" Livingstone later said that it was *that smile,* questioning and tender, which led him to make his final decision to serve his Savior as a foreign missionary.

555
Abiding Presence

When David Livingstone sailed for Africa the first time, a group of his friends accompanied him to the pier to wish him *Bon Voyage.* Some of them, concerned for the safety of the missionary, reminded him of the dangers which would confront him in the dark land to which he was journeying. In fact, one man urged Livingstone to remain in England.

In response, David Livingstone opened his Bible and read aloud the portion of our Lord's last recorded words in Matthew's Gospel, chapter 28: "Lo, I am with you always." Turning to the one who would have prevented his going, the missionary said: "That, my friend, is the word of a Gentleman. So let us be going."

— *The Pilgrim*

556
Worked for Their Freedom

Throughout his dedicated life of service in Africa, Livingstone did everything possible to end the slave trading. On one of his first trips into the jungle a tiny black girl ran out of her village and hid beneath Livingstone's wagon. She was fleeing from men who would sell her to traders for a bit of cloth or a gun. The sympathetic missionary hid the frightened child in his wagon, and she escaped. Wherever he journeyed he tried to abolish the slave trading; he reasoned that it could be done by opening up legitimate trading between the Africans and Britain, the Portuguese, and the Arabs. When he returned to England in 1856, a highly honored man, he made plans to return to Africa: "I am only buckling on my armor," he declared. "The slave trade has to be abolished, and the country opened to commerce and Christian influence."

His death in 1873 ended the long fight he made against slavery. But his influence lived on. Central Africa had been opened to legitimate commerce and missions, and he had so publicized the evil slave trade that the conscience of England was awakened. One area after another made the slave trade illegal.

557
Influence on Stanley

Henry M. Stanley found Livingstone in Africa and lived with him for some time. Here is his testimony:

> I went to Africa as prejudiced as the biggest atheist in London. But there came for me a long time for reflection. I saw this solitary old man there and asked myself, "How on earth does he stop here — is he cracked, or what? What is it that inspires him?"

For months after we met I found myself wondering at the old man carrying out all that was said in the Bible — "Leave all things and follow Me." But little by little his sympathy for others became contagious; my sympathy was aroused; seeing his piety, his gentleness, his zeal, his earnestness, and how he went about his business, I was converted by him, although he had not tried to do it.

— *The Australian Baptist*

558
Love Beareth All Things

Misjudged by a fellow missionary, Livingstone gave up his house and garden at Mabotsa, with all the toil and money they had cost him, rather than have any scandal before the heathen, and began in a new place the labor of house and school building, and gathering the people around. His colleague was so struck with his generosity that he said had he known his intention, he never would have spoken a word against him. Parting with his garden cost him a great pang. "I like a garden," he wrote, "but Paradise will make amends for all our privations here."

— Choice Gleanings Calendar

559
Dedication Calls for Sacrifice

David Livingstone is remembered as a great missionary-explorer to Africa. But his dedicated life was not without great personal loss and sacrifice. Following his heralded visit to England, he returned to Africa, and sorrow. The very trails that he had carved out of the bush were now being used to march manacled natives away as slaves; life was cheap — a man was worth only four yards of calico. The slave trade was big business, and it hurt Livingstone deeply.

Livingstone's wife died, and then his prodigal son Robert ran away from his school in England and went to America where he died fighting for the North in the Civil War. The torturous years of Africa were taking their toll on Livingstone's body. He could have returned home and retired in his own country. He did return once more, but in 1865 he left Britain for the last time, eager to find the source of the Nile. But in his last years he was often too weak to command his men. Someone stole his medicine chest, and his porters deserted him and reported his death. For four years — 1867-71 — there was no word from Livingstone. It wasn't until Henry Stanley found the weakened and sick missionary and reported it to the outside that rumors of his death could be erased. Still he would not leave his beloved Africa. And there is where he died, faithful to the last in his fight to take the gospel to Africans, to map out the dark continent, and to rid the world of the slave trade.

560
Humility

In 1856 England welcomed David Livingstone from his successful but most difficult exploration of Africa. He was invited to visit the queen and was elected as a fellow in the Royal Society. Everywhere he went he was heralded as a hero. Charles Dickens, reading of the accomplishments of Livingstone, said, "I used to think I possessed the moral virtues of courage, patience, resolution, and self control. . . . I find that these turn out to be nothing but plated goods . . . my self-esteem oozed out of me."

Livingstone's father-in-law, missionary Robert Moffat, knew that all the honors heaped on his famous son-in-law would not change the humble spirit: "The honors awaiting you would be enough to make a score of light heads dizzy, but I have no fear of their affecting your upper story."

561
A Better Home, No Separation

David and Mary Livingstone suffered many hardships, not the least of these being the long separations. Mary, daughter of another famous missionary family, the Moffats, had a home with David for only four years during their twenty years of marriage. In 1852 Mary became ill, so David sent her and the four children to England — a separation of four years. It wasn't that David didn't love his family — far from it. But his love for God and the calling on his life came first. In 1862 Mary was stricken with a sudden illness and died with her husband by her side. The next day he buried her beneath a large tree and then wrote in his journal:

> I loved her when I married her, and the longer I lived with her I loved her the more. . . . Oh, my Mary, my Mary! how often we have longed for a quiet home, since you and I were cast adrift at Kolobeng; surely the removal by a kind Father who

knoweth our frame means that He rewarded you by taking you to a better home, the eternal one in the heavens.

562
Danger in Mission Work

Near Mabsota, where Livingstone had his mission work, for a while the countryside was infested with lions. Once they went on a rampage of killing in the area; and before it was over, Livingstone himself nearly lost his life. Livingstone and some of the tribesmen were hunting the lions when they spotted a huge one seated on a knoll above them. Livingstone took careful aim and fired both barrels. While he was reloading, Livingstone heard a shout and looked around just in time to see the lion in the act of springing upon him. He later wrote about it: "He caught me by the shoulder and we both came to the ground together. Growling horribly he shook me as a terrier does a rat." The beast finally dropped Livingstone and then wounded two Africans who were nearby. Fortunately the bullets finally took their toll on the lion and a third African finished the job with his spear.

Livingstone was never known to complain about the mauled arm that hung useless at his side. He even had a sense of humor about the incident years later. When asked what he was thinking about when the lion was mauling him, he answered with a twinkle in his eye, "I was wondering which part of me he would eat first."

563
An Example to Others

Many felt no single African explorer had done so much for African geography as Livingstone during his thirty years' work. His travels covered one-third of the continent, from the Cape to near the Equator, and from the Atlantic to the Indian Ocean. Livingstone was no hurried traveler; he did his journeying leisurely, carefully observing and recording with the eye of a trained scientific observer. His example and his death acted like an inspiration, filling Africa with an army of explorers and missionaries, and raising in Europe so powerful a feeling against the slave trade that through him slavery may be considered as having received its death blow.

— Elmer L. Towns, *The Christian Hall of Fame*

564
A Man Who Kept His Word

Many stories have been told of the missionary and exploration deeds of David Livingstone, but Africans liked to tell a story about him that showed him to be a man of his word.

Livingstone had been in Africa for twelve years but had never had a chance to visit the west coast, more than a thousand miles through the jungle. He knew he would need some African helpers, so he sought the permission of the chief to take twenty-seven young men with him. The chief was concerned about the safety of the young men. Livingstone could see his anxiety. "If you give me your sons," he told him, "for the journey, I promise to return with them and deliver them to their homes and parents. My life will be as a pledge." The chief finally gave his consent.

It was not an easy trip for Livingstone and his men. They were often hungry and thirsty and they were often sick. The jungle made travel extremely slow and painful with its swollen rivers, steep hills, and the thorns and undergrowth. And at times they met unfriendly tribes.

Finally, after many long months they reached the coast. In the Luanda harbor was a British warship which had been sent to bring Livingstone back to England. The commander greeted Livingstone and proudly declared: "Queen Victoria has sent me to urge you to come home. All of England is waiting to honor you, sir. You must come."

In spite of the commander's pleas, Livingstone refused to go with him. He had made a promise to the chief, and he was going to keep it. Once again Livingstone and his party set off through the jungle for the long trip home. After an absence of two and a half years they returned safely to the village.

The Africans knew Livingstone to be an explorer, missionary, and friend; but they also knew him to be a man who kept his word.

565
Mary Second to the Lord

Marriage was certainly not in David Livingstone's plans when he applied for missionary service. He answered a question about marriage by writing: "I should prefer going out unmarried, that I might be without that care which the concerns of a family necessarily induce, and give myself wholly to the work." That was before he met Mary Moffat. The day came when he asked Mary to become Mrs. Livingstone.

Mary was soon to learn that her fiancé had his Lord in first place in his life and he urged her to do the same. He wrote: "And now, my dearest, farewell. May God bless you! Let your affection be towards Him much more than towards me. Whatever friendship we feel towards each other, let us always look to Jesus as our common friend and guide, and may He shield you with his everlasting arms from every evil!"

566
Christ Gives Peace

David Livingstone had spent sixteen years in Africa but had not faced such peril. The white man was surrounded by hostile, angry natives in the heart of Africa. He was in danger of losing his life and contemplated fleeing in the night. But something happened that changed his mind and gave him peace in his perilous situation. He recorded it in his diary that January 14, 1856.

> Felt much turmoil of spirit in prospect of having all my plans for the welfare of this great region and this teeming population knocked on the head by savages tomorrow. But I read that Jesus said: "All power is given unto Me in heaven and in earth. Go ye therefore, and teach all nations, and lo, I am with you alway, even unto the end of the world." It is the word of a gentleman of the most strict and sacred honour, so there's an end of it! I will not cross furtively tonight as I intended. Should such a man as I flee? Nay, verily, I shall take observations for latitude and longitude tonight, though they may be the last. I feel quite calm now, thank God!"

DAVID LIVINGSTONE SAID IT

567
Dedication

I will place no value on anything I have or may possess except in relation to the kingdom of Christ. If anything will advance the interests of that kingdom, it shall be given away or kept, only as by the giving or keeping of it I shall most promote the glory of Him to whom I owe my hopes in time and eternity. May grace and strength sufficient to enable me to adhere faithfully to this resolution be imparted to me, so that, not in name only, all my interest may be identified with His causes.

568
Sorrow

With many tears running down my cheeks I have to tell you that your dearly beloved mama died last night about seven o'clock. I was with her all night and trust she was tended by the all powerful arms.
— Written to Oswell, his 11-year-old son

569
Rededication

My Jesus, my king, my life, my all; I again dedicate myself to Thee. Accept me and grant, O gracious Father, that ere this year is gone I may finish my task. In Jesus' name I ask it. Amen, so let it be.
— Journal entry on his last birthday, March 19, 1873

570
Poor Imitation

God had an only Son, and He was a missionary and a physician. A poor, poor imitation of Him I am, or wish to be.

571
All for the Kingdom

It is a venture to take wife and children into a country where fever — African fever — prevails. But who that believes in Jesus would refuse to make a venture for such a Captain? A parent's heart alone can feel as I do when I look at my little ones and ask, shall I return with this or that one alive? However, we are His and wish to have no interests apart from those of His kingdom and glory. May He bless us and make us blessings even unto death.

HENRY WADSWORTH LONGFELLOW
(1807–1882)

Longfellow was the most famous and most popular American poet of the nineteenth century. Today he is best remembered for his poems, Evangeline, The Song of Hiawatha, The Courtship of Miles Standish, The Village Blacksmith, The Children's Hour, Paul Revere's Ride, The Wreck of the Hesperus, and Excelsior. He published his first poem at the age of thirteen. He became a professor at Harvard in 1836. Longfellow knew great success, but he also knew sorrow: his first wife died while they were traveling in Europe and his second wife died after accidentally setting her dress afire. His historic mansion, Craigie House, in Cambridge, Massachusetts, is open to the public.

HENRY WADSWORTH LONGFELLOW SAID IT

572
Still Work to Do

Shall we sit idly down and say
The night hath come; it is no longer day?
The night hath not yet come; we are not quite
Cut off from labor by the failing light;
Something remains for us to do or dare;
Even the oldest tree some fruit may bear.

— From *Morituri Salutamus*

573
Footprints

Lives of great men all remind us
   We can make our lives sublime,
And, departing, leave behind us
   Footprints on the sands of time.

>Footprints, that perhaps another,
> Sailing o'er life's solemn main,
>A forlorn and shipwrecked brother,
> Seeing, shall take heart again.
>   — From *The Psalm of Life*

574
Nature

>And nature, the old nurse, took
> The child upon her knee,
>Saying, "Here is a story book
> My father hath writ for thee.
>Come wander with me," she said,
> "In regions yet untrod
>and read what is still unread
> In the manuscripts of God."

575
Death

>There is a Reaper whose name is Death,
> And, with his sickle keen,
>He reaps the bearded grain at a breath,
> And the flowers that grow between.
>   — From *The Reaper and the Flowers*

576
Patience

>Though the mills of God grind slowly,
> yet they grind exceeding small;
>Though with patience He stands waiting,
> with exactness grinds He all.

577
Judging

We judge ourselves by what we feel capable of doing, while others judge us by what we have already done.

578

Ambitions

Most people would succeed in small things if they were not troubled with great ambitions.

579

Sail On

Thou, too, sail on, O Ship of State!
   Sail on, O Union, strong and great!
Humanity with all its fears,
   With all the hopes of future years,
Is hanging breathless on thy fate!
—*Building of the Ship*

580

Night

The night shall be filled with music
   And the cares that infest the day
Shall fold their tents like the Arabs,
   And as silently steal away.
—*The Day Is Done*

581

One or the Other

In this world a man must either be anvil or hammer.

582

Nature and Art

Nature is a revelation of God; art a revelation of man.

583
Singers

God sent his Singers upon earth
With songs of sadness and of mirth,
That they might touch the hearts of men,
And bring them back to heaven again.
— *The Singers*

584
Change Needed

As turning the logs will make a dull fire burn, so change of studies a dull brain.

585
God Within Us

Glorious indeed is the world of God around us, but more glorious the world of God within us. There lies the Land of Song; there lies the poet's native land.
—*Hyperion*

586
Youth

Youth comes but once in a lifetime.

587
Sounding the Alarm

So through the night rode Paul Revere;
And so through the night when his cry of alarm
To every Middlesex village and farm,
A cry of defiance, and not of fear,
A voice in the darkness, a knock at the door,
And a word that shall echo forevermore!
For, borne on the night-wind of the Past,

> Through all our history, to the last
> In the hour of darkness and peril and need,
> The people will waken and listen to hear
> The hurrying hoof-beats of that steed,
> And the midnight message of Paul Revere.

— From *Paul Revere's Ride*

588
Youthful Memories

> Often I think of the beautiful town
> That is seated by the sea;
> Often in thoughts go up and down
> The pleasant streets of that dear old town,
> And my youth comes back to me.
> And a verse of Lapland song
> Is haunting my memory still:
> "A boy's will is the wind's will,
> And the thoughts of youth are long,
> long thoughts."

— From *My Lost Youth*

589
Merciful

> Being all fashioned of the self-same dust,
> Let us be merciful as well as just.

— From *Tales of a Wayside Inn*

590
Music

Music is the universal language of mankind.

591
Excuses

We often excuse our own want of philanthropy by giving the name of fanaticism to the more ardent zeal of others.

592
Literature

No literature is complete until the language in which it is written is dead.

593
Work

The heights by great men reached and kept
Were not attained by sudden flight,
But they while their companions slept
Were toiling upward in the night.

594
No Accidents with God

Nothing is or can be accidental with God.

595
Hard Words Bruise

A torn jacket is soon mended, but hard words bruise the heart of a child.

DOUGLAS MAC ARTHUR
(1880–1964)

One of the leading American generals of World War II, MacArthur led the Allied offensive from Australia to Japan. After the war he was appointed administrator of American-occupied Japan. MacArthur won additional military fame as he led the United Nations troops in the invasion at Inchon during the Korean War. He was later recalled by President Truman when they differed on the strategy of the war. He was the son of another famous general, Arthur MacArthur, who fought in the Civil War. Douglas saw action in World War I and later became superintendent of West Point. From 1935 to 1941 he worked as a military adviser to the Philippine government, helping to prepare the Philippines for an expected attack by the Japanese. He is buried in Norfolk, Virginia.

596
Born While Parents Were Away

To read a certain newspaper headline in January 1880, it would appear that Douglas MacArthur had the most unique birth ever. The headline of a Norfolk, Virginia, newspaper announced, "Douglas MacArthur Was Born on January 26 While His Parents Were Away."

Mrs. MacArthur, a native of Norfolk, was with her husband, then Capt. Arthur MacArthur, at Little Rock, Arkansas. Her two previous children were born in Norfolk, and their plans were that Douglas would be born in Norfolk as well. However, before they could return to Norfolk, Douglas was born prematurely at Little Rock.

597
Believe in Yourself

Douglas MacArthur was preparing to take an examination for an appointment to West Point. The night before the examination he couldn't sleep. His mother spoke to him. "Doug," she said, "you'll win if you don't lose your nerve. You must believe in yourself, my son, or no one else will believe in you. Be self-confident, self-reliant, and even if you don't make it, you will know you have done your best. Now, go to it."

When the examination scores were announced, Douglas MacArthur was number one.

598
Holding Our Own

When Douglas MacArthur was a small boy, his father was transferred from Fort Wingate, New Mexico, to Fort Seldon, some sixty miles north of El Paso. Young Douglas marched along with the band of soldiers making the move. It was hot and dusty, water holes were scarce, and the water supply was low. One rancher was asked how far it was to the next water hole. "About ten miles," he replied. For almost another three hours they trudged. Finally, they met another rancher. "How far to the next water hole?" asked the first sergeant. The rancher looked off into the direction they were traveling and answered, "About ten miles." The first sergeant turned to his tired, hot, and dirty men, saying, "It's all right boys; thank God, we're holding our own."

599
I Shall Return

Gen. Douglas MacArthur and some of his key staff members were ordered from the Philippines during the heavy Japanese assaults early in World War II. They were to report to Australia where an Allied offensive would be organized. The Japanese naval forces had the area blockaded; their air force was watching the skies for an escape attempt by MacArthur.

The Americans decided to make their escape by a small fleet of PT boats under the cover of darkness. It was a desperate gamble —

"Maybe one chance in five," a sergeant guessed. The suspense mounted by the seconds as the brave PT crews zigzagged their way through the blockade. From time to time they could make out the silhouettes of huge Japanese warships. The sergeant's odds of one in five probably should have been more like one in a thousand. Any moment they could have been blown out of the water by the waiting Japanese warships.

Throughout the ordeal, MacArthur's thoughts were on the courageous troops on Bataan and Corregidor — many who would later die or suffer in prison camps — and his hopes to return with a liberation army were uppermost in his mind.

When reporters asked MacArthur on his safe arrival in Australia for a statement, he gave what was to become a battle cry for the Philippines: "The president of the United States ordered me to break through the Japanese lines and proceed from Corregidor to Australia for the purpose, as I understand it, of organizing the American offensive against Japan, a primary object of which is the relief of the Philippines. I came through and I shall return."

600
Advice

During his long military career, Gen. Douglas MacArthur had opportunity to accept or reject advice from thousands of people — military and civilians, Americans and foreigners. But his value of advice wasn't very high. "I realize," he said, "That advice is worth what it costs — that is nothing."

601
Greatness

You may not like him, but he meets the test of greatness. He fills the living space around him. He cannot be trespassed upon, or toyed with, or subtracted from. Whatever ground he stands on, it is *his*.

— Henry Luce, in tribute to MacArthur

602
Victory

One of the most thrilling moments of the 1940s came from the deck of the battleship *Missouri* in Tokyo harbor, September 2, 1945. After

Gen. Douglas MacArthur received the Japanese surrender, he went to the microphone to speak to all Americans: "And so, my fellow countrymen, today I report to you that your sons and daughters have served you well and faithfully. . . . Their spiritual strength and power have brought us through to victory. They are homeward bound — take care of them."

603
Missionaries Needed

Gen. Douglas MacArthur was made supreme commander of the occupational forces in Japan following World War II. From the beginning he desired that the Japanese have religious freedom. For that freedom to be realized, it took a renunciation by the emperor of his assumed divinity. The decision to end the assumed divinity role for the emperor was made by the emperor himself. And it helped Japan become a democracy.

MacArthur's concern, however, was that Christianity move into the spiritual vacuum. Whenever possible he told visiting Christian ministers of the need in Japan. "The more missionaries we can bring out here," he told them, "and the more occupation troops we can send home, the better." At his request, The Pocket Testament League distributed ten million Bibles translated into Japanese.

604
Sickness Not unto Death

Following his retirement, Gen. Douglas MacArthur had a serious illness that nearly took his life. While he was convalescing, he received a request from a minister in Chicago who asked his favorite Scripture text at his moment of crisis. Gen. MacArthur answered:

> It would be difficult, indeed, for me to select a single verse as the most inspirational from the myriad passages which are so immutable and everlasting in that greatest of books. But perhaps one example will suffice. I was once given but thirty-six hours of life. I remembered the Gospel of St. John where it says a certain man named Lazarus of Bethany, the town of Mary, was desperately sick even unto death. When Jesus was told he said this sickness was not unto death, and he called upon Lazarus to come forth. And Lazarus arose from the dead. And Jesus said, "I am the resurrection and the life; he that believeth in Me, though he were dead, yet shall he live." And so, I came through.

DOUGLAS MAC ARTHUR SAID IT

605
Mother

An aged, white-haired mother sat with a smile on her face, waiting for her famous son, Dwight [Eisenhower], to arrive. Someone said to her, "You must be very proud of your great and illustrious son." Upon which she asked, "Which son?" Each one was equally great to that noble mother.

My sainted mother taught me a devotion to God and a love of country which have ever sustained me in my many lonely and bitter moments of decision in distant and hostile lands. To her, I yield anew a son's reverent thanks.

606
Sorrows of War

In Essey [France, 1918] I saw a sight I shall never quite forget. Our advance had been so rapid the Germans had evacuated in a panic. There was a German officer's horse saddled and equipped standing in a barn, a battery of guns complete in every detail, and the entire instrumentation and music of a regimental band. The town was still occupied by civilians, mostly old men, women, and children. They had been there for four years, and when we came in we had great difficulty in getting them to come out of their cellars. They did not know that United States soldiers were in the war, and it was necessary for us to explain to them that we were Americans. They were started at once to the rear. Men, women, and children plodded along in mud up to their knees carrying what few household effects they could. It was one of the most forlorn sights I have ever seen. On other fields in others wars, how often it was to be repeated before my aching eyes.

— From *Reminiscences,* by General Douglas MacArthur, © 1964 Time Inc.

607
Patriotism

Only those Americans who are willing to die for their country are fit to live.

608
Peace

Could I have but a line a century hence crediting a contribution to the advance of peace, I would gladly yield every honor which has been accorded me in war.

609
Father

By profession I am a soldier and take pride in that fact. But I am prouder, infinitely prouder, to be a father.

610
Growing Old

Nobody grows old by merely living a number of years. People grow old only by deserting their ideals. Years may wrinkle the skin, but to give up interests wrinkles the soul. Worry, doubt, self-distrust, fear and despair . . . these are the long, long years that bow the head and turn the growing spirit back to dust.

Whatever your years, there is in every being's heart the love of wonder, the undaunted challenge of events, the unfailing childlike appetite for "What next," and the joy and the game of life.

You are as young as your faith, as old as your doubt; as young as your self-confidence, as old as your fear; as young as your hope, as old as your despair. In the central place of your heart, there is a recording chamber; so long as it receives messages of beauty, hope, cheer, and courage, so long you are young. When the wires are all down, and your heart is covered with the snow of pessimism and the ice of cynicism, then — and then only — are you grown old.

611
Opportunity

There is no security on this earth. Only opportunity.

612
Liberty

The inescapable price of liberty is an ability to preserve it from destruction.

613
Thank God for Victory, Peace

As I look back on the long, tortuous trail from those grim days of Bataan and Corregidor, when an entire world lived in fear, when democracy was on the defensive everywhere, when modern civilization trembled in the balance, I thank a merciful God that He has given us the faith, the courage and the power from which to mould victory. We have known the bitterness of defeat and the exultation of triumph, and from both we learned there can be no turning back. We must go forward to preserve in peace what we won in war.

— From message to American people at Japanese surrender, Sept. 2, 1945

614
Peace Through Spiritual Renewal

Men since the beginning of time have sought peace. Various methods through the ages have attempted to devise an international process to prevent or settle disputes between nations. . . . Military alliances, balances of power, leagues of nations, all in turn failed, leaving the only path to be by way of the crucible of war. We have had our last chance. If we do not now devise some greater and more equitable system, Armageddon will be at our door. The problem basically is theological and involves a spiritual recrudescence and improvement of human character that will synchronize with our almost matchless advances in science, art, literature and all material and cultural developments of the past two thousand years. It must be of the spirit if we are to save the flesh.

— From message to American people at Japanese surrender, Sept. 2, 1945

615
A Father's Prayer

Build me a son, O Lord, who will be strong enough to know when he is weak, and brave enough to face himself when he is afraid; one who will be proud and unbending in honest defeat, and humble and gentle in victory.

Build me a son whose wishbone will not be where his backbone should be; a son who will know Thee and that to know himself is the foundation stone of knowledge.

Lead him, I pray, not in the path of ease and comfort, but under the stress and spur of difficulties and challenge. Here let him learn to stand up in the storm; here let him learn compassion for those who fail.

Build me a son whose heart will be clear, whose goal will be high; a son who will master himself before he seeks to master other men; one who will learn to laugh, yet never forget how to weep; one who will reach into the future, yet never forget the past.

And after all these things are his, add, I pray, enough of a sense of humor, so that he may always be serious, yet never take himself too seriously. Give him humility, so that he may always remember the simplicity of true greatness, the open mind of true wisdom, the meekness of true strength.

Then I, his father, will dare to whisper, "I have not lived in vain."

616
Reform

The springs of human conflict cannot be eradicated through institution, but only through the reform of the individual human being.

617
Patriotism

The highest encomium you can still receive is to be called a patriot, if it means you love your country above all else and will place your life, if need be, at the service of your Flag.

618

Duty

I am closing my fifty-two years of military service. When I joined the army even before the turn of the century, it was the fulfillment of all my boyish hopes and dreams. The world has turned over many times since I took the oath on the Plain at West Point, and the hopes and dreams have long since vanished. But I still remember the refrain of one of the most popular barrack ballads of that day which proclaimed most proudly that —

"Old Soldiers never die, they just fade away."

And like the old soldier of that ballad, I now close my military career and just fade away — an old soldier who tried to do his duty as God gave him the light to see that duty.

Good-by.

HENRIETTA C. MEARS

(1890-1963)

Henrietta C. Mears began writing Sunday school lessons for her own class, and eventually saw the project expand to a service for thousands of Sunday schools. She was director of Christian education at First Presbyterian Church of Hollywood at the time. As others heard of her literature, requests were made and soon Gospel Light Publications was founded. She was the author of several study books for Sunday school pupils and workers. The literature was also translated into dozens of other languages. She began her teaching career in a Bible class in Minneapolis and was also a high school chemistry teacher at the time. After she moved to Hollywood, First Presbyterian Church Sunday school grew from four hundred to six thousand.

619
Lived to Make Jesus Known

I remember one precious experience with Henrietta Mears when we were having a sandwich in a hotel restaurant in St. Louis during a Christian bookseller's convention.

She began to reminisce about the wonderful things God had done in her life. She talked of the Lord Jesus as simply and genuinely as a new convert possessed by first love.

The tears flowed down her cheeks. It was thrilling to be with a Christian worker who hadn't become a pro. She really loved Jesus Christ, and she lived to make Him known.

— Russell Hitt, Editor, *Eternity*

620
Bible Ignorance

Is it possible that Americans can receive a good education and yet know little about the Bible? Henrietta Mears said a brilliant young man, who was working on his doctorate, told her, "I have taught in Sunday school. I consider myself a person of average intelligence, but I would flunk on a simple Bible examination."

621
Discord

Henrietta Mears told about a great organist who sat down to play the expensive church pipe organ during a service. The congregation waited for the beautiful music they knew he could produce on the instrument. But what they heard that day was only noise! It was terrible discord. The audience was as dumbfounded as the organist. Again he tried. It was even more terrible than before. It didn't take long for the organist to discover the problem: college students in the town had pulled a prank on him by rearranging the pipes.

Miss Mears likened this to God's plan for the human race. "They [the human race] are like the complicated arrangement of the pipes in an organ to make a composite whole," she explained. "How hideous it is when men rearrange that which God has arranged. It means discord instead of harmony."

HENRIETTA C. MEARS SAID IT

622
Condemned

At a United States arsenal in New York a large gun lay marked "condemned." I asked why that apparently perfect thing was condemned.

"See those marks?" the guard asked, and pointed to some little holes not more than the size of a pin head which dotted the gun in a dozen places.

These seemed insignificant. How little they were in comparison to that great gun. They did not seem to go deeper than a thirty-second of an inch, and yet the gun was condemned. Why? Because no one knew how deep those imperfections went. If they were deep, in the crisis of war this mighty engine capable of hurling half a ton of metal a dozen miles and hitting a target might, under the heat of the powder, burst into a thousand fragments.

God had to mark the human race "condemned" because of their sins. (Romans 3:23) He did not look at the thing that seemed small, but He knew that the flaw of sin weakened the whole character of man.

— *Highlights of Scripture,* Part 1

623
Keeping on the Narrow Path

One day some Americans were riding at great speed on horseback in the desert in Mesopotamia. They had left the beaten track. They were quite unconscious of the fact that in front of them, and indeed, around them on three sides, were some terrible quicksands, which would suck in a horse and his rider in a relentless way and there would be little hope of escape. An Arab suddenly seemed to lift himself out of the sand almost at their very feet, and with outstretched arms and wild eyes besought them to pull up.

Isn't this just like Christ? He sees us riding, riding fast in these days, surrounded with quicksands of temptation. He calls to us in urgent tone, "Back, back on the path. There is terrible danger all around you." Christ knows the way of our life. He knows that all around this seemingly respectable and ordinary life of ours there are those sinking sands of sin which will suck us down. He implores us to go back to the steep, and narrow, but it is a road where the feet will not slip. Christ says, "I am the way." (John 14:6).

— *Highlights of Scripture,* Part 3

624
Temptation

There is not a person in this world who will not at some time be waylaid by temptation. It is one thing a person cannot avoid. As long as we live on this earth we shall be tempted. But to deliberately walk into temptation is a different thing.

625
Bearing Fruit

Think of your life as a vineyard prepared by God in the finest possible way and loaned to you. Are you a faithful steward, or are you losing your opportunities every day to have your life count? God wants you to have returns from this vineyard every day. You do not have to wait for full manhood or womanhood, to yield Him a part of the fruit. Acknowledge Christ as your Master today, and let your life bear fruit for His glory. It is your responsibility to bear fruit for Christ, or God will choose other workmen.

626
Freedom

The sin of the prodigal not only cost him his home and its comforts, but the strangest thing of all is that it cost him his freedom. That is the very thing that he went out to seek. When he started out, he said to his father, "Give me mine inheritance." When he came back, he said, "Make me one of thy servants." Away from home, he was sent into the fields to feed swine. He was not consulted in the matter. . . . No one can have freedom apart from obedience.

627
Law

The law was broken in people's hearts before it was broken by Moses' hand.

—Quotations 627-651 are from *431 Quotes from the Notes of Henrietta C. Mears,* © Copyright 1970 by Regal Book Division, G/L Publications, Glendale, California. Used by permission.

628
Duty

The recognition of our duties is more important than the recognition of our rights.

629
Cannot Force Belief

It makes no difference who the preacher is, or how long the sermon, he cannot make his hearers believe him.

630
Authority

Nothing more impairs authority than a too frequent or indiscreet use of it. If thunder itself were to be continual, it would excite no more terror than the noise of a mill.

631
The Bible

Let the Bible fill the memory, rule the heart, and guide the feet.

632
Serving

Serving God with our little is the way to make it more; and we must never think that wasted with which God is honored, or men are blest.

633
Surrender

The greatness of a man's power is the measure of his surrender. It is not a question of who you are, or of what you are, but whether God controls you.

634
Personal Work

Personal work is one person finding another person and bringing him to the personal Savior.

635
Promises

Don't let God's precious promises just rest in the Bible; hold them close in your heart and the devil can never reach you.

636
Eternity

If you ever happen to see in the obituary column that Henrietta Mears has died, don't you believe it! This old body may die, but I'll be glad of that. I wouldn't want to have to go through eternity with this deteriorating one. I'll have a new body. And what will I do when I get to heaven? Well, I am going to ask the Lord to show me around. I'll want to get in a rocketship to inspect all the galaxies He has made. And maybe He will give me a planet of my own, so that I can start building something. Oh, it's going to be so wonderful.

637
God

A little band of Indian converts in northwest Canada came to a missionary with a strange request. "We are always hearing what God has done," they said, "now tell us what He is going to do."

638
Saving the World

It is true that Christ alone can save the world, but Christ will not save this world alone.

639
The Hardest Place

The hardest place to go is where you have been a failure.

640
Persistent Prayer

Do not use the term "importunity" in prayer as though God ever had to be hammered away at, or begged, or teased, or tired out by our much speaking before He answers. No such notion is supported by any Bible teaching, or common sense. Importunity in prayer is not pleasing to God, but persistence in prayer and unshaken confidence in God's loving wisdom, even though His answer is delayed, is very different. God honors persistent prayer.

641
Ways We Can Use Our Time for God

1. Remember, God owns all time! He just loans it to us to use.
2. Take time to read from God's Word each day.
3. Take time to pray each morning that God will keep you from evil and use you during that day.
4. Take time to be pleasant. A bright smile or pleasant words fall like sunbeams upon the hearts of those around us.
5. Take time to be polite. True politeness is to say the kindest things in the kindest ways.
6. Take time to be thoughtful of father and mother, teacher and friend.
7. You have the management of 168 hours a week. What do you do with them?

642
Youth

What your young people learn today determines what the church will know tomorrow.

643
Helping Others

The man who keeps busy helping the man below him won't have time to envy the man above him — and there may not be anybody above him anyway.

644
Solving Problems

If more problems of youth were settled in the house of the Lord, fewer problems would be settled in the house of correction.

645
A Teacher's Ten Commandments

1. I will win the personal allegiance of every one of my class to the Lord and Master.
2. I will not think my work is over when my pupil has made his decision for Christ.
3. I will see that he finds a definite place in some specific task.
4. I will bring Christianity out of the unreal into everyday life.
5. I will seek to help each one discover the will of God so the Master can work through him and use every talent.
6. I will instill a divine discontent in the mind of everyone who can do more than he is doing; not by telling him his life is petty and ordinary, but by giving him a vision of great things to be done enthusiastically, passionately.
7. I will make it easy for anyone to come to me with the deepest experiences of his inner life — not by urging, but by sympathy and understanding. I will never let anyone think I am disappointed in him.
8. I will keep the Cross of Christ central in Christian life.
9. I will pray as I have never prayed before for wisdom and power.
10. I will spend and be spent in this battle.

— Written as a young woman when she faced defeat in teaching

646
Faults

So many times the faults we see in others are our own. If we tell lies, we are watching and anxious to see another person tell an untruth. If we are selfish, we delight to see selfishness in others.

647
Friendship

Put Him in the center of the circle when you make your friends and life will hold no richer joy than your companionship. If Christ is in every heart in that circle, what a power that circle will be for Him. This is one of the reasons that we have to be careful about our choice of friends. Your other comrades have a great deal to do with your fellowship with Christ. The great Comrade cannot remain in some circles. How about yours?

648
Training Leaders

Every church should produce its own leadership — something is wrong if we are not. There are plenty in the church. They need to be enlisted and trained.

649
Teaching the Bible

I have discovered that if the Bible is taught the way it should be that it will be like a powerful magnet drawing youth unto the Lord Jesus Christ. What a supremely superb Textbook we have.

650
Definition of a Teacher

What is a teacher? God's man, in God's place, doing God's work, in God's way, for God's glory.

651
Sorrow

Sorrow in this world can become such a weight that many people go under it, entirely discouraged. To others, sorrow is a challenge and they use it to lift them to higher planes, to greater sympathy and understanding. It forces many a person to look to Christ who "always causeth us to triumph in him."

652
Can Christ Count on You?

All the disciples but John deserted Jesus in the hour of His greatest need. In that fleeing nine is James of the "inner circle," Nathanael the guileless, and Andrew the personal worker. Yet there they were, running pell-mell down the road together, away from their Friend. A sorry sight! Wait! Don't start blaming them. Suppose you look up and see where you are. Are you following closely? Remember, majorities aren't always right. Be sure you are right! Can Christ count on you?

—From *What the Bible Is All About*

DWIGHT L. MOODY
(1837–1899)

Dwight L. Moody was a famous nineteenth century American evangelist, considered one of the most successful of all time. He was born at Northfield, Massachusetts, and at the age of seventeen moved to Boston where he took a job as a shoe salesman. It was here that Edward Kimball, his Sunday school teacher, led him to the Lord. Although Moody had little formal education, he became a Bible scholar and through his simple, direct messages brought thousands to Christ in Britain and America. He also founded Northfield School for Girls, Mount Herman School for Boys, Moody Bible Institute, and Moody Press. Ira D. Sankey, a gospel singer and hymn writer, teamed with Moody in his mass evangelistic meetings.

653
The Prodigal Son

Dwight Moody's father died when Dwight was only four. A month later Mrs. Moody gave birth to twins; she now had nine mouths to feed and no income. Merciless creditors dogged the widow, claiming everything they could get their hands on.

As if Mrs. Moody didn't have enough troubles, her eldest boy later ran away from home. Certain that her son would return, Mrs. Moody placed a light for him in the window each night. Young Dwight was inspired by her faith and prayers. He wrote:

> I can remember how eagerly she used to look for tidings of that boy; how she used to send us to the post office to see if there was a letter from him. . . . Some nights when the wind was very high, and the house . . . would tremble at every gust, the voice of my mother was raised in prayer for that wanderer.

Mrs. Moody's prayers were answered. Her prodigal did eventually return. Dwight remembered the scene:

> While my mother was sitting at the door, a stranger was seen coming toward the house, and when he came to the door he stopped. My mother didn't know her boy. He stood there with folded arms and a great beard flowing down his breast, his tears trickling down his face. When my mother saw those tears she cried, "Oh, it's my lost son!" and entreated him to come in. But he stood still! "No, Mother," he answered, "I will not come in until I hear first that you have forgiven me."

Mrs. Moody was only too willing to forgive. She rushed to the door, threw her arms around him, and there the prodigal found forgiveness.

654
Moody's Conversion

At seventeen years of age, Dwight Moody left home at Northfield, Massachusetts, for Boston, where he began working for his uncle in a shoe store. He regularly attended Sunday school at the Mount Vernon Congregational Church. His teacher, Edward Kimball, took a great interest in the young Moody. Kimball desired to see Moody accept Jesus Christ as his personal Savior. One day Mr. Kimball decided the time was ready to confront Dwight about a decision for Christ. He would visit him at the shoe store. Kimball told about the experience later.

> When I was nearly there, I began to wonder whether I ought to go in just then during business hours. I thought that possibly my call might embarrass the boy, and that when I went away the other clerks would ask who I was, and taunt him with my efforts in trying to make him a good boy. In the meantime I had passed the store, and, discovering this, I determined to make a dash for it and have it over at once. I found Moody in the back part of the building wrapping up shoes. I went up to him at once, and putting my hand on his shoulder, I made what I afterward thought was a very weak plea for Christ. . . . It seemed the young man was just ready for the light that then broke upon him, and there, in the back of the store in Boston, he gave himself and his life to Christ.

655
All He Had for Christ

It is said that D. L. Moody was once preaching to a great crowd and was pouring out his very soul with great earnestness. After the service a man who was a leader in one of the fashionable churches of the city, and who had been on the platform while Moody spoke, went to the evangelist and said, "By the way, I noticed that you made eleven mistakes in grammar tonight." "I don't doubt it," said Moody. "My early education was very faulty. I have often wished that I had received more schooling. But I am using all the grammar I know in the service of Christ. How is it with you?" The man had no answer.

656
God Works in Spite of Critics

There were many who criticized Dwight L. Moody and his gigantic evangelistic meetings held in the latter part of the nineteenth century. Some objected to the excitement in the meetings; Moody met their objection by comparing his meetings with some of the nonreligious events: "Why, there is more excitement in a race course in one day than you will see in a church in fifty days. Get into a political campaign, and you will see more excitement than in a hundred religious meetings. 'Undue excitement!' they say. 'Some people will get out of their minds.' The fact is, the world is out of its mind, anyway."

When others rejected Moody's meetings because they were not of the regular church meeting type, Moody said, "God will always work in His own way. He will mark out channels for Himself. We need to learn this lesson, and just stand aside and let Him work — work as He pleases."

657
Crazy Moody

Following Moody's conversion in Boston, he went to Chicago where he became a success in two fields: business and Sunday school work. His Christian zeal often embarrassed relatives and friends. Some even called him "Crazy Moody." His uncle Zebulon Allen recalled a visit Moody made to Northfield in 1860.

> My nephew Dwight is crazy crazy as a March hare. Come on from Chicago last week. . . . I had not seen him but he drove into my yard this morning. You know how cold it was and his face was red as red flannel. Before I could say good morning he shouted "Good morning, Uncle Zebulon, what are you going to do for Christ today?" Of course I was startled and finally managed to say, "Come in, Dwight, and we will talk it over." "No, I can't stop but I want you to think about it," and he turned the sleigh around and went up the hill like a streak of lightning. I tell you he is crazy.

658
Consecration

Moody was a successful Sunday school leader, but he decided to go to Great Britain and study church methods there. A conversation he had with Henry Varley, a well-known evangelist of the day, marked a new era in his life. The two were seated in a public park in Dublin when Varley said, "The world has yet to see what God will do with and for and through and in and by the man who is fully consecrated to Him." Moody reflected on the words: "He said 'a man'; he did not say, a great man, nor a learned man, nor a smart man, but simply 'a man.' I am a man, and it lies with the man himself whether he will or will not make that entire and full consecration. I will try my utmost to be that man."

659
The Fool

In the final service of one of Moody's campaigns, an usher handed the famed evangelist a note as he entered the auditorium. Supposing it to be an announcement, Moody quieted the large audience and prepared to read the notice. He opened it to find a single word: "Fool!"

But the colorful preacher was equal to the occasion. Said he, "This is most unusual. I have just been handed a message which consists of but one word — the word 'fool.' I repeat, this is most unusual. I have often heard of those who have written letters and forgotten to sign their names — but this is the first time I have ever heard of anyone who signed his name and forgot to write the letter!"

And taking advantage of the situation, Moody promptly changed his sermon to the text: "The fool hath said in his heart, There is no God."

— *Moody Monthly*

660
Conversion Genuine

One of Mr. Moody's favorite stories was about a converted miserly farmer to whom a neighbor in distress appealed for help. The miser decided to prove the genuineness of his conversion by giving him a ham. On his way to get it the tempter whispered, "Give him the smallest one you have."

A struggle ensued and finally the miser took down the largest ham he had.

"You are a fool," the devil said.

And the farmer replied, "If you don't keep still, I'll give him every ham in the smokehouse!"

— Told by Henrietta Mears

DWIGHT L. MOODY SAID IT

661
Treasure

It does not take long to tell where a man's treasure is. In fifteen minutes' conversation with most men you can tell whether their treasures are on the earth or in heaven.

662
To Live Forever

Some day you will read in the papers that D. L. Moody of East Northfield is dead. Don't you believe a word of it! At that moment I shall be more alive than I am now. I shall have gone up higher, that is all; out of this old clay tenement into a house that is immortal — a body that death cannot touch; that sin cannot taint; a body fashioned unto His glorious body. I was born of the flesh in 1837. I was born of the Spirit in 1856. That which is born of the flesh may die. That which is born of the Spirit will live forever.

663
Good Works

Before my conversion, I worked toward the cross; then I worked to be saved; now I work because I am saved.

664
New Life

I remember the morning on which I came out of my room after I first trusted Christ. I think the sun shone a good deal brighter than it ever had before — I thought that it was just smiling upon me; and as I walked out on Boston Common and heard the birds singing in the trees, I thought they were all singing a song to me.

665
Three Classes of Christians

It seems to me we have about three classes of Christians: the first class, in the third chapter of John, were those who had got to Calvary and there got life. They believed on the Son and were saved, and there they rested satisfied. They did not seek anything higher. Then in the fourth chapter of John we come to a better class of Christians. There it was a well of living water bubbling up. There are a few of these, but they are not a hundredth part of the first class. But the best class is in the seventh chapter of John: "Out of his belly shall flow rivers of living water." That is the kind of Christian we ought to be.

666
Recipe for Revival

The best way to revive a church is to build a fire in the pulpit.

667
God's Will

Spread out your petition before God, and then say, "Thy will, not mine, be done." The sweetest lesson I have learned in God's school is to let the Lord choose for me.

668
Love

If you haven't love in your heart, you should throw your hope to the four winds and go and get a better one.

669
Atonement

I must die or get somebody to die for me. If the Bible doesn't teach that, it doesn't teach anything. And that is where the atonement of Jesus Christ comes in.

RICHARD M. NIXON
(1913–   )

Richard M. Nixon became the thirty-seventh president of the United States in 1969 by defeating Vice-Pres. Hubert H. Humphrey and Gov. George C. Wallace. His victory came seven years after his political career appeared ended when he lost the governor's race in California. Nixon was born and spent his boyhood in southern California. His parents were Quakers and attended the East Whittier Friends Meeting House. Nixon played the organ at the meeting house and taught Sunday school. After four years in the navy, Nixon was elected to the House of Representatives. As a representative he won national fame during the Alger Hiss case. He was elected to the Senate in 1950 and then became the vice-president in 1952. He was vice-president for eight years under President Eisenhower. In 1960 he was defeated by John F. Kennedy for the presidency.

670
Grandmother's Influence

Grandmother Milhous was a great influence in the life of Richard Nixon as a boy in southern California. In describing his childhood to Earl Mazo, Nixon recalled that his grandmother was a strong factor in keeping the family closely knit through the years.

The Nixon and Milhous traits — from their strict Quaker religious practice — were standards for the whole family. "Honesty, hard work, do your best at all times — humanitarian ideals," according to Nixon were his grandmother's trademarks. "She was always taking care of every tramp that came along the road, just like my own mother too. She had strong feelings about pacifism and civil liberties. She probably affected me in that respect. At her house, no servant ate at a separate table. They always ate with the family. There were Negroes, Indians, and people from Mexico — she was always taking somebody in."

671
Inspiring Second Stringer

When Richard Nixon attended Whittier College, he loved football; but he seldom played because he wasn't heavy enough. Game after game would be played as the future president sat it out on the bench. All of his varsity seasons were on the bench, but he worked hard and seldom missed a practice. "He was wonderful for morale," his college coach recalled, "because he'd sit there and cheer the rest of the guys, and tell them how well they'd played." One of his old teammates said, "Dick had two left feet. He couldn't coordinate. But, boy, was he an inspiration! He was always talking it up."

672
Encouragement

Richard Nixon as a new student found the grind and pressures in Duke University's law school tough. He was homesick, deep in studies, and worried that he wouldn't make it through. An upperclassman noticed the anxiety on his face late one night. "What's bothering you?" he asked.

"I'm scared," Nixon answered. "I counted thirty-two Phi Beta Kappas in my class. I don't believe I can stay up in that group."

"You needn't worry," the other student said. "The fact that you are studying so late shows that you're not afraid of hard work."

It was the encouragement that the young Nixon needed at that moment, and he went on to complete the tough law course and finish third in his graduating class.

673
Hard Work Brings Results

It was the Great Depression time and four law students at Duke University were sharing a room in an old ramshackle farmhouse located about a mile through the woods from the campus. They were there because they couldn't afford anything better. They had no running water and no heat other than an old laundry stove. But they worked hard at their law studies and three of the four were one, two, and three in their graduating class. The four later became successful in their chosen fields. William R. Perdue became an executive of the Ethyl Corporation; Fred S. Albrink made a career of the navy; Lyman Brownfield built a prosperous law practice in Columbus, Ohio. The fourth member of that hard working, economy minded law quartet became president of the United States — Richard M. Nixon.

674
Picture Takes on New Value

My wife, Joy, happened to be at the 1962 Seattle World's Fair when Richard Nixon, then gubernatorial candidate for California, was visiting. The next day a newspaper picture of Nixon and the crowd clearly revealed Joy standing nearby. We got a copy of the paper and an eight-by-ten-inch print. Later, Mr. Nixon lost the election, fell into near political obscurity, and the picture and clipping were filed away in an album. But then, as everyone knows, Richard Nixon made a political recovery and became our thirty-seventh president in 1969. The old picture and newspaper clipping suddenly took on increased sentimental value.

— Wayne Warner

675
Three Great Presidents

When President Nixon was asked to name the presidents he most admires and respects, he . . . named . . . Abraham Lincoln, Theodore Roosevelt, and Woodrow Wilson: Lincoln for his ability to rise to the challenges of the Civil War; Roosevelt, as the first president to be involved to any extent in the affairs of the world, and his close family relationship; Wilson because he was a great writer and orator and for his zeal for a better world.

676
Borrowed Offering

President-elect Nixon was attending a worship service at Calvary Baptist Church in New York City as a guest of evangelist Billy Graham. When the offering was announced, Mr. Nixon leaned over and whispered to Graham, "I came out this morning without any money. Could you lend me some?" Graham later told about the incident in a worship service at the White House. "You can be sure I loaned him the biggest bill I had in my pocket," he added with a chuckle.

677
Budget Limited

When Richard Nixon was Vice President, he attended the Boy Scout Jamboree at Valley Forge. Practically every scout there had a camera and was trying to get a shot of the Vice President. One little fellow was as anxious as anyone else, but after snapping three shots he closed his camera and said, "That's all my budget allows for Vice Presidents."

— Hearst Headline Service

678
Campaign's Lighter Moments

After an impressive stint as a representative, Richard Nixon threw his hat into the Senate ring and got into a hard-fought battle with Congresswoman Helen Gahagan Douglas. It wasn't an easy contest for either candidate, but it had its lighter moments for the Nixon family. It was 1950, and the Nixon children, Tricia and Julie, were too young to take an active interest in politics; but they provided the lighter moments.

At one big meeting in Los Angeles, Pat Nixon took Tricia, who was just four and a half years old. Her attention span was about normal for a child her age, so it wasn't long before she tired of her father's speech. Her father paused. Tricia took the opportunity to sound off loud and clear, "My goodness, daddy talks a long time, doesn't he?"

Julie provided her part as well when the whole family was featured on television. She soon lost interest in the event and began to probe her nose. The camera spotted it for the benefit of the viewers. Her father later remarked to her, "Julie, honey, you've either just won or just lost me the election."

RICHARD M. NIXON SAID IT

679
Isolation

America can never again live in isolation. Either we march into the future, together with other free nations, into a world of peace and prosperity, or we decline into obscurity and failure, as a people who had not the vision to see the world as it is, or who had not the courage to face up to duty.

— From speech as vice-president

680
A Cause

A man who has never lost himself in a cause bigger than himself missed one of life's mountaintop experiences. Only in losing himself does he find himself. Only then does he discover all the latent strengths he never knew he had and which otherwise would have remained dormant.

— Autobiography *Six Crises*

681
Goal

Our goal cannot and must never be to force our way of life on others. But our fundamental belief that every nation has a right to be independent must be instilled in the new generation. And we must have a crusading zeal, not just to hold our own, but to win the battle for freedom, individual dignity, and true economic progress.

682
Extra Dimensions

What I want to do more than anything else is to develop an appreciation in Americans for what I call "the extra dimensions of life." It's not enough to have peace in the world, to have safer cities, a good job, adequate medical care — these things are necessary, but there is more to life than that. What is needed, if the nation and the individuals in it are to become and remain great, is for them to have their eyes on goals beyond. It does not lie in material things. We can do better in America. But we need to regain the sense of wonder — the feeling that anything can be done — that was characteristic of us in the American Revolution. Unless this adminstration can produce that sense, it will have failed.

— From "Mr. Nixon Goes to Washington," by Allen Drury, *Reader's Digest*, February 1969. Copyright 1969 by Allen Drury, reprinted by permission of the Harold Matson Company, Inc.

683
Equality

Equality to us is basically a religious ideal. It does not refer to talent, ability, culture, or background; for we differ in those respects. It does not even refer to equality of opportunity; this is a consequence, rather than the substance, of our belief. Equality means one simple thing — in the words of Al Smith, "We believe in the common brotherhood of man under the common fatherhood of God."

684
Faith

The quiet determination of humble faith is the real secret of American strength. With this faith, the dark clouds of the moment will indeed be the darkness before the dawn, the dawn of a new future of peace, of human brotherhood, and of respect for the dignity of all men.

685
Peace

There is no greater tribute we could pay to America's war dead than to find the road to peace.

686
Fellow Man

In America there is no forgotten man, no common man, no average man. There is only our fellow man.

687
Revolution Not Ended

Our history books tell us that the American Revolution ended in Yorktown. But the American Revolution will not be complete until the ideals of independence, equality, and freedom which kept men fighting at Valley Forge are a reality not only for Americans but for peoples throughout the world.

688
Preparation

The ability to be calm, confident, and decisive in crisis is not an inherited characteristic but is the direct result of how well the individual has prepared himself for the battle.

689
Do Something

I seek the presidency not because it offers me a chance to be somebody but because it offers a chance to do something.

690
Circumstances

I have a theory that in the United States those who seek the presidency never win it. Circumstances rather than a man's ambition determine the result. If he is the right man for the right time, he will be chosen.

691
Easier Than Writing Sports

I wanted to be a sports writer, but it took me too long to turn out my stuff. I found I could become vice-president faster than I could become a newspaper man.

693
Progress Under God

I have studied the lives of all the presidents of this country of both parties. They came from different religions — some were better churchgoers than others. But there is one thing that I have noticed about every man who has occupied this office, and that is, by the time he ended his term in office, he was more dedicated to and more dependent upon his religious faith than when he entered it.

And that tells me something. This is a great office and I am proud and humble to hold it. This is an enormous responsibility, and I accept the responsibility without fear but also with great respect. But I can also tell you, America would not be what it is today, the greatest nation in the world, if it were not a nation which has made progress under God.

... I have received thousands of letters from people who say, "I pray for this country, and I pray for the president in the exercise of the powers of his office." With that kind of spiritual guidance and spiritual assistance, there is no question in my view about the long-range future of America.

— From address at Billy Graham crusade, Knoxville, Tenn., May 1970

693
Crisis of the Spirit

We find ourselves rich in goods, but ragged in spirit; reaching with magnificent precision for the moon, but falling into raucous discord on earth. We are caught in war, wanting peace. We are torn by division, wanting unity. We see around us empty lives, wanting fulfillment. We see tasks that need doing, waiting for hands to do them.

To a crisis of the spirit, we need an answer of the spirit. And to find that answer, we need only look within ourselves. When we listen to the "better angels of our nature," we find that they celebrate the simple things, the basic things — such as goodness, decency, love, kindness.

Greatness comes in simple trappings.

— From inaugural address, 1969

694
Destiny

Our destiny offers not the cup of despair, but the chalice of opportunity. So let us seize it, not in fear but in gladness — and "riders on the earth together," let us go forward, firm in our faith, steadfast in our purpose, cautious of the dangers; but sustained by our confidence in the will of God and the promise of man.

— From inaugural address, 1969

LOUIS PASTEUR
(1822–1895)

A French scientist, one of the greatest in the world's history, Louis Pasteur contributed to chemistry, medicine, and industry. He was born in Dole, France, the son of a tanner. He was the first scientist to show that living things came from living things, not from spontaneous generation as many thought. He was later credited with saving the silk industry and the wine industry in France. He pioneered in vaccination against animal and human diseases, including rabies. In spite of a brain hemorrhage that partially paralyzed him in 1868, Pasteur continued his long, hard work until his death.

695
Contribution of a Woman

In 1849, when Louis Pasteur was twenty-six, he wrote a letter to the father of the girl he loved, Marie Laurent, to ask for his daughter in marriage. His love for Marie was deep. During his courtship he wrote to her about a nightmare he had experienced: "I woke up suddenly with the thought that you did not love me and immediately started to cry." Their love was mutual and remained through the years to sustain them in several tragedies: the loss of their parents, the early deaths of two of their daughters and Louis' sister, and the paralysis which struck Louis in 1868.

Marie dedicated herself to her husband and his dreams. It was a difficult life she accepted: a professor's small salary, his odd mannerisms, and the knowledge that work came first. In 1884, she wrote to her children, "Your father is absorbed in his thoughts, talks little, sleeps little, rises at dawn, and in one word continues the life I began with him thirty-five years ago." Throughout life, until his death in 1895, she remained his faithful partner.

Alphonse de Lamartine, a contemporary of Pasteur, said, "There is a woman at the beginning of all great things." Pasteur no doubt agreed that it was true in his life — Marie Laurent Pasteur.

696
Protection Against Death

When Louis Pasteur was attempting to find a cure for a strange and deadly fever prevalent among sheep in almost all the French provinces, he was attacked by doctors and others who refused to accept his theories. Finally, after long experimentations, Pasteur evolved a culture which was a mild form of the disease itself and, instead of killing, would build up a protection against the fever. But he had the difficult job of proving it would work. In 1881 he arranged a demonstration, inoculating twenty-five sheep with his serum and placing them with twenty-five other sheep which showed symptoms of the fever. Those who watched and listened knew he was putting his career on the line when he boldly declared, "The twenty-five vaccinated ones will survive." After a period of time, he wrote further details: "We inoculated all the sheep, vaccinated and non-vaccinated, with very virulent splenetic fever. It is not forty-eight hours ago. . . . This afternoon all the non-vaccinated subjects will be dead — eighteen are already dead this morning and the others are dying. As to the vaccinated ones, all are well."

His critics were silenced; some even rushed to become his students. Through the success of that experiment countless humans and animals have been vaccinated and their lives saved from disease and death.

697
The Creator

Louis Pasteur examined the theory of spontaneous generation that was popular in his day, and rejected it. He believed that to get life, some kind of pre-existing created life must be present. He did not believe that the theory was compatible with the view of God as Creator of life. "To bring about spontaneous generation," he reasoned, "would be to create a germ. It would be creating life; it would be to solve the problem of its origin. It would mean to go from matter to life through conditions of environment and of matter.

"God as author of life would then no longer be needed. Matter would replace Him. God would need to be invoked only as author of the motions of the universe."

— From *Louis Pasteur, Free Lance of Science,* by René J. Dubos

698
Father Searches for Son

Louis Pasteur's work on viruses in human beings was interrupted by the Franco-Prussian War which began in 1870. His only son was in the army. Earlier he had suffered the personal tragedy of losing three daughters to sicknesses. But now his son was gone to the front and weeks had passed without news. Pasteur left his laboratory and set out to find him.

The war for France was a total disaster. As Pasteur made his way north he found the roads full of the defeated soldiers and stragglers — "the retreat from Moscow could not have been worse," he said. When he finally located his son's unit, he became even more disheartened and desperate; an officer told him that of the original twelve hundred men of the battalion fewer than three hundred had survived. Louis Untermeyer in *Makers of the Modern World* told of the next move by the shattered father in search of his son. "Pasteur went on through a nightmare of winding roads choked with dead horses and men suffering from freezing cold and gangrenous wounds. Finally, Pasteur recognized a gaunt soldier, weak with hunger, wrapped to his eyes in a greatcoat, and father and son, too moved for words, embraced in silence." Father and son were reunited.

699
A Stickler for Cleanliness

The great scientist, Louis Pasteur, had some social and home mannerisms which certainly must have given his associates and relatives reason to think him a bit odd. He was constantly avoiding any possible infection or germs. He avoided shaking hands as much as possible for fear of infection. At the dinner table he would wipe the dishes and silverware in an attempt to remove any dirt. A fellow scientist once described his odd behavior at mealtime. "He minutely inspected the bread that was served to him and placed on the tablecloth everything he found in it: small fragments of wool, of roaches, of flour worms. . . . This search took place at almost every meal."

700
Do Not Disturb!

Some great minds can be highly productive regardless of the clamor around them. Others, like Louis Pasteur, must have calm. René J. Dubos, in his biography, *Louis Pasteur: Free Lance of Science,* gives us a look into the great scientist's research habits.

> Pasteur's meditations could proceed only in silence, and the presence of any visitor foreign to his occupations was sufficient to disturb him; only persons working on his problems were welcome in the laboratory. Once when he had gone to visit Wurtz at the School of Medicine, he found the chemist at work amidst his pupils, in a room full of activity, like a humming beehive. "How," exclaimed Pasteur, "can you work in the midst of such agitation?" "It excites my ideas," answered Wurtz. "It would put mine to flight," retorted Pasteur.

One of Pasteur's associates, Roux, told about Pasteur's method for preventing interruptions at the laboratory:

> I can still see him turning toward the intruder, waving his hand as if to dismiss him, and saying in a despairing voice, "No, not now, I am too busy." . . . He was the most simple and most hospitable of men; but he could not understand how anyone could dare to disturb a scientist at work. . . . When Chamberlain and I were in the course of an interesting experiment, he would watch around us, and seeing from far through the window our friends coming to fetch us, he would meet them himself at the door to send them away.

701
A Tribute to Father

A French poet, Pierre Jean de Beranger, said, "He who remembers the benefits of his parents is too much occupied with his recollections to remember their faults." That was characteristic of Louis Pasteur, who loved and appreciated his mother and father.

Pasteur was busy working on silkworm diseases in 1865 when he received a telegram with the news that his father was seriously ill. But he arrived too late to see him alive. That night the great scientist wrote to his wife and children from his old boyhood home:

> I have been thinking all day of the marks of affection I have had from my father. For thirty years I have been his constant

care; I owe everything to him. When I was young he kept me from bad company and instilled into me the habit of working and the example of the most loyal and best-filled life. . . . My dear father, how thankful I am that I could give you some satisfaction!

Few people knew of the former sergeant in Napoleon's army and later a tanner, M. Jean Joseph Pasteur. But of him, Louis said, "I owe everything."

702
Theories Become Fact

Until 1885, the dreaded disease, rabies, was unchecked by man. But that year an experiment by Louis Pasteur changed all of that and gave to the world the rabies vaccination.

Pasteur began in 1882 to study the disease, a disease that destroys the nerve cells of part of the brain. He had worked many long hours in his laboratory seeking a vaccine to prevent the disease. His long hours in the laboratory were slowly wearing down his health, yet he labored on.

Then in July 1885, a peasant boy, Joseph Meister, was bitten by a mad dog. The boy was brought to Pasteur by his parents. They begged Pasteur to save their son. Pasteur hesitated to use his new vaccine on the boy because it had never been used on a human. Finally, he gave in. And then after several weeks of treatment, the vaccine proved successful and the boy's life was saved.

Again Louis Pasteur put his career on the line, and again the theories that he had reached through long research became scientific fact. Once again too the world recognized him as one of the greatest scientists who ever lived.

LOUIS PASTEUR SAID IT

703
Science and Nationalism

The conviction of having attained truth is one of the greatest joys permitted to man, and the thought of having contributed to the honor of one's country renders this joy even deeper. If science knows no country, the scientist has one, and it is to his country that he must dedicate the influence that his works may exert in the world.

704
Suffering Breaks Barriers

One does not ask of one who suffers: What is your country and what is your religion? One merely says: You suffer, this is enough for me; you belong to me and I shall help you.

705
Can't Take Time to Listen

A man of science may hope for what may be said of him in the future, but he cannot stop to think of the insults — or the compliments — of his own day.

706
Preparation

Chance favors only the mind which is prepared.

707
Fact and Faith

Too many people transfer a question of fact into a question of faith.

708
Thorough

Exhaust every combination until the mind can conceive no other as possible.

709
Peace vs. War

Two contrary laws seem to be forever wrestling for the soul of man. The one is a law of blood and death, always planning new methods of destruction, forcing nations to be constantly ready for the battlefield. The other is a law of peace, work, and health, always creating new means of delivering man from the scourges which beset him. The one seeks violent conquests; the other the relief of humanity. . . . Which of the two will ultimately prevail, God alone knows. But we may assert that science will have tried, by obeying the law of humanity, to extend the frontiers of life.

710
Keep Searching

Do not think too much about things which have already been accomplished.

711
Work

Work, love one another. Work . . . may at first cause disgust and boredom; but one who has become used to work can no longer live without it . . . with knowledge one is happy, with knowledge one rises above others.

— From letters to his young sisters

712
How to Open Doors

Action, and work, always follow will, and work is almost always accompanied by success. These three things, will, work, and success, divide between themselves all human existence; will opens the door to brilliant and happy careers; work allows one to walk through these doors; and once arrived at the end of the journey, success comes to crown one's efforts.

713
Another World

I know only scientifically determined truth, but I am going to believe what I wish to believe, what I cannot help but believe — I expect to meet this dear child in another world.

— At bedside of his dying daughter

714
The Future

The future will belong to those who will have done most for suffering humanity.

715
Evidence

I am the most hesitating of men, the most fearful of committing myself when I lack evidence. But on the contrary, no consideration can keep me from defending what I hold as true when I can rely on solid scientific proof.

716
Truth

If I have at times disturbed the calm of your academies by discussions of too great an intensity, it is only because I wanted to defend the cause of truth.

— Spoken to colleagues, 1892

JAMES C. PENNEY
(1875–1971)

James Cash Penney was born on a farm near Hamilton, Missouri. His parents eked out a living on the farm, and his father was the pastor of a small Baptist church. Penney left Missouri because of his health and moved to Colorado. After failing in a butcher shop there, he got a job in a general store. Then he bought a partnership in a store in Kemmerer, Wyoming. He later established other stores, the Golden Rule Stores, which eventually became the J. C. Penney chain. He established the James C. Penney Foundation to aid religious, scientific, and educational projects. His autobiography is Fifty Years with the Golden Rule *(1950). He wrote another book in 1960,* View from the Ninth Decade. *He was known as one of the world's greatest merchants, seeing his one store in Wyoming grow to a chain of over seventeen hundred.*

717
The Christian Family

A common tragedy throughout the history of man has been that many children grow to adulthood never giving honor to their parents. True, many parents have provoked their children to hatred rather than honor. But how inspiring to see a family relationship marked with love one for another. It's a testimony against the family which is marked by strife and hatred. J. C. Penney often thought of the happy family life he enjoyed as a boy in Hamilton, Missouri.

When young Penney became old enough to see his father and mother as they were, and to appreciate them, he wondered what gave them the qualities he admired. In time he discovered the answer.

"It was their simple and direct faith in God and their sincere love for Jesus Christ, His Son," he said. "This was the wellspring of their beauty of character, pure ideals, inexhaustible courage, and abiding trust and peace."

Mr. and Mrs. Penney believed in practicing the apostle Paul's parental advice given in his letter to the church at Ephesus: "Ye fathers, provoke not your children to wrath: but bring them up in the nurture and admonition of the Lord."

718

Love for Money

J. C. Penney was a man of advanced years before he committed his life fully to Jesus Christ. He was a good man, honest, but primarily interested in becoming a success and making money. "When I worked for six dollars a week at Joslin's Dry Goods Store back in Denver," he confessed as he looked back on his life, "it was my ambition, in the sense of wealth in money, to be worth one hundred thousand dollars. When I reached that goal I felt a certain temporary satisfaction, but it soon wore off and my sights were set on becoming worth a million dollars."

Mr. and Mrs. Penney worked hard to expand the business; but one day Mrs. Penney caught cold and pneumonia developed, which claimed her life. It was then that J. C. Penney realized having money was a poor substitute for the real purposes in living. "When she died," he said, "my world crashed about me. To build a business, to make a success in the eyes of men, to accumulate money — what was the purpose of life? What had money meant for my wife? I felt mocked by life, even by God Himself."

After several more fiery trials, J. C. Penney was financially ruined and, naturally, in deep distress. That is when God could deal with his self-righteous nature and his love for money. After his spiritual conversion he could testify of God's working.

> I had to pass through fiery ordeals before reaching glimmerings of conviction that it is not enough for men to be upright and moral men. When I was brought to humility and the knowledge of dependence on God, sincerely and earnestly seeking God's aid, it was forthcoming, and a light illumined my being. I cannot otherwise describe it than to say that it changed me as a man.

719
God's Care in Adversity

When the Great Depression broke upon America in 1929, J. C. Penney was bankrupt, as were so many other wealthy businessmen. Before he was fifty he was a multimillionaire. But it was all gone. He was discouraged and sick. Finally, his doctor sent him to the hospital after diagnosing his illness as being caused by nervous disorders. Here he was, a former multimillionaire, in the hospital with no money even to pay for his care. He was sure he wouldn't live through the night, so he wrote farewell letters to his wife and children.

But in the morning he awoke early to find that he was feeling much better. Suddenly, from down the hall he heard an old familiar song: "Be not dismayed whate'er betide, God will take care of you. . . . "

Mr. Penney slipped out of his room and made his way to a small chapel and found a seat in the back. He started to pray: "Lord," he pleaded, "of myself I can do nothing. Will you take care of me?" Later, he said he didn't really know what happened, but a weight was lifted from his spirit, and he went out of the room a different man. He began to read the Bible; he became an active Christian layman; he began to trust the Lord as he had never done previously.

It wasn't long before his business losses were recovered, and the second part of Penney's long life was better than the first. He found out that whatever happened, if he placed his faith in God, He would take care of him.

720
He Had Convictions Against Whiskey

Shortly after J. C. Penney reached success as a clerk in Hamilton, Missouri, his health failed. He left Hamilton and his family and headed west to Colorado. Although he knew nothing of the butcher business, he bought a butcher shop and went into business for himself.

Penney was told that the best customer in the meat business was a certain hotel cook. The cook, he was told, was regular and liberal so long as he was supplied each week with a quart of whiskey. Penney thought about the gift of whiskey. "It seemed to me that if this was the custom, and if it got the business, I was justified in making the investment."

He bought the quart of whiskey for the cook. Then he was convicted by the memory of his deceased father. He thought about his father's deep feelings about liquor. What would he think if he was alive?

Penney knew he could never buy another quart of whiskey for any man. He went to the cook and told him his decision. The cook, on hearing the news, took his business elsewhere. It seemed that Penney had made a mistake and failed to keep his best customer.

"That failure was one of the most fortunate experiences of my life," he said later. "I know now that it was not a failure, and that I would have been worse than a failure had I gone back with the second quart of whiskey."

721
Learning the Golden Rule

As a boy, J. C. Penney began his first business by raising hogs on his father's farm. The neighbors offered him scraps from their kitchens for his hogs. When he sold the first hog and made a profit, he bought more hogs and made more profit. But his father was soon to teach him the Golden Rule that was to guide him the rest of his life.

The neighbors began to complain about the smell and noise coming from Jim's pigpen. Mr. Penney ordered Jim to sell the pigs. He was stunned. He reasoned with his father that all pigpens smelled and all pigs were noisy. And besides, the neighbors had no business telling them what to do. Mr. Penney listened and then said, "You have no right to make money if by so doing you are taking advantage of other people."

Jim sold the pigs, much to his regret. But his godly father taught him a lesson that day — one of the most important he ever learned.

722
Beauty Only Skin Deep

Outward appearance is often deceiving. J. C. Penney learned this when he bought a colt, which he wanted to raise and sell for a profit. Penney was a boy on his father's farm when he decided to try his hand in the horse business. He settled on a handsome colt at an auction. Then he proudly walked the beautiful horse home and placed it in the barn. He then joined his family at the supper table and told them of his fine horse. All at once they heard a terrible racket from the barn. They dashed out to find the young horse had kicked out one side of the stall and was working on the other side with quick, hard kicks.

The next day was no different. Jim's prize horse was kicking everything in sight. And it continued. Jim finally realized his beautiful horse was a bad actor. He could do nothing to keep it from kicking. So he had to sell it, and for less than he paid for it.

723
A Lesson in Integrity

If it had not been for a crooked groceryman, J. C. Penney might have become the owner of a grocery store rather than the owner of a dry goods chain.

When he was a teenager, Jim worked for a groceryman in Hamilton, Missouri. He liked the work and had plans to make a career of it. One night he came home and proudly told his family about his "foxy" employer. The grocer had a practice of mixing low quality coffee with the expensive brand and thus increasing his profit. Jim laughed as he told the story at the supper table.

His father didn't see anything funny about the practice. "Tell me," he said, "if the grocer found someone palming off an inferior article on him for the price of the best, do you think he would think they were just being foxy, and laugh about it?"

Jim could see his father was disappointed in him. "I guess not," he replied. "I guess I just didn't think about it that way."

Jim's father instructed him to go to the grocer the next day and collect whatever money due him and tell the grocer he wouldn't be working for him any longer. Jobs were not plentiful in Hamilton, but Mr. Penney would rather his son be unemployed than be associated with a crooked businessman.

J. C. Penney came that close to becoming a grocer.

724
Love Our Enemies

J. C. Penney's father, a part-time minister, ran unsuccessfully for Congress. The elder Penney believed a man should be honest and honorable in every area of his life. His opponent, who was also a minister, was speaking at a political rally that Jim happened to attend. "James Cash Penney," the man roared, "hasn't got even a string for a backbone!" Jim could hardly believe his ears. He waited until the man finished his speech and then grabbed him by the coat and yanked. Penney shouted, "What you said about my father is a lie! You lied! You lied!" The man was stunned at the outburst. Then he walked away.

Penney's father heard about the incident and instead of reproving him for his action, he quietly spoke, "Jim, you remember, in the Bible, where it says we are to love our enemies, bless them that curse us, pray for them that despitefully use us?"

Mr. Penney didn't need to say anything more to young Jim. His Christian example and quiet words were enough.

725
Retirement

When J. C. Penney was fifty-six, the age when most people are making plans to retire, he lost his fortune in the Great Depression. Most men would have given up, and Mr. Penney was tempted to. But he slowly pulled out of financial ruin and built a bigger retail empire than before. Even after he reached ninety, he was still working every day. "I never think of myself as retired," he said at eighty. "The main reason is that I'm not worked out." Retirement to Mr. Penney hinted at inactivity. In that sense he did not believe in retirement. "I do most certainly believe in a change of activity, when it becomes time for what is commonly called retirement."

JAMES C. PENNEY SAID IT

726
Self-Reliance

One reason I am so continually impressed with what the country owes to groups such as the Boy Scouts and Girl Scouts, the Campfire Girls, the . . . Order of De Molay . . . the Future Farmers of America, the 4-H clubs, and the Young Men's and Young Women's Christian Associations, is that all of them teach young people self-reliance, in terms of character and the capacity for leadership.

727
God Wanted Him

God wanted to possess me, not merely my possessions.

728
Beliefs

I believe in preparation. I believe in hard work. I believe in honesty. I believe in reposing confidence in men. I believe in appealing to the spirit in men. I believe in the practical application of the Golden Rule, as taught by the Master two thousand years ago, "Therefore all things whatsoever ye would that men should do to you, do ye even so to them, for this is the law and the prophets."

729
Humility

What I have done, anyone could have done. I haven't any special attainments.

730
Grateful for Problems

I am grateful for all my problems. As each of them was overcome I became stronger and more able to meet those yet to come. I grew on my difficulties.

731
Wealthy Yet a Failure

It is possible to possess material wealth and yet to be a failure.

732
Living the Life

If it is possible to live the Christian life at any point whatever, it should be possible to live it in all relationships of one's life.

733
Making Choices

When the individual faces a question of business choice, he should ask himself, Is this worthy of my best? If the answer is yes, he should go into it to the extent not only of upholding his own self-respect, but also of holding fast to the highest Christian standards.

734
Always Room

There will always be a place for anyone with a good and practical idea, willing to work unstintingly to get it accepted and translated into terms of the service of practical use.

735
True Prayer

True prayer opens the eyes to things not seen before, the ears to things not heard before, in contrast to that prayer which has been the mere reflection of selfish desires, so colored by puny will that, only being endlessly repeated, it can bring no real answer.

736
Surprises

A few surprises — even momentarily uncomfortable ones — never hurt any businessman made of the right stuff; his quality lies in turning them to advantage, and learning from them.

737
Christ the Answer

Nothing is more clearly established in history than that, wherever the gospel of Christ and Christianity have been honored, a way out of critical circumstances, problems which may have seemed insoluble, and confusions which appeared hopeless, has been found.

738
Will of God

Each of us must undertake prayerfully to conform his private life to the will of God. We need to remind ourselves that "the fear of the Lord is the beginning of wisdom."

739
Free Enterprise

Free competition has kept us and will always keep us from becoming a stagnant nation; without it business, large or small, would not survive, without it we as a nation would not survive.

740
A Legacy

When he [father] died it was hard to believe. He had always been so alive, like the sturdiest oak.

It was said freely in the town that James Cash Penney left everything he had to his family: his blessing, his good example, and two mortgages.

They didn't mention the legacy he left me, I suppose because they didn't know about it. "Jim will make it," he said. That was my legacy. Those words gave me my goal.

— From *View from the Ninth Decade*

741
The Golden Rule

I am often asked whether the Golden Rule, obviously "a nice ideal," hasn't become obsolete as an instrument for life in a practical world. I have to answer that, in the years since the beginnings in Kemmerer [Wyoming, his first store location], I have never found any good reason to desert it.

742
Success

I am wholeheartedly committed to believing that, wherever human activity is conducted according to Christian principles of integrity, patience, unselfishness, humility, charity, diligence, and fair dealing, success cannot but follow.

743

Competition

Competition is no enemy; it is an ally, and when translated in service, it is a constant spur to betterment through more service and thus benefits all.

WILL ROGERS
(1879–1935)

An Oklahoma cowhand, Will Rogers became a stage and motion picture star with his famous homespun philosophy. But he was no drugstore cowboy; he is still considered as one of the greatest trick ropers of all time. He was born on a ranch near Oologah, Indian Territory, which is now Oklahoma. His parents were part Cherokee Indian. He capitalized on the news of the day for his humorous columns that appeared in about 350 daily newspapers. The daily news also was used in his live performances. He was killed along with Wiley Post in a plane crash near Point Barrow, Alaska, on August 15, 1935. The Will Rogers Museum is in Claremore, Oklahoma.

744
The Bible According to Rogers and Dempsey

The Rev. James W. Brougher, Sr., told about a Bible class he had in his California church that had Will Rogers and Jack Dempsey as two of its members. One Sunday he announced he would begin teaching the Epistles the next Sunday. Turning to Will, he asked, "Will, do you know what the Epistles are?" Rogers answered promptly, "You bet your life; they're the wives of the apostles." The class laughed. Turning to Jack Dempsey, Rogers said, "You don't need to laugh, Jack, I'll bet you five dollars you can't say the Lord's Prayer." Dempsey took the challenge of the comedian and said, "Now I lay me down to sleep, I pray thee, Lord, my soul to keep." According to Brougher, when Dempsey finished, Rogers handed him five dollars and said, "Jack, I didn't think you could do it."

745
Touched by Infirmities

We were at an institution where victims of infantile paralysis, broken backs and other disasters are reeducated and so trained that they can rise from their beds or wheel chairs and walk. It was wonderful to see anyone bringing such laughter to the victims of such cruel misfortunes, but I could not help wondering how anybody could be so boisterously gay with such people and show never a sign of being touched by their sufferings. Later I learned that after he had kept them all roaring and writhing with laughter Will asked where the washroom was and slipped away. A friend opened the door to hand him a towel and found him leaning against the wall, his head against his arm. He was sobbing like a child. The door was closed softly, unnoticed, and when Will came out he went back to tell the students good-by. He was laughing as hilariously as before and he left them in stitches.

— Rupert Hughes

746
Memoirs

Poor history gets a jolt every time a famous person has his memoirs published. And it isn't unusual for the memoirs of one man to disagree considerably with that of another. In his attempt to be modest, the writer often paints himself as another George Washington or Abraham Lincoln. Frequently the author will make a few enemies with his memoirs — or renew old hostilities. Will Rogers looked at the problem and said, "There ain't nothing that breaks up homes, country, and nations like somebody publishing their memoirs." Perhaps Solomom had some memoirs in his day and was thinking about it when he wrote, "Vanity of vanities; all is vanity."

747
Maybe Both Mistaken

Will Rogers and William Jennings Bryan attended a national Republican convention as writers — Rogers as the humorist writer and Bryan as the serious. Bryan, in commenting on their different roles, said to Rogers, "You have the advantage of me, you are a humorist, and I am a serious writer." Rogers laughed, "Maybe we're both mistaken."

748
Story Suited for Dirt Track

A speaker at a banquet told a story that was, as Will Rogers believed, "off color." When it came time for Rogers to speak, he commented on every speaker who had preceded him and then coming to the man who had told the story, he said, "Judging by the story my friend told, I guess his mind is like a race horse — it runs best on a dirt track."

749
Lot of Applesauce

Will Rogers enjoyed ribbing congressmen, and they took the ribbing all in fun. One congressman, he claimed, prepared a speech but then didn't have a chance to deliver it. He asked and received permission to have it printed in the *Congressional Record.* At the places where he expected applause, the congressman wrote in the word *applause.* The printer, as the story goes, had trouble reading the congressman's handwriting. Every place where it should have read *applause,* the printer had inserted the word *applesauce* instead.

750
That's Not Sin

There was a certain Irish girl, according to Will Rogers, who confessed to her priest that she thought she was guilty of the sin of pride. She said, "When I look in the mirror, I think I am beautiful." The priest said, "That's not a sin; that's a mistake."

WILL ROGERS SAID IT

751
Peter

Rome has more churches and less preaching in them than any city in the world. Everybody wants to see where St. Peter was buried, but nobody wants to try to live like him.

752
Can't Improve the Bible

There's one wonderful thing about the Bible. There was no censorship in those days. Of course now, some of our churches hold conferences and cut out certain parts they think don't belong in there, or change them to what they think should be said instead of what was said. In other words, we are always improving on the words of the Lord. That's even worse than a scenario writer brightening up Shakespeare.

753
Rogers on War

Will Rogers was at his best when he quipped about the everyday events in the news. Here are some of his cracks concerning World War I.

"I see the South American countries are comin' into the war. Let 'em come in. This is no private war. Since we give 'em the loan, they tell me Venezuela wants to cancel three revolutions to get in."

"I thought the Armistice terms read like a Second Mortgage, but the peace terms read like a foreclosure."

"Well, we finally handed Germany the Peace terms, eighty thousand words in length. It took that many to tell them what we thought of 'em."

754
Human

It's great to be great, but it's greater to be human.

755
Yesterday

Don't let yesterday use up too much of today.

756
Democracy

One of the evils of democracy is that you have to endure the man you elected, whether you like him or not.

757
Liberty

Liberty doesn't work as well in practice as it does in speeches.

758
Blowing Your Horn

Get someone else to blow your horn and the sound will carry twice as far.

759
Liked Everybody

I never met a man I didn't like.

760
Progress in War

You can't say civilization isn't advancing: in every war, they kill you in a new way.

761
Crime

We don't seem to be able to check crime, so why not legalize it and then tax it out of business.

762
Congress

This country has come to feel the same when Congress is in session as when the baby gets hold of a hammer.

763
Politics

Politics has become so expensive that it takes a lot of money even to be defeated.

764
Put and Take System

Alexander Hamilton originated the put and take system in our national treasury: the taxpayers put it in, and the politicians take it out.

765
Gossip

The only time people dislike gossip is when you gossip about them.

766
Hero

The main thing about being a hero is to know when to die.

767
Forefathers Religious

They were very religious people that come over here from the old country. They were very human. They would shoot a couple of Indians on their way to every prayer meeting.

768
Heroes

Heroes are made every little while, but only one in a million conduct themselves afterwards so that it makes us proud that we honored them at the time.

769
Arguing Religion

If they are going to argue religion in the church instead of preaching it, no wonder you can see more people at a circus than a church.

770
Man

God made man a little lower than the angels, and he has been getting a little lower ever since.

THEODORE ROOSEVELT
(1858–1919)

Theodore Roosevelt at forty-two was the youngest man ever to become president. He filled that office upon the assassination of Pres. William McKinley in 1901. He was elected in 1904 and then ran again in 1912 as the "Bull Moose" party candidate, only to lose to Woodrow Wilson. As a boy, Roosevelt loved books and the outdoors and believed in the "strenuous life." He graduated from Harvard in 1880. He gained fame in 1898 as a leader of the Rough Riders in the Spanish-American War in Cuba. In later years he hunted big game in Africa and explored in South America. He is one of the four presidents whose faces are carved on the side of Mount Rushmore; the other three are Washington, Jefferson, and Lincoln.

771
Land of Opportunity

When Theodore Roosevelt was governor of New York, he was pleased to learn of an incident in his father's life that changed the life of a homeless boy in New York City.

Roosevelt was in Portland, Oregon, where western governors were meeting. There was a special dinner in honor of Mr. Roosevelt at which the governor of Alaska, Governor Brady, greeted Roosevelt and told him of the incident.

> Your father picked me up from the streets in New York, a waif and an orphan and sent me to a western family, paying for my transportation and early care. Years passed, and I was able to repay the money which had been given me my start in life, but I can never repay what he did for me, for it was through that early care and by giving me such a foster mother and father that I gradually rose in the world, until today I can greet his son as a fellow governor.

Roosevelt later went to the lodging house for newsboys in New York to relate the inspiring story to show that America presents opportunities enough — combined with personal effort and an occasional helping hand — to take a homeless boy on the streets of New York to the governor's mansion.

772
Witty Heckler

Once when Theodore Roosevelt was making a campaign speech, a slightly tipsy heckler kept interrupting him by shouting, "I am a Democrat."

Finally, Roosevelt turned to the heckler and asked, "Just why is the gentleman a Democrat?"

"Because my grandfather was a Democrat and my father was a Democrat, so I'm a Democrat," was the reply.

"My friend," said Roosevelt, "suppose your grandfather had been a jackass, and your father had been a jackass, what would you be?"

"A Republican!" was the instant reply.

773
Heavens

Theodore Roosevelt enjoyed viewing the heavens before retiring at night. Once, after gazing at the galaxies of stars, he turned to his soldiers and remarked, "I guess we are small enough now to go to bed."

— G. Curtis Jones, *What Are You Doing?*

774
Getting Out of a Jam

With presses set to run off 3 million copies of Theodore Roosevelt's 1912 convention speech, the publisher found permission had not been obtained to use photos of Roosevelt and his runningmate, Governor Hiram Johnson, of California. Copyright law put the penalty for such oversights at $1 per copy.

The chairman of the campaign committee was equal to the situation. He dictated a telegram to the Chicago studio that had taken the pictures: "Planning to issue 3 million copies Roosevelt speech with pictures Roosevelt and Johnson on cover. Great publicity opportunity for photographers. What will you pay us to use your photographs?" An hour later the reply was back: "Appreciate opportunity, but can pay only $250."

—Jacob M. Braude

775
Advice to a Young Officer

As a young army officer in 1906, Douglas MacArthur was assigned as an aide-de-camp to President Roosevelt. MacArthur was a great admirer of the president and often had opportunity to talk with him. One day he asked the president what he felt to be the single factor for his popularity with the masses. "To put into words," the president replied, "what is in their hearts and minds but not their mouths. You just listen to the grass grow." When Washington papers criticized the president, MacArthur became angered; but the president gave his personal philosophy on editorial writers: "I like to have them talk well of me, but I would rather have them talk badly than not talk at all."

776
Proper Place for Sports

Pres. Theodore Roosevelt felt there was a time and place for everything, including sports, for his son Ted. When told that his teen-ager was playing football, the president wrote him a long letter with the advice that there were more important things to do, although he did not discourage his participation in the sport.

> I am delighted to have you play football. I believe in rough, manly sports. But I do not believe in them if they degenerate into the sole end of any one's existence. I don't want you to sacrifice standing well in your studies to any over-athleticism; and I need not tell you that character counts for a great deal more than either intellect or body in winning success in life. Athletic proficiency is a mighty good servant, and like so many other good servants, a mighty bad master.

777
The White House Gang

President Roosevelt was a dedicated family man. He loved to romp with his boys, hike, hunt, travel, and if he was separated from them, he would always take time to correspond with them. The Roosevelt children and their friends became known as the "White House Gang." One day Roosevelt learned that the children planned an "attack" on the White House. The president went along with the fun and sent a message to the children through the War Department, ordering them to call it off.

Snakes and ponies even found their way into the White House during the administration. One snake almost caused a national emergency. Roosevelt's son Quentin had a friendly but large king snake and two little ones. One day the boy burst into the president's office on roller skates to show his father the snakes. It didn't bother Quentin that his father was discussing important matters with the attorney general at the time. He eagerly deposited the snakes in President Roosevelt's lap. Since he was busy, the president suggested Quentin take the snakes into an adjoining office where four congressmen were waiting to see the president. The congressmen at first thought the snakes were toys, but recoiled promptly when it was learned that they were for real. Just about that time the king snake — all three to four feet of him — decided to go up Quentin's sleeve. The president peeked in long enough to see one congressman helping Quentin off with his jacket to let the snake out of the sleeve.

The White House was never the same after the Roosevelts moved out.

778
Patriotism

There was no hour down to the end when he would not turn aside from everything else to preach the doctrine of Americanism, of the principles and the faith upon which American government rested, and which all true Americans should wear in their heart of hearts.

He was a great patriot, a great man, above all, a great American.

His country was the ruling, mastering passion of his life from the beginning even unto the end.

— Eulogy on Theodore Roosevelt by Henry Cabot Lodge

779
Tribute to Missionaries

Theodore Roosevelt paid a high tribute to foreign missionaries as he spoke with a friend whose son was a missionary.

As high an estimate as I have of the ministry, I consider that the climax of that calling is to go out in missionary service, as your son is doing. It takes mighty good stuff to be a missionary of the right type, the best stuff there is in the world. It takes a good deal of courage to break the shell and go 12,000 miles away to risk an unfriendly climate, to master a foreign language, to adopt strange customs, to turn aside from earthly fame and salary, and, most of all, to say good-by to home and the faces of the loved ones, virtually forever.

THEODORE ROOSEVELT SAID IT

780
True Christian

The true Christian is the true citizen, lofty of purpose, resolute in endeavor, ready for a hero's deeds, but never looking down on his task because it is cast in the day of small things; scornful of baseness, awake to his own duties as well as to his rights, following the higher law with reverence, and in this world doing all that in his power lies, so that when death comes he may feel that mankind is in some degree better because he lived.

781
Service

I do not know how philosophers may ultimately define religion; but from Micah to James it has been defined as service to one's fellow men rendered by following the great rule of justice and mercy, of wisdom and righteousness.

782
Cynic

Let the man of learning, the man of lettered leisure, beware of that queer and cheap temptation to pose to himself and to others as the cynic, as the man who has outgrown emotions and beliefs, the man to whom good and evil are as one. The poorest way to face life is to face it with a sneer.

783
Average Man

I am only an average man, but, by George, I work harder at it than the average man.

784
Faithful

It is better to be faithful than famous.

785
Ideals

Some men can live up to their loftiest ideals without ever going higher than a basement.

786
Stealing

No people is wholly civilized where a distinction is drawn between stealing an office and stealing a purse.

787
Law

No man is above the law, and no man is below it.

788
Home Virtues

The first essential for a man's being a good citizen is his possession of home virtues, based on recognition of the great underlying laws of religion and morality. No piled up wealth, no splendor of material growth, no brilliance of artistic development, will permanently avail any people unless its home life is healthy.

789
Democracy

Let us be true to our democratic ideals, not by the utterance of cheap platitudes, not by windy oratory, but by living in such a manner as to show that democracy can be efficient in promoting the public welfare during periods of peace and efficient in securing national freedom in time of war.

790
Waste

To waste, to destroy, our national resources, to skin and exhaust the land instead of using it so as to increase its usefulness, will result in undermining in the days of our children the very prosperity which we ought by right to hand down to them amplified and developed.

791
Hope

We, here in America, hold in our hands the hope of the world, the fate of the coming years; and shame and disgrace will be ours if, in our eyes, the light of high resolve is dimmed, if we trail in the dust the golden hopes of men.

792
Free People

Free people can escape being mastered by others only by being able to master themselves.

793
Complete His Education

To educate a man in mind and not in morals is to educate a menace to society.

794
Evil

No man is justified in doing evil on the grounds of expediency.

795
Life of Ease

There has never yet been a man in our history who led a life of ease whose name is worth remembering.

796
Country

This country will not be a really good place for any of us to live in if it is not a really good place for all of us to live in.

797
The Strenuous Life

I wish to preach, not the doctrine of ignoble ease, but the doctrine of the strenuous life, the life of toil and effort, of labor and strife; to preach that highest form of success which comes, not to the man who desires mere easy peace, but to the man who does not shrink from danger, from hardship, or from bitter toil, and who out of these wins the splendid ultimate triumph.

798
Will Destroy America

The things that will destroy America are prosperity-at-any-price, peace-at-any-price, safety first instead of duty first, the love of soft living, and the get-rich-quick theory of life.

799
Dare Mighty Things

Far better it is to dare mighty things, to win glorious triumphs, even though checkered by failure, than to take rank with those poor spirits who neither enjoy much nor suffer much, because they live in the gray twilight that knows not victory nor defeat.

CHARLES H. SPURGEON
(1834–1892)

Probably the greatest British preacher of all time, Charles H. Spurgeon has had more sermons printed and circulated than any other preacher. At the age of twenty he accepted the pastorate of New Park Street Chapel in London. From 1854 until his death, Spurgeon preached to great crowds in London. The great Metropolitan Tabernacle, with six thousand seats, was built to hold the crowds who wished to hear him. Although his father and grandfather were preachers, Charles was converted in a church he happened to wander into one snowy Sunday in 1850 when he was sixteen. Spurgeon formed his Pastor's College, which trained hundreds of pastors during his lifetime.

800
No Thieves in Heaven

About 18 months after his conversion, the young Spurgeon was offered a pastorate in the village of Waterbeach, a notoriously drunken village, where the sober were regarded as miserly. . . . Sometimes in the excitement of preaching during those early years, his imagination ran away with him, and he used figures of speech which became the Waterbeach joke of the week. But he had the saving grace of humor and could laugh at himself. One Sunday he declared that no thief would enter heaven to spend his time picking the angels' pockets. When those who heard him afterwards inquired what sort of clothes the angels wore, he laughingly replied that he should have said, not picking the angels' pockets, but plucking the angels' feathers! There is hope for the youthful enthusiast who can laugh at his own extravagances.

— W. J. Smart, *Profiles in Christian Commitment*

801
Spurgeon Deaf?

C. H. Spurgeon, while still a young man and a village pastor, was passing the house of a woman known as the village shrew, who greeted him with a volley of words the reverse of polite. Smiling, the young man said, "Yes, thank you; I am quite well." She burst into another string of expletives. "Yes, it does look as if it's going to rain," he replied. Surprised as well as exasperated, the woman exclaimed, "Bless the man, he's as deaf as a post! What's the use of talking to him?"

802
I Shall Be Like Him

Spurgeon received one day a copy of Andrew Bonar's commentary on Leviticus. Spurgeon was greatly blessed as he read it. He returned it to its author with this request: "Dr. Bonar, please autograph this book, and paste your picture on the title page. Then return it to me." Bonar did as requested. Below the picture he wrote, "Dear Spurgeon: Here is the book with my autograph and my photograph. If you had been willing to wait a short season you could have had a better picture. When I see Christ, I shall be like Him."

— Walter B. Knight

803
Your Argument Is with Christ

Charles Spurgeon used to tell of an old farmer he often talked with, a man who would say some things that became precious to Spurgeon. One day the two were talking when the farmer told Spurgeon of a conversation he had with the devil. "The other day, sir, the devil was tempting me and I tried to answer him; but I found he was an old lawyer, and understood the law a great deal better than I did, so I gave over, and would not argue with him any more; so I said to him, 'What do you trouble me for?' 'Why,' said he, 'about your soul.' 'Oh!' said I, 'that is no business of mine; I have given my soul over into the hand of Christ; I have transferred everything to Him; if you want an answer to your doubts and queries, you must apply to my Advocate.'"

804
Witness Against Him

Charles Spurgeon's mother once called her son aside. "Charles," she said, "your father and I have trained you in righteousness. We have taught you the Word of God. We have lived a godly life before you. If you do not live a godly life, we will stand before God in the day of judgment and bear witness against you!"

805
Prayer Is the Answer

Five ministerial students were visiting in London on a hot Sunday in July. While they were waiting for the church doors to open, a man approached and asked, "Gentlemen, would you like to see the heating apparatus of the church?" They thought, "How queer he is to want to show us the heating system on a hot day in July!" Following him, they came to a door. He quietly opened it and whispered: "There, sirs, is our heating apparatus!" Some seven hundred intercessors were kneeling in prayer, seeking an outpouring of God's Spirit upon the service which was soon to begin in the Tabernacle. That unknown guide was Spurgeon himself!

— Walter B. Knight

806
Dual Personality

When Charles Spurgeon was once being shown through the library of Trinity College, Cambridge, he stopped to admire a bust of Byron. The librarian said to him, "Stand here, sir, and look at it."

"Come, now," said the librarian, "and look at it from this side."

Spurgeon changed his position and looking on the statue from that viewpoint, exclaimed, "What a demon! There stands a man who could defy the Deity!" He asked the librarian if the sculptor had secured this effect designedly.

"Yes," he replied, "he wished to picture the two characters, the two persons — the great, the grand, the almost super-genius that he possessed; and yet the enormous mass of sin that was in his soul."

— From *Macartney's Illustrations*, by Clarence E. Macartney. Copyright 1945 by Whitmore and Stone.

807
The Lord Gave It Back with Interest

Spurgeon once came to Bristol. He was to preach in the three largest Baptist chapels in the city and hoped to collect three hundred pounds needed immediately for his orphanage. He got the money. Retiring to bed on the last night of his visit, Spurgeon heard a voice which to him was the voice of the Lord saying, "Give that three hundred pounds to George Müller." "But, Lord," answered Spurgeon, "I need it for my dear children in London." Again came the word, "Give that three hundred to George Müller." It was only when he had said, "Yes, Lord, I will," that sleep came to him.

The following morning he made his way to Müller's orphanage, and found George Müller on his knees before an open Bible, praying. The famous preacher placed his hand on his shoulder, and said, "George, God has told me to give you this three hundred pounds." "Oh," said Müller, "dear Spurgeon, I have been asking the Lord for that very sum." And those two prayerful men rejoiced together. Spurgeon returned to London. On his desk a letter awaited him; he opened it and found it contained three hundred guineas.

"There!" he cried with joy. "The Lord has returned my three hundred pounds with three hundred shillings interest."

— *Power*

808
We Are Brothers

It is related of Spurgeon that on one occasion he found a boy on the streets, ragged and hungry. Taking him along with him home, the good pastor fed and clothed him, and then, kneeling down, prayed for the friendless boy as only he could pray. Several times in the prayer he referred to the Almighty as "Our Father." When the prayer was finished, the boy said, "Did you say, 'Our Father'?" "Yes, my boy, yours and mine," was the reply. "Then we are brothers." "Yes," gravely replied the pastor, and then he talked to him of the Lord Jesus Christ, and finally, as he left him, gave him a letter to a certain shoe shop for a pair of boots. A few days after, Mr. Spurgeon was passing the shop when the dealer saw him and called to him. "I had a strange thing the other day," he said. "A boy came into the shop and asked for a pair of boots, saying that his brother had sent him, and when I asked him who his brother was he said you were." "That is right," said Mr. Spurgeon, "and he is your brother, too, and if you like we will share the cost of the boots."

— *Gospel Herald*

809

Prayer Is Secret of Success

Wilbur Chapman, an American preacher, received some good advice in London that he never forgot. Chapman was a young man when he went to London to visit the famous Metropolitan Tabernacle where Charles Spurgeon preached. Chapman was anxious to discover Spurgeon's secret of success. Spurgeon told him what it was.

> Every day and night thousands of men and women here in London pray for the work of the Tabernacle, and for me. All around the world, day after day, hundreds of thousands of God's people ask for His blessing on me and my sermons. In answer to those prayers the Lord opens the windows of heaven and pours out so many blessings that there is not room in our hearts and lives to receive them all. Young man, try this way of running your church!

CHARLES H. SPURGEON SAID IT

810

Victory Possible

The lesson of wisdom is, be not dismayed by soul trouble. Count it no strange thing, but a part of ordinary Christian experience. Should the power of depression be more than ordinary, think not all is over with your usefulness. Cast not away your confidence, for it hath great recompense of reward. Even if the enemy's foot be on your neck, expect to rise and overthrow him. Cast the burden of the present, along with the sin of the past and the fear of the future, upon the Lord. Live by the day — aye, by the hour.

811

Gentleness

A Christian is the gentlest of men; but then *he is a man.*

812
A Christian's Testimony

I would not give much for your religion unless it can be seen. Lamps do not talk, but they do shine.

813
Affliction

The Lord gets His best soldiers out of the highlands of affliction.

814
Faith, Love, Hope

Faith goes up the stairs that love has made and looks out of the windows which hope has opened.

815
Gospel

We can learn nothing of the gospel except by feeling its truths. There are some sciences that may be learned by the head, but the science of Christ crucified can only be learned by the heart.

816
Home

When home is ruled according to God's Word, angels might be asked to stay with us, and they would not find themselves out of their element.

817
Sin

Sin is sovereign till sovereign grace dethrones it.

818
Speed of a Lie

A lie travels around the world while Truth is putting on her boots.

819
Wives

God save us all from wives who are angels in the streets, saints in the church, and devils at home.

820
Perseverance

By perseverance the snail reached the ark.

821
Definitions

Impatient people water their miseries and hoe up their comforts; sorrows are visitors that come without invitation; and complaining minds send a wagon to bring their troubles home in.

822
The Same Bundle

Faith and obedience are bound up in the same bundle. He that obeys God trusts God; and he that trusts God obeys God. He that is without faith is without works; and he that is without works is without faith.

823
Wisdom

The doorstep to the temple of wisdom is a knowledge of our own ignorance.

824
Great Faith

Brethren, be great believers. Little faith will bring your souls to heaven, but great faith will bring heaven to your souls.

825
Christ

Christ is the great central fact in the world's history; to Him everything looks forward or backward.

826
Say No

Learn to say no. It will be of more use to you than to be able to read Latin.

827
Oyster Slandered

I heard one say the other day that a certain preacher had no more gifts for the ministry than an oyster, and in my judgment this was a slander on the oyster, for that worthy bivalve shows great discretion in his openings, and knows when to close. If some men were sentenced to hear their own sermons it would be a righteous judgment upon them, and they would soon cry out with Cain, "My punishment is greater than I can bear." Let us not fall under the same condemnation.

828
Illustrations

Illustrations, like windows, let light into the chamber of the mind. Mere bald statements are soon forgotten, but an apt illustration sticks in the soul like a hook in a fish's mouth.

ADLAI E. STEVENSON
(1900–1965)

Twice the Democratic nominee for president against Dwight D. Eisenhower, Adlai E. Stevenson became noted for his speaking ability and wit that he used in those 1952 and 1956 campaigns. He was a grandson of Vice-Pres. Adlai E. Stevenson I (with President Cleveland). He worked for his family newspaper, the Daily Pantagraph, *in his native Bloomington, Illinois, and later practiced law in Chicago. After government service during World War II, he became governor of Illinois (1948). He was urged to seek the presidential nomination in 1952, but he would not campaign. He was later pressured to change his mind. He served as United States ambassador to the United Nations from 1961 until his death in 1965.*

829
Lulled to Sleep

William Jennings Bryan had the distinction of being one of the greatest public speakers in American history. But he put Adlai Stevenson to sleep in a big Democratic rally in Bloomington, Illinois. Adlai was just a boy and too young to appreciate, or endure, political speeches.

Adlai's sister Elizabeth recalled the meeting as their grandfather had given them a prominent place on the speakers' platform. Adlai Stevenson I, who had been vice-president under President Cleveland, introduced Bryan with a lengthy speech of praise. Then Bryan captivated the audience with his thunderous speech and dramatic gestures. Explosive applause rippled through the great crowd. Elizabeth stole a glance at her brother to see how he was taking his first political rally. She was disgraced! Adlai was sound asleep.

830
Never Promise Too Much

A lesson Adlai Stevenson learned while attending Choate Prep School in Connecticut was a lasting one, according to his sister, Elizabeth Ives, who told about it in her book *My Brother Adlai.*

Adlai had his grandfather's love for newspaper work and landed a spot on the *Choate News,* reporting news and soliciting merchants for advertisements. Once Adlai persuaded a reluctant Italian, who had only recently opened his own candy firm, to advertise in the newspaper. He convinced the proprietor Choate students would rush into the store to buy his candy once they saw the advertisement. Unfortunately, Choate students were unaffected by the advertisement. Later Adlai returned to the shop to collect the money due for the advertisement space. The proprietor, in a burst of Latin indignation, grabbed a large iron ladle and threatened Adlai, shouting, "Nobody come buy. I don't pay!"

Adlai's sister said she didn't think Adlai ever promised too much after that incident.

831
Duty and Loyalty

One of the most reluctant men in history to accept his party's presidential nomination was Illinois Gov. Adlai Stevenson in 1952. He was running for a second term as governor and discouraged every attempt politicians made at getting him to be a candidate. One fervent supporter in Wisconsin followed him around one day, begging him to consider the nomination. Finally, as Stevenson was getting into his plane, the man called out: "Well, what'll you do if we nominate you anyway?" One close by said the governor turned in weary exasperation. "Guess I'd have to shoot myself," he said and disappeared into the plane. Although he continued to resist any attempts to nominate him, the reluctant governor was drafted at the Democratic national convention, and nominated. Then with the characteristic Stevenson dedication to serving the people, he said, "Better we lose the election than mislead the people; and better we lose than misgovern the people."

Lost, he did — and again four years later — but it was always duty and loyalty above politics, as indicated in the speech he made shortly after the outcome of the 1952 election was known: "I urge you all to give to General Eisenhower the support he will need to carry out the great tasks that lie before him. I pledge him mine."

832
Political Longevity

Adlai Stevenson was the namesake of his grandfather, who was vice-president under President Cleveland. It was a well-known name in Illinois politics — and still is, as Adlai Stevenson III took up his father's political mantle. An elderly farmer approached Adlai when he was running for governor of Illinois in 1948. The farmer came up to him after a speech, shook hands, inquired about his health. When told he was fine, the old man seemed relieved to hear it. "I been wonderin'," he muttered. "Ain't seen you since I voted for you last time you run, in 1908."

Adlai didn't have the heart to tell the farmer that he was only eight years old in 1908 and that the other Adlai was his grandfather.

833
Most Valuable Citizens

In a talk to the graduating class at Smith College, Adlai Stevenson once told his listeners that the "self-adjusted" people who fit painlessly into the social pattern may not be the most valuable citizens.

> While I am not in favor of maladjustment, I view this cultivation of neutrality, this breeding of mental neuters, this hostility to eccentricity with grave misgiving.
>
> One looks back with dismay at the possibility of Shakespeare perfectly adjusted to bourgeois life in Stratford, Wesley contentedly administering a county parish, George Washington going to London to receive a barony from George III, or Abraham Lincoln prospering in Springfield with nary a concern for the preservation of the crumbling union.
>
> What is needed is not just well-adjusted, well-balanced personalities, not just better groupers and conformers but more idiosyncratic, unpredictable characters; people who take open eyes and open minds out with them into the society which they will share and help to transform.
>
> —Jacob M. Braude, in *New Treasury of Stories for Every Speaking and Writing Occasion*

834
Correct Story, Wrong Photo

During World War II, Adlai Stevenson was an assistant to the secretary of the navy. At the end of the war he was awarded the Distinguished

Civilian Service Award, the navy's highest civilian award. Next morning the *Washington Post* illustrated its story of the award with a photograph — of the first Adlai E. Stevenson, Adlai's grandfather, in his last years. Stevenson was understandably irritated by the mistake. He clipped out the story and mailed it to a friend on the newspaper staff with this brief note: "Ho hum, I've a white moustache and a wing collar and I'm 70, and all the time I thought I was a young man and in the very mould of fashion. But then perhaps it's just as well we see ourselves as 'ithers see us,' and the resemblance would be very surprising to grandfather, dead these 35 years."

It isn't likely the *Post* ever repeated that mistake.

835
A Good Father

Pres. Harry Truman was speaking at a Boston campaign meeting in 1952 for his fellow democrat, Adlai Stevenson. Nineteen-year-old Borden Stevenson, the candidate's son, was a student at Harvard, and somebody spotted him in the audience and took him to the platform and insisted he say a few words. He put his hands into his pockets and said earnestly, "If my dad is elected and can be as good a president as he's been a father, I know the country's safe."

836
You Ain't Big Enough

When Adlai Stevenson was governor of Illinois, he took great delight in attending the state fair, meeting people from all over the state and chatting with them. He once told a fair crowd about the time he had to substitute for the Kentucky senator, Alben Barkley, in a speech in Indiana. He felt he was a poor substitute. "I felt like the motorist who ran over a hog on the highway. The farmer was very irate, but the motorist finally calmed him down and said, 'Don't worry, I'll replace your pig.' 'Replace him!' the farmer shouted. 'You can't. You ain't big enough.'"

837
A Tribute from the President

Many crises have threatened the peace of the world since Adlai Stevenson became the United States Ambassador to the United Nations.

The force, eloquence and courage with which he has advanced the American viewpoint have played no small part in helping to confine these crises to the council chambers where they belong. . . . During his presidential campaigns Governor Stevenson raised the level of our national political dialogue. As our representative in the United Nations he has similarly raised the level of the international political dialogue.

> — President Kennedy, in preface to Stevenson's *Looking Outward: Years of Crisis at the United Nations*

838
Apprehensive of Danger

Adlai Stevenson had apprehensions about President Kennedy's plans to go to Dallas in November 1963, but a presidential aide didn't feel he should alarm Kennedy by passing on Stevenson's fears to the president.

A month before President Kennedy was gunned down in Dallas, Stevenson was there to deliver a United Nations Day address. He had seen some ugly things in Dallas; he was booed and heckled, surrounded by a mob, and struck in the head with a sign. He felt a presidential visit would be unwise.

When the news came that the president was shot, Stevenson was in his office in the UN Mission building. Several others were in his office watching the news from Dallas on television. One of the men turned to look at Stevenson. "For a moment he held his head in his hands," the man said; "then he began quietly giving instructions on what had to be done before finally reaching for a pad and slowly writing the statement that had to be made."

ADLAI E. STEVENSON SAID IT

839
Democracy

I yield to no man in my belief in the principle of free debate. The sound of tireless voices is the price we pay for the right to hear the music of our own opinions. But there is also a moment at which democracy must prove its capacity to *act*. Every man has a right to be heard; but no man has the right to strangle democracy with a single set of vocal cords.

293

840
America

When an American says that he loves his country, he means not only that he loves the New England hills, the prairies glistening in the sun, the wide and rising plains, the great mountains, and the sea. He means that he loves an inner air, an inner light in which freedom lives and in which a man can draw the breath of self-respect.

841
America

Let us present once more the true face of America — warm and modest and friendly, dedicated to the welfare of all mankind, and demanding nothing except a chance for all to live and let live, to grow and govern as they wish, free from interference, free from intimidation, free from fear.

842
Life

There is nothing so fine as to be twenty-one and an American. One is for a fleeting instant — and the other is forever. So live — decently, fearlessly, joyously — and don't forget that in the long run it is not the years in your life but the life in your years that counts!

843
United Nations

The whole basis of the United Nations is the right of all nations — great or small — to have weight, to have a vote, to be attended to, to be a part of the twentieth century.

844
Accuracy and Virtue

Accuracy is to a newspaper what virtue is to a lady, but a newspaper can always print a retraction.

845
New America

There is a New America every morning when we wake up. It is upon us whether we will it or not.

846
Strangers

On this shrunken globe, men can no longer live as strangers.

847
Communism

Communism is the death of the soul. It is the organization of total conformity — in short, of tyranny — and it is committed to making tyranny universal.

848
Hypocrite

A hypocrite is the kind of politician who would cut down a redwood tree, then mount the stump and make a speech for conservation.

849
Words

Journalists do not live by words alone, although sometimes they have to eat them.

850
Man in Charge

To me, there is something superbly symbolic in the fact that an astronaut sent up as assistant to a series of computers, found that he worked more accurately and more intelligently than they. Inside the capsule, *man* is still in charge.

851
Peace

Peace is the one condition of survival in this nuclear age.

852
Ignorance and Prejudice

Ignorance is stubborn and prejudice is hard.

853
Discern the Time

I hope you will think on the mighty problems of your time.

In St. Luke it is written: "Ye can discern the face of the sky and of the earth; but how is it that ye do not discern this time?"

You must discern this time, for your own sake, and for your country's sake. You have had the advantage of education; it is therefore your right and privilege to sustain the sovereignty of intelligence and imagination against the assaults of stupidity and vulgarity. I hope you can do it with gentleness and humility, with tolerance and good humor.

— To college seniors

854
Government

It seems to me that government is like a pump, and what it pumps up is just what we are, a fair sample of the intellect, the ethics, and the morals of the people, no better, no worse.

855
Peace

If the pursuit of peace is both old and new, it is also both complicated and simple. It is complicated, for it has to do with people, and nothing in this universe baffles man as much as man himself.

856
Moral Base

Military power without a moral base is always intolerable.

857
Truth and Brotherhood

The world is now too dangerous for anything but the truth, too small for anything but brotherhood.

858
Evil

There is no evil in the atom; only in men's souls.

859
Power

It is the whole history of mankind that power lacking the inner strength of self-restraint will be eventually cast down.

THOMAS À KEMPIS
(1380?–1471)

Thomas à Kempis, a medieval Christian writer, is best remembered for his devotional classic, Imitation of Christ. *He was born Thomas Hamerken in Kempen, Germany, and in school he was called Thomas from Kempen. Later, he was known as Thomas à Kempis. He entered the Augustinian monastery of Mount St. Agnes, near Zwolle, The Netherlands, about 1400. In 1425 he became a superior there. He lived such a devout life that friends claimed when he prayed his countenance seemed completely transfigured. A biographer said of him, "He stood, with his feet barely touching the earth, as if he would fly away to heaven, where were his thoughts and his desires."*

THOMAS À KEMPIS SAID IT

860
Love

He who loves with purity considers not the gift of the lover, but the love of the giver.

861
Humility

God walks with the humble; He reveals Himself to the lowly; He gives understanding to the little ones; He discloses His meaning to pure minds, but hides His grace from the curious and the proud.

862
Influence

The life of a faithful Christian man is a guide to paradise.

863
Obedience

The only safe ruler is he who has learned to obey willingly.

864
Reflections

The reflections on a day well spent furnish us with joys more pleasing than ten thousand triumphs.

865
Self-Control

No conflict is so severe as his who labors to subdue himself.

866
Self-Knowledge

The highest and most profitable learning is the knowledge of ourselves. To have a low opinion of our own merits, and to think highly of others, is an evidence of wisdom. All men are frail, but you should consider none so frail as yourself.

867
Absence

When a man is out of sight, it is not too long before he is out of mind.

868
Caution

Caution in crediting, and reserve in speaking, and in revealing one's self to but very few, are the best securities both of a good understanding with the world, and of the inward peace of our own minds.

869
Judging Others

He that well and rightly considereth his own works will find little cause to judge hardly of another.

870
The Test of a Man

Occasions do not make a man either strong or weak, but they show what he is.

871
Pure Conscience

He will easily be content and at peace, whose conscience is pure.

872
Carrying One's Cross

Carry the cross patiently, and with perfect submission; and in the end it shall carry you.

873
The Difference

Man proposes, but God disposes.

874
Faults

Endeavor to be always patient of the faults and imperfections of others; for thou hast many faults and imperfections of thine own that require forbearance. If thou art not able to make thyself that which thou wishest, how canst thou expect to mold another in conformity to thy will?

875
Choose Less

Choose rather to want less, than to have more.

876
Vanity

It is vanity to seek after perishing riches and to trust in them.

877
Understand and Conform

Whosoever will fully and with relish understand the words of Christ must endeavor to conform his life wholly to the life of Christ.

878
Temptations and Adversities Everywhere

There is no order so holy, or place so secret, where there are not temptations or adversities.

879
Deaf Ear

There are many things to which it is your duty to pass by with a deaf ear, and be rather mindful of those which belong to peace.

880
Secret Place

Seek a secret place, love to dwell alone, desire the conversation of none; but rather pour out devout prayer to God, that you may keep a contrite mind and a pure conscience.

LEO TOLSTOY
(1828–1910)

Count Leo Tolstoy was one of Russia's greatest writers of fiction. He was also considered an important moral thinker and social reformer, especially in the latter half of his life. He inherited a large family estate and never lacked money. As a young man he joined the Russian army and was involved in the Crimean War in 1855. He was cited for his bravery in the famous siege of Sevastopol. Tolstoy's two most famous novels, War and Peace and Anna Karenina, were written between 1863 and 1877. Following a religious experience in 1880, Tolstoy's life was largely devoted to religious, moral, and social themes. He gave up his estate, renounced the copyrights to his writings. He became a pacifist, gave up tobacco and intoxicating liquors, and became a vegetarian. He died in a tiny railway station at Astapovo a few days after he secretly left his home because of family differences.

881
The Folly of Sin

In the novel *Anna Karenina* Tolstoy tells the powerful story of an unhappy woman and the folly of sin. Anna Karenina is married and has an eight-year-old son. She falls in love with Count Vronsky and is unfaithful to her husband. She confesses her guilt to her husband and then becomes deathly sick. Her husband is ready to forgive her for her infidelity. But Anna recovers and leaves the country with Count Vronsky. As it often happens, the novelty soon wears off. Anna begins to suffer, and Vronsky misses the military career he left to follow her. Anna secretly visits her son who is in his father's care. But the meeting only increases her despair. She goes from one disillusionment to another. In the end her life is unbearable and she throws herself under a train and dies. Vronsky is filled with remorse, enlists to fight the Turks, and then himself commits suicide.

882
Refused to Give Pride a Chance

After Leo Tolstoy's novel *Anna Karenina* was widely praised, the author wrote to a friend how pleased he was that the story was well received. Later the friend sent him two reviews praising the book. Most authors would have framed the reviews. Tolstoy burned them. "I was too afraid," he wrote the friend, "that those articles would turn my head."

883
No Human Perfection

The book *War and Peace* is a historical novel written by Leo Tolstoy, and has a setting during Napoleon's invasion of Russia in 1812. The novel is considered the greatest in Russian fiction. Tolstoy's marvelous ability as a storyteller is unsurpassed. But it isn't perfect. Even though it was read over a hundred times by Tolstoy, his wife, and proofreaders, the author's biographer, Henri Troyat, points out glaring errors.

> It is a little silver icon that Princess Marya gives her brother Andrey as he is going off to war, but it is a little golden icon that the French soldiers remove from his neck when they pick him up wounded at Austerlitz. Natasha Rostov is thirteen years old in August 1805, fifteen in 1806 and sixteen in 1809. After gambling away his money late in December, Nicholas Rostov leaves Moscow in mid-November. Minor characters change their first names from one chapter to the next. Pierre Bezukhov sees the comet of 1812 in February 1811.

Man's greatest works can always be improved and often his errors haunt him the rest of his life. Alexander Pope, the great English poet, wrote:

> Whoever thinks a faultless piece to see,
> Thinks what ne'er was, nor is, nor e'er shall be.

884
Greed

In Tolstoy's *Man and Dame Fortune* the hero is told he can have the right to all of the land around which he can plow a furrow in a single day. The man started off with great vigor, and was going to encompass only that which he could easily care for. But as the day progressed he desired more and more rights. He plowed and plowed, until at the end of the day he could in no possible way return to his original point of departure, but struggling to do so, he fell, the victim of a heart attack. The only right he secured was the right to 18 square feet of land in which to be buried.

— Russell T. Loesch

885
Have Done It unto Me

The Russian writer, Count Tolstoy, tells a story about a lonely cobbler who was unhappy because his wife and children had died. Then a good priest gave him a New Testament, and after reading it he changed, and became contented. One day he heard a Voice saying, "Martin, look tomorrow on the street: I am coming." The next day he watched and waited, but no stranger appeared. An old soldier whom he knew came in and the cobbler gave him a cup of tea. Later a poor woman and her little child came in out of the cold, and they were given food, clothing, and money. Finally the cobbler rescued a poor apple woman from a bad boy who was robbing her, gave the boy an apple and persuaded him to apologize.

When evening came he lighted his lamp, and still no stranger had come. Then he heard a Voice again, "Martin, it is I!" and he saw in a vision all the people he helped that day. They smiled and vanished. The happy cobbler now saw at the top of the gospel page the words, "I was an hungered, and ye gave me meat; . . . thirsty, and ye gave me drink; . . . a stranger, and ye took me in. . . . Inasmuch as ye have done it unto one of the least of these my brethren ye have done it unto me."

— Amy L. Person, in *Illustrations from Literature*

886
Wild Oats Remain

Knowing death would eventually catch up with him, Count Tolstoy decided his wild youthful escapades recorded in his diaries should be destroyed. Then he had a change of mind and ordered they remain as he wrote them. "That way, at least," he wrote, "it may be seen that in spite of the degradation and shamelessness of my youth, God had not forsaken me and that — late in life, it is true; on the very threshold of old age — I did begin to understand him a little, and to love him."

887
Solution for Temptations

Reading of Leo Tolstoy's youth reminds one of the sins of Augustine. But Tolstoy was sincerely looking for a way out of the dilemma he faced. He wrote his personal "rules of life," but then saw how far short he fell in life itself. He tried repeatedly to reform, all to no avail. Just as soon as he thought he had victory over his vices, he would be tempted. And more times than not he would repeat a sin he had vowed he would never do again. Once he wrote: "I knew where these voices came from, I knew they were destroying my happiness; I struggled, I lost. I fell asleep dreaming of fame and women . . . it was stronger than I."

Who hasn't experienced some of Tolstoy's frustrations! But the apostle Paul gives the answer to the human dilemma in a letter he wrote to Christians at Corinth: "There hath no temptation taken you but such as is common to man: but God is faithful, who will not suffer you to be tempted above that ye are able; but will with the temptation also make a way to escape, that ye may be able to bear it" (I Cor. 10:13).

888
The Secret of Happiness

When Leo Tolstoy was five years old, he heard his older brother Nicholas declare he knew the secret of happiness. The secret, according to Nicholas, was everybody love everybody else. It would bring the kingdom of heaven to every man, he reasoned. Then Nicholas said the rules for such a blessed life were written on a green stick buried in the forest under oak trees near a deep, dark ravine. Symbolically Leo was to seek the green stick all his life. And so have countless others. It isn't Nicholas' green stick for which they search. Men have been searching for other "green sticks" in quest of love and peace.

The search goes on, and ironically the only answer, the Lord Jesus Christ, is too often overlooked or disregarded.

LEO TOLSTOY SAID IT

889
The Goal of Life

The goal of our life should not be to find joy in marriage, but to bring more love and truth into the world. We marry to assist each other in this task. The most selfish and hateful life of all is that of two beings who unite in order to enjoy life. The highest calling is that of the man who has dedicated his life to serving God and doing good, and who unites with a woman in order to further that purpose.

890
Do Christians Obey Christ?

Not long ago I was reading the Sermon on the Mount with a rabbi. At nearly each verse he showed me very similar passages in the Hebrew Bible and Talmud. When we reached the words, "Resist not evil," he did not say, "This too is in the Talmud," but asked, with a smile, "Do the Christians obey this command?" I had nothing to say in reply, especially as at that particular time, Christians, far from turning the other cheek, were smiting the Jews on both cheeks.

891
Conduct

Everybody lives and acts partly according to his own, partly according to other people's ideas.

892
Life

The idea shared by man that life is a vale of tears is just as false as the idea shared by the great majority, the idea to which youth and health and riches incline you, that life is a place of entertainment.

893
Money

Money is a new form of slavery, and distinguishable from the old simply by the fact that it is impersonal — that there is no human relation between master and slave.

894
Value of Writer

A writer is dear and necessary for us only in the measure in which he reveals to us the inner working of his soul.

895
Happy Families

All happy families are alike, but each unhappy family is unhappy in its own way.

896
No Opinion

He never chooses an opinion; he just wears whatever happens to be in style.

897
No Help to the Poor

He will do almost anything for the poor, except get off their backs.

898
Faith

Faith is the force of life.

899
Goals in Life

The man whose only goal is his own happiness is bad; he whose goal is the good opinion of others is weak; he whose goal is the happiness of others is good; he whose goal is God, is great!

900
Two Opposites

The revolutionary and the Christian are at opposite ends of an open circle. Their proximity is only apparent. In reality, no two points could be farther apart. To meet, they would have to turn around and travel back over the entire circumference.

901
Serving Others

The simplest and shortest ethical precept is to be served by others as little as possible and to serve others as much as possible.

WERNHER VON BRAUN

(1912–   )

When he was twenty years of age, Wernher von Braun was placed in charge of Nazi Germany's rocket program. With other German scientists he developed the famous V-2 rocket which Germany used to bomb London. When the Russian and American armies were closing in from two directions on Peenemünde, the German rocket center, von Braun and other scientists made their way toward the Americans. He directed the team that launched the Explorer, *the first United States earth satellite, on January 31, 1958. According to von Braun, the basic idea of the old German V-2 is still being used in rockets of today. Today he is considered the foremost rocket engineer in the world.*

902
His First Blast-off

Young Wernher von Braun's aristocrat father was disturbed at his son's interest in rockets and hoped it was only a passing fancy. When Wernher was thirteen, he tied six skyrockets to his coaster wagon and lit the fuses; the wagon shot down the street out of control. Wernher chased the racing wagon, but not everyone was as excited about the incident as he. Later, he recalled the experience: "The rockets burned out in a magnificent thunderclap, and the police quickly took me into custody. But I was ecstatic." That was in 1925 in Germany. Wernher von Braun's rocket career had its first blast-off.

903
Providence

Wernher von Braun's greatest fear as Germany surrendered in 1945 was not living in a conquered nation; he was fearful that he and his associates at the Peenemünde rocket center would fall into the hands of Stalin and thus be the tool of another dictator. The scientists sat together and discussed their fate. It was unanimous: they wished to join the Americans. Von Braun said, "I was strongly convinced that since we had this treasure it was our duty to put it in the right hands." He and several other German rocketeers fled Peenemünde just hours ahead of the advancing Russian army. Magnus, Wernher's younger brother, spoke English well, so he rode ahead on a bicycle with an offer to surrender to the Americans. Pvt. Fred Schneiker of the United States Army confronted Magnus and was told that Germany's leading rocket scientists were waiting on a mountain to surrender. A few hours longer at Peenemünde and the entire group would have been in the hands of the Russians. Von Braun believes it was providential that he and his coworkers came to America. He won't have any arguments in America.

904
God Creator and Master

It seemed as if all seven hundred reporters from newspapers, radio stations, and television networks wanted to talk to Wernher von Braun following the successful launching of the mighty Saturn V. The Cape Kennedy noise was at a high decibel range. And von Braun wanted to escape it all for the moment. He grabbed the arm of a newspaper friend, Adon Taft. "Come on, let's get away where we can talk." Taft, religion writer of the *Miami Herald,* pushed away from the crowd with the space scientist and made his way toward the shoreline. Pacing rapidly back and forth, von Braun seemed to be in deep thought. Taft waited for his companion to speak. "We must learn to consider God as creator of the universe and master of everything," von Braun began. "We need a greater Lord than we have had in the past." It would have been difficult for the reporters back at the launching site to understand this talk; they had just watched the unleashing of twice as much hydroelectric power as all the rivers on the North American continent could provide if run through turbines at once. They would probably think that the brilliant mind of von Braun also contained mysticism or superstition. Who needs God? Wernher von Braun is one of the "brains" behind the United States space program, but he believes in a God and as revealed through the Lord Jesus Christ.

905
Rivalry Causes Delay

Service rivalries in the United States gave the Russians the time they needed to put the first rocket into orbit around the earth. Over a year before the Russians sent their Sputnik into orbit, Wernher von Braun and his space team launched a Jupiter C rocket. But Washington, not wanting to create hard feelings between the army, navy, and air force, ordered von Braun not to fuel the last stage which would have placed the rocket into earth orbit. About a year after the Jupiter C was fired, on October 4, 1957, the Russians launched Sputnik, much to the consternation of Washington. At Huntsville, Alabama, a frustrated von Braun asked Secretary of Defense Neil H. McElroy to let Washington know "we have the hardware down here to put up a satellite any time." But it took a dog, finally, and another Russian satellite before von Braun was told to put his hardware into operation. The Defense Department, after the Russians sent their dog into orbit, ordered von Braun's team to put something into orbit within ninety days. They did just that with an orbiting 30.8-pound torpedo-shaped object called Explorer I. The American space program was on its way, but not until rivalries here had permitted the Russians a big jump on our program.

906
Found a Personal God

During his youth in Germany, Wernher von Braun was reared in a devout Lutheran home and was confirmed at 12 or 13. But as he grew older he noticed that few people attended church services in the big cathedrals of Europe. Later, during the war years, worship in Germany was almost at a standstill due to the government's discouragement. It wasn't until he was brought to the United States that he detected a vibrant church life. "I immediately saw a difference in church life," he said. "I saw thriving congregations everywhere. There seemed to be spiritual life. Then one day I saw a Church of the Nazarene bus in the desert near El Paso. I had never heard of the church before, so I investigated. I discovered that the pastor drove the old bus 50 miles to pick up people and they worshiped in a wooden barracks. I was impressed by their simplicity and their missionary spirit. They seemed like the early Christians."

Later, after much searching and study of religious books, von Braun and his family united with the Episcopal Church. His earlier doubts and agnosticism have been exchanged for a firm belief in a personal God who created the universe and reveals himself to man.

—Reprinted by permission from *Christian Life* magazine, copyright 1969, Christian Life Publications, Inc., Gundersen Drive and Schmale Road, Wheaton, Illinois 60187.

907
A Scientist's Belief in God

Many scientists have scoffed at the idea of a God behind the complex universe. Some of these men are in the space program. The Soviet cosmonauts tried to settle the question of God when they returned to earth with the less than scientific statement that they did not find God out there.

Wernher von Braun can't understand such rationale. He finds it as difficult "to understand a scientist who does not acknowledge the presence of a superior rationality behind the existence of the universe as it is to comprehend a theologian who would deny the advances of science. And there is certainly no scientific reason," he continues, "why God cannot retain the same position in our modern world that He held before we began probing His creation with telescope and cyclotron."

David's trust in God was known by friend and foe alike. And he considered the poor misguided individual who didn't believe in God a fool: "The fool hath said in his heart, There is no God" (Ps. 14:1).

WERNHER VON BRAUN SAID IT

908
Science and Religion

I deplore the attitude that scientific enlightenment and religious belief are incompatible. I consider it one of the greatest tragedies of our times that this is so widely believed.

909
Creation and Creator

Through a closer look at creation, we ought to gain a better knowledge of the creator; and a greater sense of man's responsibility to God will come into focus.

910
Ethical Values

It was during the latter part of Hitler's regime, near the end of the war, that it became apparent to me that there is a need for ethical values in the material world. Particularly as I was growing older and we were unleashing more and more power that need become apparent.

911
Research

Basic research is what I am doing when I don't know what I am doing.

912
Science and Religion

Science and religion are not antagonists, but sisters. Both seek ultimate truth. Science helps to reveal more about the creator through His creation.

913
God and Space

God has built man with curiosity. God expects man to use this gift. I do not think the process should ever stop. Now we have tools to explore space. I believe this: if it were not the creator's intent for us to explore celestial bodies He would not have permitted us to have acquired the tools. Something else is apparent. God has not placed any visible obstacles in our way. I believe we have His permission and His blessing.

—Interview with C. M. Ward, 1966

914
Reason for Science

Because of the wonderful things it has done for society, we are tempted to place too high value on science. We should remember that science exists only because there are people, and its concepts exist only in the minds of men. Behind these concepts lies the reality which is being revealed to us — but only by the grace of God.

915
Space

There is beauty in space, and it is orderly. There is no weather, and there is regularity. It is predictable. . . . Everything in space obeys the laws of physics. If you know these laws and obey them, space will treat you kindly. And don't tell me man doesn't belong out there. Man belongs wherever he wants to go.

916
Man Needs Faith

The materialists of the 19th century and their Marxist heirs tried to tell us that as science shows us more knowledge about the creation, we could live without faith in a Creator. But with every new answer from science, we have discovered new questions. The more we know about the nature of life, the master plan for the galaxies, and the intricacies of the atomic structure, the more reason we have found to marvel at the greatness of God's created works. But beyond awe, we know that man needs faith just as he needs food, water, or air.

Quotations 916-920 are taken from *Lift-Off!* by James C. Hefley, © 1970 by Zondervan Publishing House, Grand Rapids, and are used by permission.

917
Science and Religion

Science in its drive to understand the creation, and religion in its drive to understand the Creator, have many common objectives. Nevertheless, there have been conflicts in the relationships between science and religion. Today, at best, we can say there is peaceful coexistence between the two.

Personally, I find this state of affairs unsatisfactory, for I regard the Creator and His creation as an entity. "The heavens declare the glory of God, and the firmament sheweth His handiwork," we read in the beautiful 19th Psalm.

918
Evil and Good

The same forces of nature that enable us to fly to the stars also enable us to destroy our home planet. Nuclear energy when harnessed in a reactor can produce cheap electrical power for human benefit, but may kill untold numbers when abruptly released in a bomb.

919
Existence of God

The public has a deep respect for the amazing scientific advances made within our lifetime. There is admiration for the scientific process of observation, experimentation, of testing every concept to measure its validity. But it still bothers some people that we cannot prove scientifically that God exists. Must we light a candle to see the sun?

920
Jesus Christ the Secret

In our search to know God . . . Jesus Christ should be the focus of our efforts, and our inspiration. The reality of that life and His resurrection . . . is the hope of mankind.

GEORGE WASHINGTON
(1732–1799)

For almost twenty years George Washington guided his country, first in the army, then as president of the convention that wrote the United States Constitution, and then for two terms as president of the United States. He is often referred to as the "Father of His Country." As a teen-ager, George wanted to be a sailor; but his mother would not have it. At fifteen, he got a job as an assistant to a surveyor. In 1753, at the age of twenty, he began his military career. He led the colonies in the long Revolutionary War (1775-1783). After the Independence was won, Washington spent five quiet years on his farm. He was elected to the presidency in 1789.

921
I Was Wrong

Early in Washington's army career he had a dispute with a Mr. Payne in Alexandria, Virginia. Washington was a colonel at the time and was stationed in Alexandria with some troops. An election dispute occured, and in the argument Washington called Payne a liar. Payne reacted with a blow that knocked Washington down. The incident could have meant a duel — a common way to end arguments in that day — if it were not for the qualities Washington possessed. He displayed those qualities the next day when he met Payne. Washington greeted him with outstretched hand, saying, "I believe I was wrong yesterday . . . here is my hand; let us be friends!"

922
Close Call

Gen. George Washington had several close calls during the Revolutionary War. One incident could have cost him his life if it were not for a British officer's decision not to fire on him. Washington and a French soldier were making a reconnaissance near the British lines. A British officer, Major Ferguson, and his men spotted Washington and the Frenchman. Ferguson ordered three good marksmen to creep near and fire at them; but, as he said later, "the idea disgusting me, I recalled the order." As they came closer, the major advanced from the woods where they were concealed and called upon them to stop. But Washington and the Frenchman turned and retreated. Ferguson said, "By quick firing we could have killed them easily; but, as it was not pleasant to fire at their backs, I let it alone." It wasn't until the next day that Ferguson learned that the American was George Washington.

923
Prayer of Washington

The sublimest figure in American history is Washington on his knees at Valley Forge.

He was in that hour and place the American personified, not depending on their own courage or goodness, but asking aid from God, their Father and Preserver.

Washington knew that morals are priceless, but he knew that morals are from within. And he knew that in that dread day when all, save courage, had forsaken the American arms, appeal must be to that Power beyond ourselves, eternal in the heavens, which after all, in every crisis of the lives of men and nations, has been their surest source of strength.

— Albert J. Beveridge

924
Profanity

General Washington's Orderly Book of August 3, 1776, included a note to his men concerning the use of profanity:

> The general is sorry to be informed that the foolish and wicked practice of profane swearing, a vice hitherto little known

in the American army, is growing into fashion; he hopes the officers will by example as well as influence endeavor to check it and that both they and the men will reflect that we can have little hope of the blessing of heaven on our arms if we insult it by our impiety and profanity. Added to this, it is a vice so mean and low, without temptation, that every man of sense and character detests and despises it.

925
Traitor's Plan Misfires

As can be expected, the type of war that the British and the colonies fought made traitors on both sides. One elderly man attempted to turn General Washington over to the British but was outwitted by Washington. One day Washington received an invitation from the man to dine with him in his mansion, something Washington had done several times previous. But when the host insisted this time that Washington be at his home precisely at two and that he would be safe without a guard, Washington was suspicious.

The next day Washington arrived at one o'clock — an hour earlier — and saw immediately that his host was nervous. While walking around the grounds, Washington had an opportunity to bring up the subject of traitors. Suddenly a company of red-coated men approached the mansion on horses. Washington acted shocked and questioned the man, "What cavalry are these? What does this mean?" The man acted relieved to see the red coats and answered, "A party of British light horses sent for my protection." Then, as the calvary dismounted and approached Washington and his host, the man said, "General, you are my prisoner!" "I believe not," Washington answered calmly, "but, sir, I know that you are mine! Arrest this traitor, officer!" Finally, it dawned on the traitor that the troopers were actually American cavalrymen whom Washington had disguised in British uniforms.

Later the prisoner confessed that he had been bribed to deliver Washington to the enemy. Afterward he was pardoned by Washington at the pleading of his family.

— Adapted from *Boys and Girls Bookshelf*, by H. A. Ogden

926
Faith

It is my conviction that faith is stronger than disbelief; faith can overcome fear and hopelessness, just as the history of mankind has been lighted up by the faiths that have triumphed over the forces of darkness.

George Washington prayed to God through bitter winters from 1775 to 1780 when his soldiers were cold, hungry, tattered and barefoot — their marches through the snow traced by blood from their bleeding feet. Yet faith carried Washington's ragged band of patriots to victory for American independence and the values of the spirit that enter into the pursuit of genuine happiness.

— Henry J. Kaiser

927
Tribute to Washington

Washington, the brave, the wise, the good,
Supreme in war, in council, and in peace.
Valiant without ambition, discreet without fear,
Confident without presumption.
In disaster, calm; in success, moderate; in all, himself.
The hero, the patriot, the Christian.
The father of nations, the friend of mankind,
Who, when he had won all, renounced all,
And sought in the bosom of his family and of nature, retirement,
And in the hope of religion, immortality.

— Mount Vernon inscription

GEORGE WASHINGTON SAID IT

928
Virtue

Few men have virtue to withstand the highest bidder.

929
Freedom of Worship

The liberty enjoyed by the people of these states, of worshiping Almighty God agreeably to their consciences, is not only among the choicest of their blessings, but also of their rights.

930
Providential Guidance

In tendering this homage to the great Author of every public and private good, I assure myself that it expresses your sentiments not less than my own; nor those of my fellow citizens at large, less than either. No people can be bound to acknowledge and adore the invisible Hand, which conducts the affairs of men, more than the people of the United States. Every step by which they have advanced to the character of an independent nation seems to have been distinguished by some token of Providential agency.

— From first inaugural address

931
Associations

Associate yourself with men of good quality if you esteem your own reputation; for 'tis better to be alone than in bad company.

932
Preparation

To be prepared for war is one of the most effectual means of preserving peace.

933
Thanksgiving Day

I do recommend and assign Thursday, the Twenty-Sixth Day of November next, to be devoted by the people of these states, to the service of that great and glorious Being, who is the beneficent Author of all the good that was, that is, or that will be.

— Thanksgiving Day proclamation, November 26, 1789

934
Go Together

Reason and experience both forbid us to expect that national morality can prevail in exclusion of religious principle.

— From farewell address, 1796

935
Constitution Obligatory

The basis of our political systems is the right of the people to make and to alter their constitution of government. But the Constitution which at any time exists, 'till changed by an explicit and authentic act of the whole People, is sacredly obligatory upon all.

— From farewell address, 1796

936
Prayer for Nation

Almighty God: we make our earnest prayer that Thou wilt keep the United States in Thy holy protection; that Thou wilt incline the hearts of the citizens to cultivate a spirit of subordination and obedience to government; and entertain a brotherly affection and love for one another and for their fellow citizens of the United States at large. And, finally, that Thou wilt most graciously be pleased to dispose us all to do justice, to love mercy and to demean ourselves with charity, humility, and pacific temper of mind which were the characteristics of the Divine Author of our blessed religion, and without an humble imitation of whose example in these things we can never hope to be a happy nation. Grant our supplication, we beseech Thee, through Jesus Christ our Lord. Amen.

— Inaugural prayer

937
Literature and Knowledge

Cultivate literature and useful knowledge, for the purpose of qualifying the rising generation for patrons of good government, virtue, and happiness.

938
Conscience

Labor to keep alive in your heart that little spark of celestial fire called conscience.

939
Happiness and Moral Duty

The consideration that human happiness and moral duty are inseparably connected, will always continue to prompt me to promote the former by inculcating the practice of the latter.

940
United States of Europe

Some day, taking its pattern from the United States, there will be founded a United States of Europe.

941
Friendship

Friendship is a plant of slow growth, and must undergo and withstand the shocks of adversity before it is entitled to the appellation.

DANIEL WEBSTER
(1782–1852)

America's best known orator and one of its ablest lawyers was Daniel Webster. He supported the idea of a strong national government. He was elected to represent Massachusetts in the House of Representatives in 1823, and in 1827 was elected to the Senate. Historians call Webster's speech favoring the Compromise of 1850 as the "Union-saving" speech. He served as secretary of state under three presidents — Harrison, Tyler, and Fillmore. Webster's great unfilled goal was to be president. Although Webster did not live long enough to see the Civil War, such words of his as "Liberty and Union now and forever, one and inseparable!" became battle cries for many Northern soldiers.

942
Reward of Good Work

When Daniel Webster was a young lawyer in Portsmouth, an insurance case was brought to him. Only a small amount was involved, and a twenty-dollar fee was all that was promised. Webster saw to it that his client received justice, even though it meant, at his own expense, making a trip to Boston to consult the law library.

Years later, Webster, who had meanwhile become famous, was asked to take a case for the next day because the attorney had become sick. Money was no object and Webster was asked to name his terms and conduct the case. He told about it later.

> I told them that it was preposterous to expect me to prepare a legal argument at a few hours' notice. They insisted, however, that I should look at the papers; and this I finally consented to do. It was my old twenty-dollar case over again; . . . I was handsomely repaid both in fame and money for that journey to Boston; and the moral is that good work is rewarded in the end.

943
Say Only What's Necessary

An important case was being argued by two of the most famous orators of the nineteenth century, Daniel Webster and Henry Clay. Webster argued that a certain machine violated the patent rights of his client. For hours Clay held the court spellbound with his eloquence as he argued for his client; it seemed almost certain that his argument convinced everyone that the two machines no more resembled each other than a daisy and a tulip. When Webster rose to answer, the courtroom was still. The excitement was high. The case for Webster's client would mean millions of dollars — lost or saved. He gravely placed the two machines before the jury and said, "There they are. If you can see any difference between them it is more than I can." And then Webster sat down. The jury was convinced and Webster won.

944
A Vast Difference

Every Sunday morning and evening in a small New England church there was seen among the few worshipers a man whose great head and cavernous eyes were in keeping with his great distinction. Someone who knew him in Washington asked him how it was that there in the village he was so regular in going to the small church and listening to the ungifted minister, whereas in Washington he paid little attention to great churches and distinguished preachers. The man with the great head and the wonderful eyes answered: "In Washington they preach to Daniel Webster the statesman and the orator. Here in this village this man preaches to Daniel Webster the sinner."

— From *Macartney's Illustrations,* by Clarence E. Macartney. Copyright 1945 by Whitmore and Stone.

945
Sue Me, but Don't Starve Me

A butcher once sued Daniel Webster for a long-standing bill. One day Webster met the butcher on the street and asked why he had stopped sending for his meat order.

"Well, Mr. Webster, I didn't think that you would want to deal with me after I had sued you."

"Tut, tut!" exclaimed Webster, "sue me all you want; but for heaven's sake, don't try to starve me to death."

946
Superhuman Savior

In a company of literary gentlemen, Daniel Webster was asked if he could comprehend how Jesus Christ could be both God and man. "No, sir," he replied and added, "I should be ashamed to acknowledge Him as my Savior if I could comprehend Him. If I could comprehend Him He could be no greater than myself. Such is my sense of sin, and consciousness of my inability to save myself, that I feel I need a superhuman Savior, one so great and glorious that I cannot comprehend Him."

947
Encouragement

Daniel Webster left his country home and went to Boston to study law. He entered, without invitation, the office of Christopher Gore, then head of the Massachusetts bar. There he was looked upon as an intruder, and nobody paid any attention to him. One day Rufus King saw the lonely, solitary student. He warmly shook his hand and said, "I know your father well. Be studious and you will win. If you need any assistance or advice, come to me." Years later, after he had achieved greatness, Webster said: "I can still feel the warm pressure of that hand, and hear those challenging words of encouragement."

— *God's Revivalist*

DANIEL WEBSTER SAID IT

948
An American

I was born an American; I live an American; I shall die as an American; and I intend to perform the duties incumbent upon me in that character to the end of my career. I mean to do this with absolute disregard of personal consequences. What are the personal consequences? What is the individual man, with all the good or evil that may betide him, in comparison with the good or evil which may befall a great country, and in the midst of great transactions which concern that country's fate? Let the consequences be what they will, I am careless. No man can suffer too much and no man can fall too soon, if he suffer, or if he fall, in the defense of the liberties and constitution of his country.

949
Eternal Value

If we work upon marble, it will perish; if on brass, time will efface it; if we rear temples, they will crumple into dust; but if we work upon immortal minds, and imbue them with principles, with the just fear of God and love of our fellow men, we engrave on those tablets something that will brighten to all eternity.

950
Our Country

Let our object be our country, our whole country, and nothing but our country. And, by the blessing of God, may that country itself become a vast and splendid monument, not of oppression and terror, but of wisdom, of peace and of liberty, upon which the world may gaze with admiration forever.

951
Liberty

God grants liberty only to those who love it, and are ready to guard it and defend it.

952
Bible Principles

If we abide by the principles taught in the Bible, our country will go on prospering and to prosper. But if we and our posterity neglect its instruction and authority, no man can tell how suddenly a catastrophe may overwhelm us and bury our glory in profound obscurity.

953
Christian Origin

Let us not forget the religious character of our origin. Our fathers were brought here by their high veneration for the Christian religion. They journeyed by its light, and labored in its hope. They sought to incorporate its principles with the elements of their society, and to diffuse its influence through all their institutions — civil, political, and literary. Let us cherish these sentiments, and extend this influence still more widely, in the full conviction that this is the happiest society, which partakes in the highest degree of the mild and peaceable spirit of Christianity.

954
Farmers

When tillage begins, other arts follow. The farmers, therefore, are the founders of human civilization.

955
Lies

Falsehoods not only disagree with truths, but usually quarrel among themselves.

956
Christian Literature

If religious books are not widely circulated among the masses in this country and the people do not become religious, I do not know what is to become of us as a nation. And the thought is one to cause solemn reflection on the part of every patriot and Christian. If the truth be not diffused, error will be; if God and His Word are not known and received, the devil and his works will gain the ascendancy; if the evangelical volume does not reach every hamlet, the pages of corrupt and licentious literature will.

957
Veracity of the Gospel

Philosophical argument, especially that drawn from the vastness of the universe, in comparison with the apparent insignificance of this globe, has sometimes shaken my reason for the faith which is in me; but my heart has always assured and reassured me that the gospel of Jesus Christ must be Divine Reality. The Sermon on the Mount cannot be a mere human production. This belief enters into the very depth of my conscience. The whole history of man proves it.

—Epitaph dictated day before his death

JOHN WESLEY

(1703–1791)

One of the great religious leaders in Christian church history, John Wesley successfully took Christianity to the masses of the eighteenth century. Wesley traced his conversion to May 24, 1738, after he had been trained as a preacher and had worked as a missionary in Georgia. He began forming small religious societies in 1739 that eventually became the Methodist Church. But as long as he lived, Wesley remained a member of the Church of England. When forbidden to speak in the state churches, Wesley preached in the open, attracting great crowds and bringing many to conversion. He was a prolific writer, and preached several times each day most of his life.

958

A Special Child

When John Wesley was just a child, the house caught fire; and he was nearly burned alive. Throughout his long life he never forgot his narrow escape and was grateful to God for keeping him from death. In later years, when he thought he was dying, he wrote his own epitaph, in which he described himself as "a brand plucked out of the burning."

After the narrow escape, Susanna Wesley felt she must take special care of her young son; she wrote in her private meditations: "I do intend to be more particularly careful of the soul of this child, that Thou hast so mercifully provided for, than ever I have been, that I may do my endeavor to instil into his mind the principles of Thy true religion and virtue. Lord, give a grace to do it sincerely and prudently, and bless my attempts with good success!"

959
Building Friendships

As a young man, John Wesley believed that his close associates should be those who had an interest in spiritual things. He adopted an effective plan to rid himself of undesirable associates.

> I resolved to have no acquantance by chance but by choice, and to choose only such as would help me on my way to heaven. In consequence of this, I narrowly observed the temper and behavior of all that visited me. I saw no reason to think that the greater part of these truly loved and feared God; therefore, when any of them came to see me I behaved as courteously as I could, but to the question, "When will you come to see me?" I returned no answer, and when they had come a few times and found I still declined the visit, I saw them no more, and I bless God this has been my invariable rule for about three-score years.

960
Wesley's Conversion

Susanna Wesley was one of the most remarkable women in history. She gave John and Charles and her other children a well-rounded education. John went on to Oxford University where he was a diligent student. He formed a small religious society for Bible study and prayer and social help. But with all of his good works and attempts at righteous living, John Wesley came to a point in his life where he realized he was not really converted. It was after he and Charles spent time in America that John began to doubt his salvation. After almost two years of fruitless ministry in Georgia, John confessed, "I went to America to convert the Indians; but oh! who shall convert me!"

Wesley's conversion came after he returned to England. "I went very unwillingly to a society in Aldersgate Street, where one was reading Luther's preface to the Romans. About a quarter before nine, while he was describing the change God works in the heart through faith in Christ, I felt my heart strangely warmed. I felt I did trust in Christ alone, for salvation; and an assurance was given me, that He had taken away my sins, even *mine,* and saved *me* from the law of sin and death."

961
God's Man for the Hour

Throughout church history there periodically were men God raised up to lead in revival and reform. Eighteenth-century England found itself in such desperate need and Wesley was the man God used. America's Pres. Woodrow Wilson saw in Wesley that answer: "The church was dead and Wesley awakened it; the poor were neglected and Wesley sought them out; the gospel was shrunken into formulas and Wesley flung it fresh upon the air once more in the speech of common men."

962
Praying for Persecutors

John Wesley was often viciously persecuted as he preached the gospel in the fields or wherever he could find an audience. Ruffians would try to break up his meetings by driving cattle through the crowds or by throwing rocks at Wesley or by other means. One day a bully hit him with a club, and others knocked him to the ground with rocks. Lying on the ground, Wesley prayed for the persecutors. The gang leader was touched by the prayer. He said, "Sir, get up. Not one man will harm a hair on your head." The gang leader accepted Christ that day and later became a preacher himself.

963
A Life of Service

John Wesley was an undersized man of delicate appearance, he yet had nerves of iron, could ride horseback twenty to sixty miles a day — once he rode a hundred miles in twenty-four hours. He rose at four in the morning, retired at ten p.m. and never wasted a minute. He read hundreds of volumes while traveling — would drop the reins on the horse's neck and with both hands would hold the big books to his nearsighted eyes. In later years, when friends had given him a chaise (two-wheel carriage), he boarded up one side of it, put in book shelves and a writing board and so kept up his incessant work. He wrote voluminously, published 233 original works besides editing and translating others. For sixty years he kept a diary which accounted for every hour of every day, and kept besides a full-length journal. He could read Hebrew, Greek and Latin and could not only read but preach in German, French and Italian. At the age of 83 he was piqued to discover that he could not write more than 15 hours a day without hurting his eyes; and at the age of 86 he was ashamed to admit that he could not preach more than twice a day. In his 86th year he preached in almost every shire in England and Wales and often rode thirty to fifty miles a day.

— Albert Edward Bailey

964
Holiness

Late in John Wesley's long career he said he thanked God for the advice given to him fifty years before by Dr. Potter, then archbishop of Canterbury. "If you desire to be extensively useful," Dr. Potter told Wesley, "do not spend your time and strength in contending for or against such things as are of a disputable nature, but in testifying against open and notorious vice and in prompting real spiritual holiness."

Wesley urged his ministering brethren to heed the advice of Dr. Potter: "Let us keep to this, leaving a thousand disputable points to those that have no better business than to toss the ball of controversy to and fro, and let us bear a faithful testimony in our several stations against all ungodliness and unrighteousness, and with all our might recommend that inward and outward holiness without which no man shall see the Lord."

965
Schedule Unchanged

What would he do if he knew he would die the next day? someone asked John Wesley. The eighty-year-old Mr. Wesley displayed what later generations might term "cool" as he answered.

"What should I do? Exactly what I shall do now. I shall call and talk to Mr. So-and-so, and Mrs. So-and-so; and dine at such an hour, and preach in the evening, and have supper, and then I should go to bed and sleep as soundly as ever I did in my life."

966
Lay Preachers

When laymen of Wesley's day began to preach the gospel, he was shocked and said he would stop them. His wise mother, however, warned him against taking action, but to observe the results. Wesley took the advice of his mother and was later amazed at what the "untaught" preachers were able to accomplish.

Four years later he wrote about laymen in the pulpit.

> I am bold to affirm that these unlettered men have help from God for the great work of saving souls from death. But, indeed, in the one thing which they profess to know, they are not

ignorant men. I trust there is not one of them who is not able to go through such an examination in substantial, practical, experimental divinity, which few of our candidates for holy orders even in the university are able to do.

JOHN WESLEY SAID IT

967
Love

For God's sake, if it be possible, let us not provoke one another to wrath. Let us not kindle in each other this fire of hell. If we could discern truth by that dreadful light, would it not be loss rather than gain? For how far is love, even with many wrong opinions, to be preferred before truth without love! We may be without the knowledge of many truths, and yet be carried to Abraham's bosom. But if we die without love, what will knowledge avail? Just as much as it avails the devil and his angels!

968
Don't Scream

Speak as earnestly as you can, but do not scream; speak with all your heart, but with a moderate voice. . . . I often speak loud, often vehemently; but I never scream. I never strain myself. I dare not. I know it would be a sin against God and my own soul.

— To a preacher friend

969
Cleanliness

Let it be observed, that slovenliness is no part of religion; that neither this, nor any text of Scripture, condemns neatness of apparel. Certainly this is a duty, not a sin. "Cleanliness is, indeed, next to godliness."

970
Reading Means Growing

Reading Christians are growing Christians. When Christians cease to read, they cease to grow.

971
Fashion

As to matters of dress, I would recommend one never to be first in the fashion nor the last out of it.

972
Opinions

A string of opinions no more constitutes faith, than a string of beads constitutes holiness.

973
Experience

When I was young I was sure of everything; in a few years, having been mistaken a thousand times, I was not half so sure of most things as I was before; at present, I am hardly sure of anything but what God has revealed to me.

974
Duty

>Do all the good you can,
>By all the means you can,
>In all the ways you can,
>In all the places you can,
>At all the times you can,
>To all the people you can,
>As long as ever you can.

975
Differing View

I have no more right to object to a man holding a different opinion from mine, than I have to differ from a man because he wears a wig and I wear my own hair. But if he takes his wig off, and shakes the powder in my eyes, I shall consider it my duty to get rid of him as soon as possible.

976

Money

When I have any money, I get rid of it as quickly as possible, lest it find a way into my heart.

977

Religion

Some people have just enough religion to make them uncomfortable.

978

Mystery

Tell me how it is that in this room there are three candles and but one light, and I will explain to you the mode of the divine existence.

WOODROW WILSON
(1856–1924)

The twenty-eighth president of the United States (1913-1921), Wilson is considered by many historians as one of the greatest. He not only achieved fame as president and world leader; he was also a successful educator and legislator. Historian Arthur S. Pink said that "Wilson would have won a place in history even if he had been active in only one of his three careers." Son of a Presbyterian minister, he became president of Princeton University in 1902, governor of New Jersey in 1910, and president of the United States in 1912. He was reelected president in 1916 and led the nation during World War I. But his disappointment in the United State's rejection of membership in the League of Nations was great. He suffered a stroke while on a tour of the states and remained partially paralyzed the rest of his life. He is the only president buried in Washington, D.C.

979
Dealing with Cheating

When Woodrow Wilson was at Princeton, where he was a popular teacher and later president of the school, he cracked down on students who were not attending school for an education. One boy was expelled for cheating. His mother made a trip to Princeton to talk with Wilson. She had a sad tale of personal sickness and worry, and pled with Wilson to reinstate her boy because of the possible adverse reaction it would have on her. Wilson heard the woman's plea. "Madam," he began, "you force me to say a hard thing; if I had to choose between your life or my life or anybody's life and the good of this college, I should choose the good of the college." The boy was not reinstated and the woman left disappointed. Because of the decision he had to make that morning, Wilson could eat no lunch.

980
Importance

Woodrow Wilson was once the guest speaker at a women's club meeting in a midwestern city. The president of the club gave a lengthy and flattering introduction which Mr. Wilson acknowledged: "Madam President, Ladies and Gentlemen. Last fall I was much troubled with dizziness. My physician said it was due to my liver. I now know it was my eminence."

981
Golfing in Peace

Once, when Pres. Woodrow Wilson decided to play a game of golf, the Secret Service herded a group of photographers into a shack near one of the greens, explaining that the walls were full of holes through which they could take their pictures without disturbing the president. Once inside, however, the photographers found no holes — and also that the door had been padlocked from the outside.

— Peter Lisago, *Coronet*

982
Profanity

Woodrow Wilson liked to speak of his godly ministerial father, Dr. Joseph R. Wilson, for many years a distinguished Presbyterian minister in the South. Among the anecdotes he related of him was this: "He was once in a company of men where they were having a heated discussion. In the midst of it one let out a profane expletive. Then, seeing Dr. Wilson there, he offered him an apology, saying, 'Sir, I had forgotten that you were present. Please pardon me.' Dr. Wilson's reply was, 'It is not to me that you owe your apology, but to God.'"

— From *Macartney's Illustrations*, by Clarence E. Macartney. Copyright 1945 by Whitmore and Stone.

983

Peace, an Elusive Dream

Few presidents could match Woodrow Wilson's efforts for peace and overall success in that office. He hated war and tried unsuccessfully to keep the United States out of World War I. It disturbed him to know that America would have to send soldiers to Europe and that many would never return. After the bloody and costly war he went to Europe amid one of the most tumultuous receptions ever given any leader. He was hailed as the hope of humanity by Europeans who had suffered tragically during the war. He went to Paris with a dream of bringing nations together in a League of Nations. He had painstakingly tooled out a plan to prevent the horror of another war. London and Paris rocked with cheers; millions lined the streets to see him. He was Peace personified.

But one day the cheering stopped. Mr. Wilson returned to America to sell his idea, but the Senate wouldn't buy it. He then went to the American people by train. To St. Louis, Kansas City, Des Moines, Omaha, and then to the Northwest, Wilson went to the people. But when it was over, Wilson's health was broken. The cheering had ended. And before long, his dream for a League of Nations — with the United States as a member — was gone. Another admirable but futile attempt for man to bring peace among nations.

984

Justice

It was inauguration day, 1921. A sick Woodrow Wilson was ending two terms as president. Warren G. Harding was to be inaugurated within a short time. Wilson's secretary, Joseph Tulmulty, who had been with him for eleven years, stopped by to see Wilson. In his hand he held a pardon for an aged Nebraska man who had been convicted of a federal crime. The criminal had persuaded Tulmulty to help get him a presidential pardon. "I know," said Tulmulty to Wilson, "some day, that when you need mercy this last act will be remembered for you." The president looked at the paper. He could grant the pardon with his signature. Then he shook his head. "No, Joe, that case has been reviewed. The country needs a just government more than the old man needs a pardon or I need an act of mercy." Wilson took his pen and wrote "Disapproved" across the paper.

WOODROW WILSON SAID IT

985

National Renewal

When I look back on the processes of history, when I survey the genesis of America, I see this written on every page: that the nations are renewed from the bottom, not from the top; that the genius which springs up from the ranks of unknown men is the genius which renews the youth and energy of the people.

986

Judgment

One cool judgment is worth a thousand hasty councils. The thing to do is to supply light and not heat.

987

Freedom of Speech

I have always been among those who believe that the greatest freedom of speech has the greatest safety, because if a man is a fool the best thing to do is to encourage him to advertise the fact by speaking. It cannot be so easily discovered if you allow him to remain silent and look wise, but if you let him speak the secret is out and the world knows that he is a fool.

988

Liberty

Liberty has never come from government. Liberty has always come from the subjects of it. The history of liberty is a history of resistance. The history of liberty is a history of limitations of governmental power, not the increase of it.

989
America

America does not consist of groups. A man who thinks of himself as belonging to a particular national group in America has not yet become an American.

990
Democracy

I believe in democracy because it releases the energies of every human being.

991
Free People

Only free peoples can hold their purposes and their honor steady to a common end, and prefer the interests of mankind to any narrow interest of their own.

992
Honor

The nation's honor is dearer than the nation's comfort; yes, than the nation's life itself.

993
Providence

I firmly believe in divine providence. Without belief in providence I think I should go crazy. Without God the world would be a maze without a clue.

994
Duty

It is just as hard to do your duty when men are sneering at you as when they are shooting at you.

995
Eventual Triumph

I would rather fail in a cause that someday will triumph than to win in a cause that I know someday will fail.

996
Loyalty

Loyalty means nothing unless it has at its heart the absolute principle of self-sacrifice. Loyalty means that you ought to be ready to sacrifice every interest that you have, and your life itself, if your country calls upon you to do so; and that is the sort of loyalty which ought to be inculcated into these newcomers, that they are not to be loyal only so long as they are pleased, but that, having once entered into this sacred relationship, they are bound to be loyal whether they are pleased or not; and that loyalty which is merely self-pleasing is only self-indulgence and selfishness. No man has ever risen to the real stature of spiritual manhood until he has found it is finer to serve somebody else than it is to serve himself.

997
Silent Gospel

It is in our life and conduct that we must show our devotion to Christ. The silent gospel reaches further than the grandest rhetoric.

998
Purpose

A nation which does not remember what it was yesterday does not know what it is today, nor what it is trying to do. We are trying to do a futile thing if we do not know where we came from or what we have been about.

999
Opportunity

The beauty of democracy is that you never can tell when a youngster is born what he is going to do with you, and that, no matter how humbly he is born, he has got a chance to master the minds and lead the imaginations of the whole country.

1000

Democracy

It is for this that we love democracy: for the emphasis it puts on character; for its tendency to exalt the purposes of the average man to some high level of endeavor; for its just principle of common assent in matters in which all are concerned; for its ideals of duty and its sense of brotherhood.

BIBLIOGRAPHY

Archer, Jules. *Fighting Journalist: Horace Greeley*. New York: Julian Messner, 1966.
Barker, William P. *Who's Who in Church History*. Old Tappan, N.J.: Fleming H. Revell Company, 1969.
Bocca, Geoffrey. *The Adventurous Life of Winston Churchill*. New York: Julian Messner, Inc., 1958.
Boreham, F. W. *A Bunch of Everlastings*. Nashville: The Abingdon Press, 1920.
Boyd, Forest. "From the President's Pew." *Christian Life*, November 1969.
Boys and Girls Bookshelf. New York: The University Society, Inc., 1920.
Bradley, John P.; Daniels, Leo F.; and Jones, Thomas C. *The International Dictionary of Thoughts*. Chicago: J. G. Ferguson Publishing Company, 1969.
Braude, Jacob M. *New Treasury of Stories for Every Speaking and Writing Occasion*. Englewood Cliffs, N.J.: Prentice-Hall, Inc., 1959.
──────. *Speaker's Desk Book of Quips, Quotes, and Anecdotes*. Englewood Cliffs, N.J.: Prentice-Hall, Inc., 1963.
Brockway, Wallace, ed. *High Moment*. New York: Simon and Schuster, 1955.
Bunyan, John. *Visions of Heaven and Hell*. Reprint. Swengel, Pa.: Reiner Publications, 1966.
Collier, Richard. *The General Next to God*. New York: E. P. Dutton Company, Inc., 1965.
Cooper, Lettice. *A Hand upon the Time, A Life of Charles Dickens*. New York: Pantheon Books (Random House, Inc.), 1968.
Davis, Kenneth S. *The Politics of Honor, A Biography of Adlai E. Stevenson*. New York: G. P. Putnam's Sons, 1957, 1967.
De Toledano, Ralph. *One Man Alone: Richard Nixon*. New York: Funk & Wagnalls, 1969.
Disney, Roy. "The Unforgettable Walt Disney." *The Reader's Digest*, February 1969.
Doan, Eleanor. *The Speaker's Sourcebook*. Grand Rapids: Zondervan Publishing House, 1960.
Donovan, Robert J. *Eisenhower, The Inside Story*. New York: Harper & Brothers, 1956.

Drakeford, John W. *This Insanity Called Love.* Waco, Tex.: Word Books, 1970.

Drury, Allen. "Mr. Nixon Goes to Washington." *The Reader's Digest,* February 1969.

Dubos, René J. *Louis Pasteur: Free Lance of Science.* Boston: Little, Brown, and Company, 1950.

Edman, V. Raymond. *They Found the Secret.* Grand Rapids: Zondervan Publishing House, 1960.

Eisenhower, Dwight D. *In Review.* Garden City, N.Y.: Doubleday & Company, Inc., 1969.

Elliott, Lawrence. *George Washington Carver: The Man Who Overcame.* Englewood Cliffs, N.J.: Prentice-Hall, Inc., 1966.

Fay, Paul B., Jr. *The Pleasure of His Company.* New York: Harper & Row Publishers, 1966.

Fishwick, Marshall. *Illustrious Americans*: *Clara Barton.* Dallas: Silver Burdett Company, 1966.

Haines, Charles. *Charles Dickens.* New York: Franklin Watts, Inc., 1969.

Hall, Gordon Langley. *The Sawdust Trail.* Philadelphia: Macrae Smith Company, 1964.

Hart, William J. *600 Sermon Illustrations.* Grand Rapids: Baker Book House, reprinted 1969.

Hefley, James C. *Lift-off!* Grand Rapids: Zondervan Publishing House, 1970.

————. *A Dictionary of Illustrations.* Grand Rapids: Zondervan Publishing House, 1971.

Henry, Lewis C. *Five Thousand Quotations for All Occasions.* Garden City, N.Y.: Doubleday & Company, 1945.

————. *Humorous Anecdotes about Famous People.* Garden City, N.Y.: Halcyon House, 1948.

Hines, Jerome. *This Is My Story, This Is My Song.* Old Tappan, N.J.: Fleming H. Revell Company, 1968.

Holt, Rackam. *George Washington Carver*: *An American Biography.* New York: Doubleday and Company, 1943.

Hoover, J. Edgar. *J. Edgar Hoover Speaks Concerning Communism.* Edited by James D. Bales. Nutley, N.J.: The Craig Press, 1970.

Ives, Elizabeth Stevenson, and Dolson, Hildegarde. *My Brother Adlai.* New York: William Morrow & Company, 1956.

Jacobs, J. Vernon. *450 True Stories from Church History.* Grand Rapids: Wm. B. Eerdmans Publishing Company, 1955.

Johnson, Lyndon B. *My Hope for America.* New York: Random House, Inc., 1964.

Johnson, Sam Houston. *My Brother Lyndon.* New York: Cowles Book Company, Inc., 1969.

Kennedy, John F. *Profiles in Courage.* New York: Harper & Row Publishers, 1956.

————. *The Quotable Mr. Kennedy.* Edited by Gerald Gardner. New York: Popular Library, 1963.

Knight, Walter B. *Knight's Master Book of New Illustrations.* Grand Rapids: Wm. B. Eerdmans Publishing Company, 1956.

──────. *Knight's Treasury of Illustrations.* Grand Rapids: Wm. B. Eerdmans Publishing Company, 1963.

──────. *Knight's Illustrations for Today.* Chicago: Moody Press, 1970.

Lawson, James Gilchrist. *Deeper Experiences of Famous Christians.* Anderson, Ind.: The Warner Press, 1911, 1971.

MacArthur, Douglas. *Reminiscences.* New York: McGraw-Hill Book Company, 1964.

Macartney, Clarence E. *Macartney's Illustrations.* Nashville: Abingdon Press, 1946.

McCall, Donald. *Twice upon a Time*: *Aesop's Fables for 20th Century Christians.* Chicago: Moody Press, 1971.

Mears, Henrietta C. *Highlights of Scripture.* Glendale, Calif.: Gospel Light Publications, 1937.

──────. *431 Quotes from the Notes of Henrietta C. Mears.* Edited by Eleanor L. Doan. Glendale, Calif.: Gospel Light Publications, 1970.

Miller, Diane Disney. *The Story of Walt Disney.* New York: Henry Holt and Company, 1957.

Paul, Doris A. "From Met to Mission." *Christian Life,* September 1964.

Penney, J. C. *View from the Ninth Decade.* New York: Thomas Nelson & Sons, 1960.

Person, Amy L. *Illustrations from Literature.* Grand Rapids: Baker Book House, 1966.

Pippert, Wesley. "Billy Graham: Prophet or Politician?" *Christian Life,* May 1971.

Plumb, Beatrice. *J. C. Penney, Merchant Prince.* Minneapolis: T. S. Dennison, Inc., 1963.

Pollock, John. *Billy Graham.* New York: McGraw-Hill Book Company, 1966.

Redding, David A. *What Is the Man?* Waco, Tex.: Word Books, 1970.

Robinson, Corinne Roosevelt. *My Brother Theodore Roosevelt.* New York: Charles Scribner's Sons, 1921.

Ross, Walter S. *The Last Hero*: *Charles A. Lindbergh.* New York: Harper & Row, Publishers, 1968.

Silverberg, Robert. *Light for the World*: *Edison and the Power Industry.* Princeton: D. Van Nostrand Company, Inc., 1967.

Smith, Gene. *When the Cheering Stopped.* New York: William Morrow & Company, Inc., 1964.

Taft, Adon. "Why Has God Allowed Us into Space?" *Christian Life,* July 1969.

Thomas à Kempis. *The Imitation of Christ.* Reprint. Chicago: Moody Press, n.d.

Tomlin, E. W. F., ed. *Charles Dickens.* New York: Simon and Schuster, 1969.

Treadway, Charles and Ruby. *Fifty Character Stories.* Nashville: Broadman Press, 1969.

Troyat, Henri. *Tolstoy.* Garden City, N.Y.: Doubleday & Company, Inc., 1967.
Untermeyer, Louis. *Makers of the Modern World.* New York: Simon and Schuster, 1955.
Wall, Joseph Frazier. *Andrew Carnegie.* New York: Oxford University Press, 1970.
Wallis, Charles L., ed. *The Treasure Chest.* New York: Harper & Row, Publishers, 1965.
—————. *Words of Life.* New York: Harper & Row, Publishers, 1966.
—————. *Our American Heritage.* New York: Harper & Row, Publishers, 1970.
Ward, C. M. "The Farther We Probe into Space, the Greater My Faith." Springfield, Mo.: Assemblies of God, tract, 1966.
White, Theodore H. *The Making of the President, 1964.* New York: Atheneum Publishers, 1965.
World Book Encyclopedia. Chicago: Field Enterprises Educational Corporation, 1970.

INDEX

*Number following entry indicates number of story or quotation, not page number. Contents page lists the famous people by page number and in alphabetical order.

A

Abilities, 69, 142
Accidents, 219, 223, 278, 282, 594
Accomplishments, 268, 271, 272, 476, 560
Accuracy, 844
Adversity, 53, 258, 285
Advice, 11, 27, 47, 307, 416, 494, 600, 775, 964
Affection, 204, 222. *See also* Love
Afflictions, 52, 813. *See also* Sickness
Africa. *See* David Livingstone
Age of Reason, The, 307
Aging, 212, 610. *See also* Old Age
Agnostic, Difficult to Be, 537
Airplane. *See* Charles Lindbergh
Alcohol, 86, 97, 349, 351, 376, 379, 720
Ambition, 99, 384, 394, 396, 460, 578, 718
America, 286, 287, 297, 298, 299, 300, 301, 303, 305, 357, 429, 430, 435, 436, 402, 407, 408, 409, 410, 416, 495, 501, 503, 536, 579, 602, 606, 607, 682, 684, 685, 686, 687, 692, 739, 771, 778, 791, 796, 798, 840, 841, 845, 930, 948, 950, 952, 953, 985, 989
American Revolution, 306, 682, 687
Ancestors, 477
Angels, 800, 816, 819
Anger, 326, 921
Anxiety, 566, 599. *See also* Fear

Apathy, 91, 377
Applause, 749
Appreciation, 280, 311, 483, 605, 701, 717. *See also* Gratitude; Thankful
Arguing Religion, 769
Art, 283, 582
Associations, *See* Friendships
Astronaut, 850
Atheism, 64, 307, 409, 417, 557, 907
Atonement, 669
Authority, 359, 630
Avarice, 460. *See also* Greed

B

Beauty Skin Deep, 722
Bible, 307, 332, 360, 373, 401, 411, 416, 426, 474, 557, 603, 620, 631, 635, 649, 669, 724, 744, 752, 804, 816, 952. *See also* Word of God
Birds, Preserving, 541
Blessings, 205, 357, 505, 571, 619, 809
Blindness. *See* Helen Keller
Boer War, 171
Boldness, 387
Books, 48, 213, 295, 478, 479, 956
Bravery. *See* Courage
Brotherhood, 683, 684, 857
Brothers in Christ, 808
Budget, Limited, 677
Bully, 71
Burden for Others, 90, 91, 93, 94, 97, 99, 102, 105, 107, 347. *See also* Clara Barton; Compassion

353

C

Calamity, 243, 464
Capitalism, 185
Capital Punishment, 199, 288
Cares, 580, 718, 719. *See also* Problems; Troubles
Cause, A, 680
Cedar Mountain, 74
Censorship, 295
Challenge, 71, 153
Chance, 706
Change, 584
Changed Life, 31, 111, 195, 348, 349, 351, 362, 384, 387, 397, 557, 616, 653, 664, 718. *See also* Conversion; Transformation
Character, 285, 411, 465, 518, 622, 726, 1000
Charity. *See* Love
Cheated, 450
Cheating, 979
Children, 206, 345, 405, 410, 411, 412, 415, 416, 417, 778
Choices, Making, 733
Christ. *See* Jesus Christ
Christian, 358, 361, 406, 665, 780, 812, 900
Christianity, 65, 110, 158, 250, 327, 335, 357, 603, 665, 737. *See also* Religion
Christmas, 195, 203, 223, 322
Church (members, attendance, etc.), 353, 365, 372, 410, 417, 418, 419, 490, 906, 944
Church and State, 501
Circumstances, 251, 290, 810
Citizens, Good, 833
Civilization, 546, 551, 760
Civil Rights, 441, 511, 516
Civil War, 73, 74, 81, 83, 266, 366, 560, 675
Cleanliness, 699, 969
Clock Watching, 269
Commandments, 322, 645
Committee, 532
Common Sense, 378
Communicate, 492
Communism, 193, 402, 406, 409, 417, 436, 847
Compassion, 52, 73, 74, 76, 78, 79, 81, 83, 87, 97, 347, 401, 550, 745. *See also* Burden
Competition, 739, 743, 905
Complaining, 3, 336, 562, 821
Compliments, 705
Concentration, 147, 369
Condemnation, 622
Conduct, Human, 891
Confession, 44
Confidence, 810
Conformed to Christ, 54, 90, 665, 877
Confusion, Name, 832, 834
Conscience, 556, 720, 871, 880, 938
Consecration. *See* Dedication
Consent, 524
Conservation, 541
Constitution, U.S., 935
Contentment, 4, 22, 129
Conversion, 35, 88, 111, 348, 349, 351, 356, 362, 384, 397, 557, 654, 660, 664, 960. *See also* Changed Life; Transformation
Conviction of Spirit, 35, 92
Convictions (about whiskey), 720
Cooperation, 679
Counsel. *See* Advice
Counterfeit, 519
Courage, 73, 148, 187, 285, 291, 406, 407, 480, 503, 560, 599, 613, 696
Courteous, 52
Cowards, 17
Creation, 542, 697, 907, 909, 916, 917
Creator, 697
Credit, 211
Crime, 86, 263, 404, 411, 412, 413, 415, 510, 761, 786. *See also* Lawlessness
Crisis, 391, 392, 604, 688, 693, 718, 719
Criticism, 95, 168, 184, 226, 253, 366, 419, 513, 655, 656, 696, 775
Curiosity, 463, 469, 913
Custom, 58
Cynics, 207, 538, 782

D

Dare, 799

Danger, 73, 182, 188, 223, 391, 392, 425, 499, 503, 507, 552, 555, 562, 564, 566, 599, 604, 623, 702, 838, 918, 922, 958, 962
Death, 78, 83, 87, 119, 196, 201, 215, 346, 347, 475, 493, 496, 552, 560, 561, 562, 563, 568, 571, 575, 636, 662, 669, 696, 698, 718, 740, 965
Deceit, 5, 723
Decency, 295, 302, 404, 412, 693
Decision, 440, 535, 554, 718, 719
Declaration of Independence, 526
Dedication, 153, 155, 159, 188, 542, 556, 671
Dedication to God, 88, 90, 98, 103, 105, 119, 125, 554, 561, 565, 567, 569, 571, 655, 658, 718, 889, 962, 963
Defeat, 613, 719, 831, 983
Democracy, 603, 756, 789, 839, 990, 999, 1000
Destiny, 694
Determination, 74, 81, 105, 180, 467, 494, 506, 508, 556, 672, 820, 963
Devil, The, 391, 395, 660, 803
Dirty Jokes, 232, 748
Disappointment, 200, 559, 613, 719, 721, 722, 983
Disaster, 78, 79, 719. *See also* Tragedy
Discerning Times, 853
Discipline, 84, 294, 334, 335, 405, 407, 411, 412, 416
Discord, 621
Discouragement, 393, 651
Discovery, 275, 282
Discretion, 55
Disease in Animals, 696, 702
Dishonesty, 208, 420, 723, 979
Dispute, 921
Dreams, 549
Drunkenness. *See* Alcohol
Dual Personality, 806
Duty, 139, 170, 181, 188, 242, 288, 328, 417, 495, 528, 618, 628, 831, 939, 969, 974, 994. *See also* Responsibility
Dying for Another, 201, 669

E

Eating Words, 186, 849
Education, 224, 258, 265, 793. *See also* Study
Election, Political, 420, 427, 493, 674, 678, 724, 831, 832
Emancipation Proclamation, 366, 516
Embarrassment, 553, 657
Encouragement, 126, 393, 538, 573, 599, 610, 671, 672, 719, 740, 947
Enemy, 171, 194, 242, 425, 442, 499, 547, 810
Enthusiasm, 270, 657
Envy, 136, 643
Epitaph, 309
Equality, 72, 135, 242, 305, 388, 526, 556, 670, 683, 687
Errors, 883
Eternal, 561, 636, 662, 713, 802, 949
Ethics, 910
Evangelism, 91, 92, 93, 97, 99, 100, 101, 102, 104, 107, 349, 351, 655, 656, 659. *See also* Personal Work; Soul Winner; Witness
Evidence, Scientific, 715
Evil, 31, 35, 44, 404, 499, 556, 794, 858, 890, 918
Evolution, 96
Exaggeration, 509
Example, 28, 47, 81, 313, 401, 520, 525, 563, 573, 670, 717, 724, 740, 751
Excuses, 15, 163, 591
Execution, 199, 201, 288
Experience, 973
Experiment, 270, 272, 275, 308, 538, 696
Exploration. *See* David Livingstone

F

Fact, 707
Failure, 173, 226, 240, 270, 350, 384, 386, 400, 432, 553, 639, 645, 720, 731, 799, 995 (temporary)
Faith, 39, 77, 91, 345, 362, 407,

470, 480, 540, 684, 707, 717, 814, 822 (and works), 824, 898, 916, 926, 972
Faithful, 602, 625, 652, 695, 784
Fame, 382, 384, 531, 535, 552, 560, 784. See also Popularity
Family, 237, 296, 401, 740, 777, 895. See also Home
Family Training, 100, 401, 405, 410, 411, 520, 701, 804. See also Home
Famine, 76
Famous Daddy, 228, 539
Fanatic, 189, 591
Farmers, 954
Fashion, 971
Father, 345, 539, 609, 615, 698, 701, 740, 771, 835
Faults, 241, 466, 646, 874. See also Imperfections
Favoritism, 9, 370
FBI. See J. Edgar Hoover
Fear, 49, 53, 126, 392, 566, 579, 613. See also Anxiety
Flag, U.S., 287
Flattery, 329
Folly, 26, 60, 432, 547, 881
Food, 456
Fool, 659, 660
Football, 138, 671, 776
Force, 522, 681
Forget, 553
Forgiveness, 80, 110, 203, 209, 653
Forgotten 867
Fortune, 60, 136, 138, 140, 272, 718, 719. See also Money; Wealth
Franco-Prussian War, 81, 698
Freedom, 116, 170, 373, 407, 416, 495, 498, 511, 514, 523, 526, 530, 556, 603, 626, 681, 687, 792, 929, 987. See also Liberty
Free People, 792, 991
French Revolution, 201
Friendly, 554
Friendships, 2, 71, 329, 354, 392, 446, 449, 514, 539, 565, 647, 931, 941, 959
Fruit, Christian, 625
Future, 110, 139, 240, 360, 382, 402, 475, 498, 579, 713, 714

G

Generous, 76, 195, 558
Genius, 241, 277, 806
Gentleman, 220, 253, 555, 724
Gentleness, 557, 558, 724, 811
Gettysburg, 512
Gift, 138, 140, 195, 531, 676 (offering), 807 (offering), 808
Goals, 681, 682, 899
God, 36, 61, 62, 111, 118, 126, 197, 388, 389, 408, 481, 505, 511, 537, 540, 551, 565, 585, 594, 613, 621, 625, 632, 633, 637, 650, 658, 667, 692, 697, 718, 719, 727, 738, 770, 804, 808, 822, 904, 906, 907, 913, 919, 930, 978
Golden Rule, 426, 721, 728, 741. See also J. C. Penney
Goodness, 293, 461, 558, 660, 693, 885. See also Kindness
Good Works, 32, 44, 461, 660, 663, 885
Gospel, 101, 104, 406, 815, 957
Gossip, 765
Government, 427, 692, 854
Gracious, 52, 82
Grandmother, Influence of, 670
Gratitude, 6, 8, 52, 78, 178, 183, 194, 241, 280, 296, 311, 401, 511, 701, 730, 930. See also Appreciation; Thankful
Greatness, 601
Greed, 1, 195, 460, 884. See also Avarice
Grief, 514, 561. See also Sorrow
Growing Old, 610
Guidance, 129, 134, 151 154, 158, 160, 166, 366, 384, 391, 401, 408, 468, 548, 565, 631, 692, 721, 930

H

Habit, 40
Handicaps, 486
Happiness, 364, 405, 409, 453, 473, 481, 527, 664, 717, 888, 895, 939
Hardship, 182, 188, 559, 561, 562, 571, 606, 613

Hate, 165, 170, 199, 345, 355, 404
Healing, 317, 389
Health, 59, 89, 133, 175
Heaven, 110, 135, 561, 583, 636, 713, 824
Heavens, 773, 800, 916, 917
Hell, 110, 353
Helping Others, 643, 660, 704. *See also* Clara Barton; William Booth
Hero, 171, 201, 292, 416, 476, 536, 560, 766, 768
History, 173, 285, 429, 505, 825, 859, 923
Holiness, 964
Holy Spirit, 38, 88, 110, 406
Home, 100, 280, 363, 411, 412, 561, 788, 816, 895. *See also* Family; Family Training; Marriage
Honesty, 34, 147, 291, 416, 517, 531, 564, 670, 718, 723, 724, 728
Honor, 99, 142, 155, 291, 441, 552, 560, 608, 717, 992
Hope, 286, 360, 445, 561, 579, 713, 791, 814
Horseback, 443
Human, 754
Humility, 20, 33, 37, 115, 129, 159, 292, 386, 390, 494, 512, 550, 560, 570, 729, 742, 773, 861
Humor, 131, 135, 136, 137, 156, 172, 175, 177, 178, 229, 243, 306, 368, 370, 372, 385, 418, 420, 422, 423, 424, 443, 444, 445, 489, 491, 502, 509, 513, 515, 532, 539, 562, 596, 598, 659, 660, 676, 678, 691, 744, 747, 749, 750, 753, 772, 800, 801, 836, 945, 981. *See also* Will Rogers
Hymns. *See* Music; Singing
Hypocrites, 819, 848, 890

I

Ideals, 785
Idleness, 214

Ignorance, 442, 457, 620, 823, 852
Illustrations, 828
Imitation, 26
Immortality, 215, 359, 364, 561, 662, 713
Impatience, 821
Imperfections, 622, 655, 874, 883. *See also* Faults
Importance, 980
Improvement, 544
Inconveniences, 255
Independence Day, 357
Inequity, 496
Infidel, 96
Infidelity, 881
Influence, 143, 151, 280, 313, 401, 402, 501, 556, 557, 573, 670, 758, 862, 997
Inhumane, 290, 503, 556
Initiative, 130, 132
Injury to Others, 14
Innovator, 77, 101
Inspiration, 277, 293, 557, 563, 573, 599, 604, 671
Insults, Disregard, 705
Integrity, 407, 550, 723, 742
Intellect, 62
Interruptions, Preventing, 700
Invent, 68
Invention, 264, 268, 271, 272, 273, 274, 275, 278, 282, 284, 312, 547, 902
Iron Curtain, 290
Isolation, 679

J

Jail Service, 344
Jealousy, 11, 24, 203
Jesus Christ, 54, 110, 112, 335, 481, 565, 566, 570, 571, 604, 619, 623, 625, 638, 647, 649, 652, 657, 669, 737, 802, 803, 808, 815, 825, 920, 946
Jew, 242, 244
Johnstown Flood, 78
Joy, 348
Judging, 68, 577, 869, 986
Judgment Day, 92, 120, 804
Just, 589
Justice, 210, 288, 339, 341, 984

K

Kindness, 158, 289, 339, 367, 370, 390, 447, 556, 643, 660, 670, 693, 771, 808, 885, 942. *See also* Goodness
Kings, 477
Knowledge, 63, 256, 458, 473, 937
Korean War, 288, 503
Ku Klux Klan, 409

L

Labor, 109, 268, 269, 277, 459. *See also* Work
Lawlessness, 404. *See also* Crime
Laws, 315, 627 (Ten Commandments), 787
Leadership, 174, 176, 179, 292, 293, 304, 419, 421, 494, 648
Learn, 190, 471, 642, 826
Lecture, 7, 368
Legacy, 231, 314, 330, 740
Liar, 25, 420, 724, 921. *See also* Lie
Liberate, 180, 188, 193
Liberty, 316, 332, 409, 529, 612, 757, 951, 988. *See also* Freedom
Lie, 818, 955. *See also* Liar
Life, 248, 290, 343, 394, 400, 409, 447, 468, 469, 473, 475, 484, 496, 535 (or death), 625, 664 (new), 732 (Christian), 795, 797 (strenuous), 804, 842, 892, 899
Listener, Good, 239
Literature, 478, 512, 592, 956, 937
Look before Leaping, 12
Love, 41, 206, 210, 257, 320, 348, 355, 393, 416, 466, 471, 472, 475, 481, 558, 605, 619, 668, 693, 695, 701, 717, 718, 724, 742, 814, 860, 888, 889, 967. *See also* Affection
Loyalty, 420, 831, 996

M

Marriage, 267, 364, 385, 445, 565, 695, 889. *See also* Family; Family Training; Home

Materialism, 455
Memoirs, 746
Memory, 337, 375, 382, 588, 701, 720, 755
Merciful, 589
Military Life, 496, 618. *See also* Dwight D. Eisenhower; Douglas MacArthur
Millionaire, 133, 140, 718, 719. *See also* Fortune; Money; Wealth
Minister's Life, 462
Miracle, 389
Misery, 49, 394
Misfortune, 205, 243
Misrepresentation, 23
Mission, Skid-Row, 387, 390
Missionary, 570, 603, 779. *See also* David Livingstone
Mistake, 749, 750, 832, 834
Mob, 199, 217, 534
Money, 131, 133, 136, 137, 138, 140, 149, 155, 196, 222, 264, 266, 272, 314, 318, 324, 325, 337, 370, 382, 453, 531, 676, 718, 719, 763, 764, 807, 893, 976. *See also* Fortune; Wealth
Moon Travel, 538
Moral Force, 550
Morality, 332, 359, 364, 788, 793, 856, 923, 934
Mother, 28, 280, 294, 605
Murder, 86
Music, 101, 384, 580, 590, 621. *See also* Singing

N

Nail, For Want of, 333
NATO, 292
Nature, 574, 582
Nazi Germany, 173, 193, 409, 550
New Birth, 111, 308. *See also* Conversion
Newspaper, 332, 340, 370, 381, 382, 389, 830, 844
Night, 572, 580
Nursing. *See* Clara Barton

O

Obedience, 322, 626, 822, 863, 890

358

Oblivion, 377, 382
Offering, 137, 424, 676, 807
Old Age, 452, 469. *See also* Aging
Opinion, 896, 972, 975
Opportunities, 50, 72, 104, 141, 246, 451, 611, 771, 999
Optimism, 238, 240, 485, 610
Orphan, 771
Orphanage, 807

P

Pardon, 52, 88, 510, 984 (denied)
Parents, 701, 717, 804. *See also* Father; Mother
Past, 56, 374, 475
Patience, 247, 254, 261, 285, 319, 560, 576, 742, 872
Patriotism, 287, 301, 503, 605, 607, 617, 703, 778, 948, 950
Peace, 124, 173, 286, 300, 321, 349, 425, 437, 438, 439, 566, 608, 613, 614, 684, 685, 709, 851, 868, 888, 981, 983
Permissiveness, 359, 364
Persecution, 99, 116, 503, 962
Perseverance, 820. *See also* Determination
Persistent Prayer, 640
Personal Work, 634. *See also* Evangelism
Philanthropy, 137, 138, 140, 591
Philosophy, 64, 301, 396, 548
Phonograph, Invention of, 273, 274
Phrenology, 82
Plagiarism, 46
Pleasure, 460
Pledge, 564, 599, 645 (Sunday school teachers')
Point of No Return, 535
Poor, 88, 89, 90, 91, 97, 100, 101, 105, 198, 225, 303, 367, 653, 897. *See also* Poverty
Popularity, 382, 560. *See also* Fame
Poverty, 152, 427, 653. *See also* Poor
Power, Seeking, 497, 550
Praise, 448, 701
Prank, 621

Prayer, 28, 122, 127, 154, 160, 161, 296, 300, 305, 343, 351, 354, 361, 387, 388, 389, 391, 392, 414, 418, 440, 513, 569, 615, 640, 653, 692, 719, 735, 805, 807, 808, 880, 890, 923, 936, 963
Prayer Breakfast, 388
Preaching, 89, 91, 92, 96, 104, 116, 308, 344, 352, 353, 827
Prediction, 940
Prejudice, 85, 135, 158, 242, 244, 301, 355, 409, 557, 852
Preparation, 587, 688, 707, 728
Present (time), 56
Presidents, Great, 675
Pride, 19, 37, 115, 129, 196, 202, 245, 249, 371, 372, 386, 396, 605, 609, 750, 882
Principles, 373, 375, 742, 934, 952
Prison, 114, 116, 117, 197, 201, 290, 503
Problems, 433, 644, 653, 730. *See also* Cares; Troubles
Procrastinate, 346, 461
Prodigal, 626, 653
Profanity, 924, 982
Progress, 279, 546, 598, 692, 760
Promise, God's, 391, 395, 555, 635
Proof, Scientific, 715
Property, Private, 525
Prophesy, 110
Proposal, Marriage, 267
Prosperity, 53
Protection, God's, 391, 408, 555, 565
Providential, 903, 958, 993
Purpose, 353, 394, 411, 447, 998

Q

Quiet Life, 218

R

Rabies, 702
Racial Issues, 355, 441, 511, 556. *See also* Prejudice
Reading, 57, 478, 479, 970
Reality, 549
Rebellious, 118, 345

Red Cross, 75, 76, 78, 81, 224
Reflections, 864
Reform, 616
Regeneration, 102, 110. *See also* Conversion; New Birth
Rejection Notice, 350
Religion, 64, 65, 110, 128, 158, 216, 335, 359, 398, 412, 415, 419, 481, 977. *See also* Christianity
Remembered, 521, 701
Reminisce, 619, 701
Repentance, 110
Reputation, 518, 521
Rescue Drowning, 7
Research, 911. *See also* George Washington Carver; Thomas Edison, Louis Pasteur
Reservations, 103
Responsibility, 242, 286, 417, 625, 692. *See also* Duty
Results, 270, 275
Resurrection, 604, 636
Retirement, 725
Reunion, Father and Son, 698
Revelation, 582
Revenge, 66
Revival, 666, 961
Revolutionary, 900
Reward, 505, 942
Ridicule, 538
Right, 528
Righteousness, 112, 118
Rivalry, 905
Rockets, 538. *See also* Wernher von Braun
Rudeness, 71
Rumor, 492, 560

S

Sacrifice, 153, 155, 182, 201, 285, 298, 558, 559, 567, 571, 996
Salvation, 102, 104, 110. *See also* Conversion; New Birth; Regeneration
Salvation Army, 386, 389. *See also* William Booth
Saved. *See* Conversion; New Birth; Regeneration; Salvation
Science, 540, 542, 546, 547, 548, 551. *See also* George Washington Carver; Louis Pasteur; Wernher von Braun
Security, 488, 499, 547, 611
Self-Confidence, 494, 597
Self-Control, 240, 294, 560, 865
Selfishness, 383
Self-Knowledge, 866
Self-Reliance, 726
Self-Restraint, 859
Senses, Five, 483
Separation, Church and State, 501
Sermon, 553, 827
Serving, 632, 704, 734, 781, 901, 963
Sex, 359, 364
Sharing, 10, 75, 76, 367
Sickness, 59, 75, 389, 559, 561, 564, 604, 698, 718, 719
Silence, 700
Sin, 28, 29, 92, 94, 97, 111, 118, 120, 198, 359, 361, 364, 622, 623, 626, 750, 806, 817, 881, 886
Singing, 30, 101, 384, 386, 390, 392, 583, 719. *See also* Jerome Hines; Music
Sinner, 101, 102, 104, 111, 120
Slavery, 135, 150, 366, 477, 511, 516, 556, 559, 563, 893 (to money)
Sleeping During Speech, 829
Smile, 554
Social Concern, 198, 367, 441, 442, 556, 704. *See also* Clara Barton; William Booth
Socialism, 185
Soldiers, 290, 291, 425, 598, 606, 608, 618, 698. *See also* Military Life
Son, 615, 698
Sorrow, 291, 487, 559, 561, 568, 606, 651, 698, 701, 718, 821. *See also* Grief
Soul Winner, 90, 91, 92, 93, 99, 100, 102, 107, 387, 634, 654. *See also* Evangelism; Personal Work; Witness
Sour Grapes, 21
Sowing and Reaping, 165
Space Travel. *See* Wernher von Braun
Spanish-American War, 75

Speech, 55, 58, 240, 368, 422, 423, 512, 553, 724, 749, 772, 774, 827, 829, 943, 968, 987
Spirit of St. Louis. See Charles Lindbergh
Spiritual Need, 614, 718
Spiritual Power, 90, 408
Spiritual Training, 401, 410, 415, 416, 417, 804
Spontaneous Generation, 697
Sports, 776
Starving, 76
Stealing, 786
Steward, 625, 641
Strangers, 846
Study, 69, 308, 394, 410, 672, 776. See also Education
Success, 134, 145, 166, 233, 240, 368, 560, 578, 657, 696, 702, 712, 718, 742, 771, 797, 809. See also Victory
Suffer, 450, 464, 503, 559, 561, 564, 568, 606, 704, 719
Suicide, 121, 346, 347, 881
Sunday Religion, 216
Sunday School, 410, 417, 620, 645, 654, 657, 658
Superstition, 67, 493
Surprises, Benefits of, 736
Surrender, 90, 98, 554, 567, 602, 633, 658
Sympathy, 557, 606, 704

T

Tact, 259
Teacher, 650
Teacher's Commandments, 645
Teaching, 71, 72, 645, 649
Temper, 294
Temperance, 404
Temptation, 338, 624, 660, 878, 887
Terrorism, 404
Test, 870
Testimony, 348, 387, 389, 390, 394, 399, 619, 718, 719, 812
Testings, 167, 168, 182, 188, 258, 624, 718, 719
Thankful, 52, 183, 486, 511, 605, 701, 730. See also Appreciation; Grateful

Thanksgiving Day, 933
Thrift, 276
Time, 262, 535, 641, 853
Tolerance, 480
Torture, 503
Totalitarianism, 498
Tragedy, 421, 435, 547, 695, 698, 718. See also Disaster
Traitor, 925
Transformation, 195, 348, 349, 351, 355, 362, 384, 387, 718. See also Changed Life; Conversion; New Birth; Regeneration; Salvation
Treason, 46, 925
Treasure, 661, 718
Trials. See Testings
Trick, 534, 621, 925
Triumph. See Success; Victory
Trouble, 126, 393, 474, 653, 718, 774, 810, 821, 878. See also Cares; Problems
Trust, 91, 450, 468, 471, 718, 719, 822
Truth, 170, 262, 381, 542, 548, 551, 716, 818, 857, 889
Tuskegee Institute. See George Washington Carver

U

United Nations, 843
United States. See America
United States of Europe, 940
Universe, Marvels of, 537
Unrest, 394. See also War

V

Vainglory, 51
Valley Forge, 677, 687, 923
Value, 264, 290, 417, 448, 674, 910
Vanity, 876
Victory, 123, 179, 180, 467, 468, 475, 602, 613, 651, 799, 926, 995. See also Success
Virtues, 53, 198, 221, 332, 542, 560, 788, 844, 928
Vision, 407, 556, 559
Vote, 420, 501
Vulgarity, 232, 236

W

War, 73, 74, 75, 81, 83, 87, 171, 176, 179, 180, 181, 182, 188, 191, 193, 194, 290, 292, 321, 341, 366, 425, 439, 440, 499, 500, 503, 515, 599, 606, 608, 613, 614, 675, 698, 709, 753, 760
Warning, 587, 623
Waste, 276, 790
Wealth, 133, 136, 140, 149, 272, 342, 382, 428, 731, 788. *See also* Fortune; Millionaire, Money
Weapons, 284, 392, 414, 428, 432, 547, 622, 760, 918. *See also* War
White House, 418, 488, 491, 514, 676, 777
Will, 29, 144, 331, 667, 712, 738
Wisdom, 70, 157, 161, 738, 823
Wit, 331, 772
Witness, Christian, 387, 388, 390, 397, 619, 804. *See also* Evangelism; Personal Work; Soul Winner
Wives, 819
Women, 106, 695. *See also* Mother; Wives
Word of God, 111, 112, 113, 126, 401, 804, 816. *See also* Bible
Words, 454, 595 (hard), 849
Work, 109, 268, 269, 277, 278, 343, 459, 556, 572, 593, 670, 671, 672, 673, 700, 711, 712, 728, 734, 783, 795, 797, 822, 963. *See also* Labor
World, 507, 679, 791
World War I, 606, 752
World War II, 176, 179, 290, 292, 599, 613
Worship, 116, 929, 944
Writer, Value of, 894
Writing, 57
Wrong, Confessing, 921

X

X-Rated Films, 235, 236

Y

Young Men, 68, 139
Youth, 345, 353, 362, 364, 401, 402, 410, 417, 452, 540, 586, 588, 642, 644, 649, 726, 886
Youthful Initiative, 130, 132, 902

Z

Zeal, 152, 557, 591, 657